URBAN UPGRADING

Prepared for the ODA by WEDC and GHK/MRM International

URBAN
UPGRADING

OPTIONS AND PROCEDURES FOR PAKISTAN

◆ **Kevin Tayler and Andrew Cotton**

WEDC

GMI

GHK / MRM INTERNATIONAL

Prepared by
The Water, Engineering and Development Centre (WEDC),
Loughborough University of Technology, Leicestershire, LE11 3TU, UK.
and GHK/MRM International, St James Hall, Moore Park Road, London SW6 2JW, UK.

Published in Great Britain by WEDC

ISBN 0 906055 31 8

First edition: January 1993
Reprinted: April 1994

Book designed by Rod Shaw

Typeset and illustrated by WEDC/Transcribe, Loughborough.
Printed by Quorn Litho, Loughborough, Leicestershire, LE11 1HH, UK.

ACKNOWLEDGEMENTS

This document was prepared for the Overseas Development Administration, whose support is gratefully acknowledged. The authors would also like to thank Richard Franceys and Hilary Byrne for supplying material which has been incorporated into the manual. Information provided and comments made on earlier drafts of the manual by staff of the ODA, GHK/MRM International, WEDC and colleagues in Pakistan, particularly from the Lahore Development Authority, Faislabad Development Authority and the Orangi Pilot Project (Karachi) have been gratefully received and incorporated.

Figures 2.1 and 2.3 are based on figures in the SEARO Regional Health Paper No.9, WHO, New Delhi 1985.

Figure 8.1 is based on the intensity–duration curves produced for Lahore by NESPAK, (National Engineering Services, Pakistan) from Meteorological Dept. Data.

TABLE OF CONTENTS

LIST OF FIGURES

LIST OF TABLES

LIST OF BOXES

FOREWORD

BACKGROUND

The urban populations of developing countries are growing at unprecedented rates. This is partly due to natural population increase and partly due to in-migration. Pakistan is no exception in this regard; its urban population in 1989 was estimated to be 35.1 million with a growth rate of 4.1% or about 1.45 million per annum. Forecasts indicate that the growth rate may increase to perhaps 4.7% per annum in coming years.

Officially sanctioned housing provision has been unable to cope with this rate of growth. This is true for both conventional housing units and serviced plots on which allottees can build their own houses. As a result of this failure, a high proportion of housing is provided without regard to official rules and procedures. It has been estimated, that this housing, which we will refer to collectively as the informal sector, accounts for around 40% of the new housing provided in Pakistan each year. A recent study concluded that 49% of the urban population of the Punjab, the largest province, live in informal areas.

Informal housing is rarely planned in any overall sense, although individual schemes often have a degree of internal planning. It is almost unknown for services to be provided at the time that schemes are laid out and houses are built. The subsequent provision of services severely strains the resources of the concerned government departments and is often complicated by the lack of overall planning of informal areas.

One response to this situation is to refuse recognition to the informal sector and concentrate government efforts on increasing the supply of formally sanctioned housing, provided in the form of conventional housing units and serviced plots. Experience and the figures quoted above show that this approach is untenable. The Government in Pakistan accepts this and considerable resources are used each year to extend services into informal areas. Despite this, conditions in many areas remain poor and much remains to be done before the situation can be deemed to be satisfactory.

PROVISION OF SERVICES

Services are provided to informal areas in various ways. The most common at present is a rather piecemeal approach in which individual services are provided by municipalities and other concerned agencies and government departments with little coordination or overall planning. From the late 1970's, the recognition of the need to plan and coordinate actions led to the development of upgrading. **Upgrading may be defined as a systematic attempt to improve living conditions for people residing in informal settlements.** It is often taken to include only infrastructure improvements but a wider definition would include improvements to some or all of the following:

◆ housing (both improvements in fabric and additional rooms);

◆ on-plot facilities (particularly sanitation);

◆ social facilities (schools, health facilities etc.);

◆ environment (tree planting, parks).

Integrated upgrading programmes have been implemented in Lahore and Karachi with finance provided by the World

Bank and the Asian Development Bank and similar projects are planned in other cities. These projects deal almost exclusively with physical infrastructure but a more wide ranging approach is planned for Faisalabad with support from ODA. With the exception of Karachi, where the implementing agency is the Karachi Metropolitan Corporation Department of Katchi Abadis, all these projects have been organised through Development Authorities. While individual projects are large, integrated projects at present account for less than 20% of service provision in informal areas.

Services are also provided by residents of informal areas. The most obvious examples are facilities such as WCs, septic tanks and shallow on-plot wells. There are also many examples of local sewers provided by community action, most notably in Orangi, Karachi where the Orangi Pilot Project (OPP) acted as a catalyst for action to sewer around 50,000 plots by self-help action in the period 1981-1991. OPP is now working in other areas both in Karachi and in other towns and cities.

PURPOSE AND STRUCTURE OF THE MANUAL

The manual is intended primarily for use by engineers responsible for the planning, design and construction of upgrading schemes. However, it provides information which should be useful to other professionals working in the field of upgrading. It is not intended specifically for conmmunity activists and other community members who are interested in upgrading their environment. It is planned that complementary materials intended for community members will be produced at a later date.

There are three parts to the manual. The first part comprises Chapters 1-3 which provides an introduction to the subjects of informal development and upgrading, examines the scope for community involvement in infrastructure provision and suggests an approach, referred to as action programming, to the planning of areas requiring upgrading. Much of the information contained in this section should be of interest to policy and decision makers.

Part 2, comprising Chapters 4-10, covers the technical aspects of upgrading. It includes chapters on site appraisal and survey, water supply, sanitation and sewerage, street and lane paving, drainage, solid waste collection and street lighting. The emphasis is on the planning and design of facilities but information is also included on good construction practice. Charts and tables are used wherever possible in order to provide information in an accessible form and it is hoped that this will enable the manual to be used by non-engineers.

Part 3, comprising Chapters 11 and 12, covers contract documentation, costing and affordability. Adequate documentation is essential if upgrading works are to be implemented properly. The need to match the level of documentation provided to the size and complexity of the proposed work is emphasised, as is that for an appropriate approach to documentation for community managed schemes.

A digest of each chapter, including a summary of contents and a list of the key points is included at the beginning of the chapter. The main body of the text follows and contains essential information relating to the planning, design and construction of the service. Additional useful information is included in annexes at the end of each chapter.

I.

THE BACKGROUND

SUMMARY

This chapter provides an introduction to informal land development processes in Pakistan. It identifies two main types of informal development, unauthorised settlements on public land (katchi abadis) and unregulated subdivision of private land. The processes by which land is assembled, sub-divided, developed and serviced are then briefly examined. Consideration of the legal status of informal development and its important physical and social characteristics follows.

The second part of the chapter provides an introduction to upgrading. The reasons for upgrading informal settlements are given and briefly discussed and some key points relating to upgrading are made. Finally, the relative merits of different approaches to upgrading are considered, bearing in mind the key points already made.

KEY POINTS

◆

Informal development in the form of both unregulated land subdivisions and katchi abadis makes an important contribution to housing provision in Pakistan.

◆

Services are rarely provided in informal areas at the time they are developed. Upgrading, defined as a systematic attempt to improve the living conditions of the people in informal settlements, offers an alternative to ad-hoc provision of services.

◆

The objectives of upgrading are to provide greater convenience for residents of informal areas and improvements in both heath and environmental conditions.

◆

A degree of overall planning is essential if upgrading projects are to be fully effective.

◆

Upgrading schemes must be affordable to both government and beneficiaries, acceptable to the latter and provide discernable benefits.

◆

Construction standards should be appropriate to the conditions found in upgrading areas.

◆

Operation and maintenance requirements of upgrading schemes should always be matched to available resources and institutional capabilities at the planning stage.

◆

Integrated upgrading projects, controlled by a specialist upgrading unit, are appropriate in rapidly developing fringe areas. Elsewhere, the aim should be to coordinate the actions of the various organisations, groups and individuals involved with upgrading, making use of community resources wherever possible.

INFORMAL DEVELOPMENT

Informal land development processes

Informal land development processes vary from country to country and from city to city, depending on the scale of housing demand, land ownership patterns and the workings of the housing market. Informal development in Pakistan falls into two main categories. These are:

◆ unauthorised settlements on public land. These are known and in many cases legally defined as katchi abadis; and

◆ settlements formed by sub-division and sale for housing of private land without reference to official planning and building regulations. These will be referred to as unregulated land sub-divisions.

In both cases, most development is initiated by land dealers who gain control of land, sub-divide it and sell it. In the case of katchi abadis, the dealers do not own the land but they reach agreements with the authorities that sub-divisions will be tolerated and eventually provided with services. This costs money and the costs are passed on to those who acquire plots in the developments. In the case of unregulated land sub-divisions, land has to be purchased, resulting in rather higher plot prices than those in katchi abadis.

The relative importance of the two types of development depends on the availability of public land and the attitude of the authorities to unauthorised settlement of this land. In Karachi, which is surrounded by Government owned desert land, sub-division of the land has been condoned by the authorities with the result that almost all informal settlements are katchi abadis. The Punjab, in contrast, has much less public land and about 75% of informal settlement is in unregulated subdivisions of private land.

Once land has been acquired, plots are sold and houses are built on them. In many instances, subdividers employ local estate agents to sell plots. Not all plots are developed immediately, either because they are not sold or because owners choose to delay house construction, with the result that full development of informal settlements usually takes several years. This has some implications for infrastructure provision in that facilities must be designed to allow for future connections.

There is a degree of uniformity in the order in which services are provided to informal settlements. In Pakistan, electricity is usually the first to be provided. Where shallow ground water is available, many people install tubewells on their plots, fitted either with hand-pumps or, in the case of the more affluent, with electrically powered mechanical pumps. Where groundwater is not accessible, water may be obtained from standpipes or from water vendors in the first instance. Street paving, open sullage drains and piped water supplies follow. Sewerage, street lighting and gas supply are usually the last services to be provided. Until recently, most sanitation in informal settlements was provided by unsatisfactory dry latrines but there has been a strong move towards the use of pour-flush latrines. Most of these discharge to open drains, some via septic tanks located in streets and lanes in front of plots.

There are some instances of groups of plot-holders banding together to provide their own services. These have mostly been aimed at the provision of sewers but there are also examples of community action to provide other services. There is a strong argument for increasing the scale of community action and the subject will be considered in more detail later.

Legal status of informal development

The legal status of unauthorised development on public land at the time of subdivision and initial development is clear; plotholders do not have any legal right to occupy the land and could in theory be evicted and their houses demolished. In practice, there are very few cases of eviction and demolition. The legal position is altered if the Government officially recognises a settlement as a katchi abadi. Once this has been done, the settlement has some legal standing although plotholders still have no official claim on their plots. The latter is provided through the process known as regularisation by which plotholders are provided with basic services and a 99 year lease in return for a payment based on the size of their plot. At present, lease charges do not meet the cost of the services provided, let alone the value of the land.

The situation regarding unregulated land sub-divisions is rather different. In these, the plotholders normally hold documents showing that they have legally purchased their plots. This means that they cannot be deprived of their land but that their houses could in theory be demolished because there is no official sanction for the development of the land. Again, there are very few examples of demolition being carried out and the existence of most unregulated land subdivisions is tacitly accepted by Government.

Main characteristics of informal development

Although there are variations between individual informal settlements, there are some physical and social features that are characteristic. These are summarised below.

Physical characteristics

◆ Layouts are usually regular and reasonably efficiently planned, often in a grid-iron pattern.

◆ Access widths often do not meet official building and planning regulations. This is not universal. There are examples in Karachi of subdivisions being laid out in accordance with Karachi Metropolitan Corporation (KMC) standards in order that there will be no problems in having the development regularised in the future. In general, rights of way are narrower where land prices are higher.

◆ Informal settlements are frequently located on low-lying land which suffers from flooding problems. To overcome this problem, streets and plots are raised, often using poor quality material as fill. However, flooding problems remain because of the lack of overall planning.

Social characteristics

◆ Informal settlements vary in the degree of their social cohesion. In some settlements, particularly in Karachi, whole areas are inhabited by people from one ethnic background. Elsewhere, settlements tend to be more mixed although there does appear to be a tendency for individual lanes to be occupied by people from similar backgrounds. Nevertheless, it is probable that there is often a lack of social cohesiveness in informal settlements, particularly those which are of recent origin. This has to be taken into account when planning to involve the community in upgrading works.

◆ In katchi abadis, the original subdividers may continue to retain an interest in an area, often acting as middlemen between the residents and government officials when improvements are sought.

◆ The social and religious life within almost all informal housing areas are linked and centred on the mosque, land for which is often designated in the original layout.

UPGRADING

As stated in the introduction, upgrading can be defined as a systematic attempt to improve the living conditions of the people living in informal settlements. This manual is concerned primarily with infrastructure but it must be recognised that infrastructure improvements may form only part of an overall upgrading programme. The remainder of this chapter provides basic information on the process of upgrading and is intended to provide a context for the consideration of specific services in later chapters. A review of the reasons for upgrading will be followed by an examination of some key features of successful projects and a brief analysis of various approaches to upgrading.

Throughout this manual, references will be made to primary, secondary and tertiary infrastructure. These are not exact terms but are used for convenience in defining the various levels of infrastructure provision. Figure 1.1

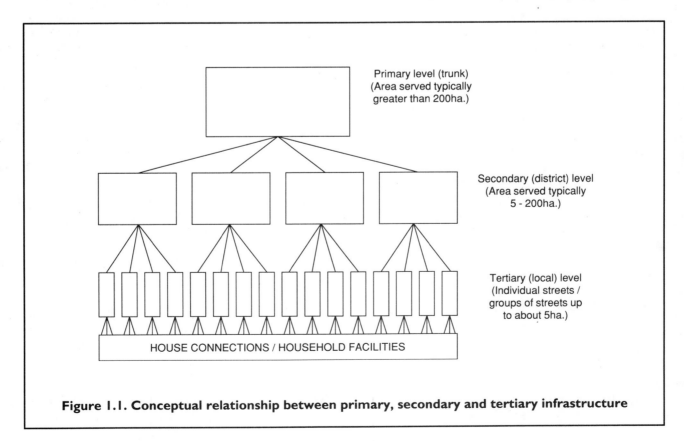

Primary level (trunk)
(Area served typically greater than 200ha.)

Secondary (district) level
(Area served typically 5 - 200ha.)

Tertiary (local) level
(Individual streets / groups of streets up to about 5ha.)

HOUSE CONNECTIONS / HOUSEHOLD FACILITIES

Figure 1.1. Conceptual relationship between primary, secondary and tertiary infrastructure

Improvements in health	Improvements in convenience/ reduction in expenditure	Improvements in environment
Water supply	Water supply	Solid waste collection
Sanitation	Sanitation	Sanitation
Solid waste collection	Electricity supply	Street surfacing
Drainage	Gas supply	Drainage
	Street surfacing	Street lighting
	Street lighting	

Table 1.1. Effects of infrastructure improvements on health, convenience and environment

shows the relationship between the different levels of infrastructure diagrammatically and gives rough limits on the area which each level will serve.

Reasons for upgrading

Three basic reasons for upgrading can be identified. These are:

◆ to improve the health of the residents;

◆ to make life easier for the residents, ie. to improve convenience; and

◆ to improve the environment.

There may also be social benefits in that the community organisation developed through participation in upgrading schemes may remain after completion of the schemes, to the general benefit of the community.

Different groups of people will attach varying degrees of importance to these aims. Health professionals will obviously be primarily concerned with improvements in health. Residents of informal areas may also be concerned about health but their main interests are likely to be in improved convenience and a better environment. Politicians will wish to satisfy the perceived needs of the people who elect them and will therefore have similar concerns to residents. Economists will tend to look beyond the three basic objectives noted above to the effect of upgrading measures on the income and productivity of the people living in the upgraded settlements. It is always important to realise that there are these differences in perceptions and priorities. **Failure to take the interests of residents into account may mean that the facilities provided are under-used or even misused so that they fail to achieve their intended objectives.**

Table 1.1 groups the various services in terms of their effect in producing improvements in health, convenience and environment.

At present, the overt aim in most upgrading schemes is to improve the environment. Health benefits are rarely taken into account implicitly when planning schemes although it is often assumed that they will be an automatic consequence of upgrading efforts. In fact, this is not the case; improvements in health cannot be brought about by physical improvements alone but also require changes in behaviour patterns, for instance washing hands after defecating. There is perhaps a need to consider the health aspects of upgrading schemes more explicitly and with this in mind the manual will briefly explain the relevance of good water supply, sanitation, drainage and solid waste disposal facilities to improved health.

Key points regarding upgrading projects

In this section, some key requirements for successful upgrading projects are introduced. When planning a project, it is essential to ensure that account is taken of these requirements.

Overall planning

All upgrading measures depend to a greater or lesser extent on off-site facilities and conditions. For example, a scheme to improve piped water supply will be ineffective if water production facilities and trunk mains are inadequate. Similarly, local measures to improve drainage will have little effect if the underlying problem is caused by deficiencies outside the area to be upgraded. It is therefore essential that there is a degree of planning so that upgrading measures are seen in an overall context. The action programming approach presented in Chapter 3 is one option for ensuring satisfactory overall planning.

Levels of service

Levels of service can be specified in terms of where services are provided, for instance water supply at a public standpost rather than on-plot. They can also be gauged in terms of the regularity of services, the time for which they are available and the quality of the service supplied. The service levels provided must be related to :

- ◆ affordability and willingness to pay;
- ◆ the levels below which there will be no discernable benefits;
- ◆ the limits set by public bodies. and
- ◆ their acceptability to the intended beneficiaries.

In general, it is better to provide a basic level of service to everyone than to provide a better level of service to part of the population.

Methods of assessing affordability, willingness to pay and acceptability are outlined in Chapters 4 and 12. The chapters on specific services include coverage of the links between the level of service provided and the benefits achieved.

Design and construction standards

The purpose of design and construction standards is to ensure that facilities fulfil their intended functions and will continue to do so over their intended lifetimes. **They should therefore be related to the location and required functions of facilities rather than being set arbitrarily on the basis of standards adopted in another quite different set of circumstances.** For example, the minimum cover over a sewer in a pedestrian lane can be much less than that under a heavily trafficked main road. Specific construction standards are discussed at the appropriate places in the chapters on individual services. However, it should be noted that many of the standards presently followed in Pakistan are not based on function and location but are adapted from those applied in the very different conditions of Europe and North America. Efforts should be made to ensure that a rational approach to the setting of appropriate standards is generally introduced. It is unwise in the long term to adopt special standards, differing from those in general use, for individual upgrading projects.

Cost recovery

The limited resources available to government mean that the scope and extent of upgrading work will be restricted unless the intended beneficiaries contribute something towards its costs. This contribution may be made in various ways including:

- ◆ as direct expenditure in schemes managed directly by individuals or community groups;
- ◆ as a contribution to some form of government or NGO run matching grant scheme;

- ◆ as standard service connection and user charges;
- ◆ as a payment in return for regularisation of tenure. This is only an option in katchi abadis;
- ◆ as some form of betterment tax; and
- ◆ in the form of increased property tax.

In practice, some of the above do not appear to be an option in Pakistan at present while others do not recover full costs. The issue of cost recovery is one that should always be addressed at initial meetings with the community to discuss upgrading proposals. In principle, the aim should be that, above an agreed basic standard, higher levels of service should be provided in return for increased contributions from the beneficiaries.

Operations and maintenance

Improved facilities will only bring lasting benefits if they are properly operated and maintained. When appraising upgrading options, it is therefore always important to consider their operation and maintenance requirements in relation to the available resources and institutional capabilities.

In general, the least satisfactory aspect of many upgrading projects completed to date has been the lack of adequate maintenance subsequent to completion. In the light of this, an aim of upgrading schemes should be to minimise the need for maintenance by public bodies. Options for achieving this by devolving maintenance responsibilities for local facilities to the community will be considered shortly.

APPROACHES TO UPGRADING

As has already been noted, services are eventually provided to most informal areas. The main shortcoming of this activity is that it is piecemeal in nature, can often take many years and is rarely integrated into any overall plan. At worst, the provision of one service may result in a deterioration of conditions because of the absence of a related service. The most obvious example is the provision of on-plot water supplies in the absence of adequate drainage facilities, resulting in ponding of waste water and mosquito breeding. It can be seen that, in order to be effective, improvements must be coordinated, hence the emphasis on the systematic nature of upgrading in the definition given in the introduction.

From the above, it can be deduced that any successful approach to upgrading must ensure that there is a degree of coordination between the actions undertaken in different sectors. However, the coordination of a wide range of concerns is likely to require a high degree of organisation.

Government organisations in developing countries have limited resources and it is unwise to burden them with the control of projects which are unduly complex. It is therefore arguable that it is counterproductive to attempt to coordinate activities other than those which have obvious close links with each other. If this principle is accepted, it is legitimate to coordinate a sanitation improvement programme with health education initiatives but questionable whether either should be linked directly with income generation efforts. (There will always be exceptions to such rules. For instance, income generation is likely to be the prime concern where income levels are so low that no effective improvements can be afforded). This is not to say that an upgrading initiative should not concern itself with a wide range of issues provided that responsibility is devolved to the appropriate organisations with control from a central project unit kept to the minimum necessary to ensure essential coordination. Bearing this point in mind, the three basic approaches to upgrading will now be examined.

Integrated project approach

This makes one organisation, usually a specialist upgrading unit, responsible for the provision of a range of services, including water supply, sewerage and/or drainage and street surfacing and perhaps solid waste collection and street lighting. In Pakistan, most integrated projects have been implemented through development authorities, often with financial assistance from lending institutions such as the World Bank. Projects in Karachi are implemented by the Karachi Metropolitan Corporation Department of Katchi Abadis rather than the Karachi Development Authority.

Advantages

The advantages of the integrated approach are that it is relatively easy to administer and that it ensures that action on the various services is coordinated. We have already noted however that these advantages may be negated if a project tries to cover too wide a spectrum of actions. Because of its relative administrative simplicity, the integrated approach has been widely advocated by international lending agencies. Despite this, the approach does present some fundamental problems and it is important to be aware of these when deciding whether to adopt it.

Problems

The most fundamental problem stems from the fact that specialist upgrading units are responsible for a range of services. Since there are few informal areas where there is no action to improve services, either by government departments or by self-help action, this can lead to a duplication of responsibilities and activities. This in turn can increase maintenance problems as facilities are pro-

vided by the upgrading unit and then handed over to another organisation for operation and maintenance.

Another shortcoming of many integrated projects is that they fail to influence other initiatives. This shortcoming is a direct consequence of the setting up of special units outside the normal government structures. There is a danger that such units and the projects for which they are responsible will cease when external funding stops.

Conditions for success of approach

In view of the above, care is needed at the identification stage of any integrated project to ensure that it meets the following conditions:

◆ that there is general consensus among all affected government and non-government organisations on the need for a specialist upgrading unit and the extent of its responsibilities;

◆ that there is an agreement with the organisations responsible for maintenance that they will take over facilities once they have been commissioned and it has been established that they have adequate funds for this purpose; and

◆ that the powers of the upgrading unit are clearly set out in accordance with current legislation and generally accepted practice.

In general, these conditions are most likely to be met in fringe areas where the existing level of servicing is very low and needs are such that they cannot be met from normal budgets. Where an integrated project approach is adopted, it is important to consider from the outset how the upgrading unit will eventually be accommodated by or absorbed within the overall administrative structure.

Coordinated approach

This approach aims to coordinate the efforts of all those individuals, groups and organisations working to improve conditions in informal areas. The organisations include municipalities, specialist infrastructure agencies and possibly NGOs. The approach is theoretically very attractive because by working through existing organisations it helps to strengthen those organisations and enhance their powers. It should also reduce problems caused by duplication of efforts and responsibilities between different organisations.

Conditions for success of approach

If the coordinated approach is to be successful ,it is necessary that there should be generally agreed procedures to ensure that actions are coordinated. There must also be a structure which allows decisions to be made and conflicts to be resolved. At the district level, this might be achieved by a working group, comprising local councillors, community representatives and officers of the various concerned government departments and agencies. The action programming process described in Chapter 3 could form a basis for agreeing priorities and monitoring progress.

The local municipality must take a lead role in any coordinated improvement scheme. This may present problems where the municipality has limited financial and technical resources. For example, a small municipal committee with one diploma engineer, perhaps shared with other municipalities, and limited funds would seem to be capable of achieving only limited goals. Two conclusions follow from this situation, that:

◆ tasks must be assigned to the various involved organisations in a way which matches responsibility to capability; and

◆ there is a need to provide support services to organisations, groups and individuals with limited resources.

As a general rule, tasks should be assigned as follows:

On-plot facilities - Individual households;

Local services - Local offices and representatives of municipalities and specialist agencies and/or community groups;

District/town/city level services - central design/construction sections of specialist agencies.

Involvement of non-specialists

For technical and safety reasons, non-specialists should not be involved with the installation of electricity and gas services. Provision of these services at the local level should therefore remain the responsibility of specialist agencies, ideally through their local area offices. The same is generally true of water supply although there is scope for some provision of local services by non-specialists, using materials such as galvanised steel which are relatively easy to install. Sewerage, drainage, street surfacing, street lighting and solid waste disposal all offer scope for involvement by non-specialist organisations.

Issues relating to legislation

A potential problem with the division of responsibilities suggested above is that existing legislation may not allow the provision of local facilities by organisations other that the concerned specialist agencies. Even where existing legislation does not present problems, the specialist agencies may be reluctant to accept the connection of facilities provided by other organisations to their systems. These potential problems must be examined at the start of any new upgrading initiative. Where changes in practice are

thought to be necessary, agreement must be reached with the concerned parties and any necessary changes in legislation must be enacted before the changes are made.

The need for support services

Support services are essential if effective improvements are to be extended to the smaller municipalities. These services should include, among others, the following:-

◆ supply of standard details and documents;

◆ provision of advice on specific problems;

◆ where necessary, assistance in preparing schemes; and

◆ where appropriate, provision of financial assistance.

A point that is often overlooked is that there is a need to provide support for community based and self-help activity. Where community organisation is well established, this support may be purely technical in nature. However, the more general situation will be that there is a need to provide institutional support to community organisations. These points will be considered further in Chapter 2.

In general, the coordinated approach should always be the preferred option where the budgets of municipalities and local groups can finance the demand for services. This will usually be the case in established, slow-growing areas. It may also be appropriate in areas where rapid growth results in a need for external funding. The critical issue in such areas will be the way in which funds are allocated and distributed to the various organisations involved. One option will be to set up a special co-ordination unit. This will result in an administrative structure that has similarities to that suggested for the integrated approach, the crucial difference being that the unit in the coordinated approach would not undertake work directly.

Provision of services by community action

A certain amount of community involvement is essential in projects are to result in long-term benefits. At the very least, there must be provision for community involvement in decision making. Provision of services by community action implies something more, the involvement of the community as the major actors in the upgrading process. For technical reasons, this involvement is likely to be possible mainly at the local level although decisions made about local facilities will have an influence on the primary and secondary level facilities required.

Given the present situation in Pakistan in which the capacity of local government to provide and maintain services is limited, there is a strong argument for trying to devolve some responsibilities to the local communities. Because of the importance of the subject, Chapter 2 will be devoted entirely to community involvement.

2.

COMMUNITY INVOLVEMENT

SUMMARY

This chapter looks at the important subject of community involvement in upgrading schemes. It distinguishes between community involvement through participation in government or other schemes and community management and control of schemes. Participation must be present, at the very least, if upgrading schemes are to be appropriate to needs and respected by the community. Community management potentially offers more, the chance to provide services in a way that reduces the demand on scarce government resources. However, there are preconditions for the success of attempts to involve the community, particularly when the aim is to achieve community management. Where these preconditions are not met, any project or programme must be preceded by efforts to bring about the conditions required for the appropriate level of community involvement.

The community management option is most appropriate for tertiary level works and the chances to use it in a wider context will usually be limited. Where it is being introduced for the first time, a demonstration phase should be followed by a consolidation phase, during which the emphasis should be on institutional arrangements, and an expansion phase, aimed at the general introduction of the approach.

If effective community involvement is to be achieved, there must be good channels of communication between government officials and community members. Facilitators or motivators can help the communication process and are particularly important in ensuring that the concerns of women, children and disadvantaged groups are considered. Community meetings also provide a means of communication.

KEY POINTS

◆

Community involvement in upgrading schemes and in particular in deciding priorities and objectives is essential if there are to be lasting benefits.

◆

There are two basic approaches to community involvement in upgrading work, community participation and community management. In the former, control of the scheme remains with the appropriate government authorities. The latter is a more radical approach which devolves power and responsibilities to the community.

◆

Both approaches require acceptance of the need for community involvement by government and a demand for involvement from the community.

◆

For the community management approach to be successful, additional conditions must be met; it must offer clear benefits to both government and the community, legislation and by-laws must allow for it and adequate support services must be provided.

◆

Best results are obtained if community action is organised at the level of the lane, typically in groups of 15-30 households.

BACKGROUND

Many agencies and organisations involved in upgrading work state their commitment to the principle of community involvement. Despite this, levels of community involvement in upgrading schemes remain generally low. This is often because little thought has been given at the beginning of a project to what community involvement is, what is its purpose and how it is going to achieve this purpose. The aim of this chapter is to give answers to these questions, to give an introduction to the various approaches to community involvement and to highlight some key features of these approaches.

A fundamental question concerns what is meant by the term community in the context of community involvement. Some sense of community exists at all levels of society from the family, through the street and district levels to the country or ethnic group. Thus, community involvement could have a wide range of meanings. The main concern of this manual is with communities at the street and local district (mohalla)level although the need for umbrella organisations to coordinate the activities of such local groups will also be considered.

A possible model for community involvement in upgrading is provided by the Orangi Pilot Project (OPP) in Karachi. Another possible model is that of the community development councils (CDCs) in Sri Lanka. Concepts from both

are included in the present chapter. The OPP experience shows that community management of local schemes can work in Pakistan but this management has been achieved for sewers which are not connected to government-owned facilities. It therefore leaves some questions about the relationship between communities and government to be answered. This relationship is a central concern of the chapter.

The first part of the chapter gives the possible objectives of community involvement in upgrading projects and relates these objectives to two approaches to community involvement. Attention is then focused on the preconditions for involvement and the action required in advance of programmes which aim to involve the community. The second part of the chapter provides an introduction to the processes and organisational structures required for community involvement.

OBJECTIVES

The objectives of community involvement can extend to any one of the following levels:

Basic level
◆ to ensure that facilities provided are appropriate to needs and to ensure that they are properly used;

a: Top-down approach: Community not consulted resulting in rigid and often inappropriate assumptions in project design. Result: Alienation of the community

b: Consultation with the community can lead to more fluid process with community involved at every stage Result: Successful project

Figure 2.1. Comparison of top-down approach with that of involving the community

Second level
- ◆ to achieve basic level objectives plus a reduction in costs and/ or an increased rate of implementation;

Third level
- ◆ to strengthen community organisation and capabilities, achieving the basic and second level objectives in the process.

Every upgrading project should aim to achieve the basic level of community involvement and the higher levels should be achieved whenever possible. Figure 2.1 provides a visual illustration of the benefits of involving the community in services provision.

The most important factor in ensuring that basic level objectives are met is the involvement of the community in the decision making process and in particular in the setting of goals. This involvement must allow the community to put forward its views on its needs and priorities and in this respect professionals involved in upgrading need to be able to listen and avoid preconceived ideas. Where necessary, they must then be able to act as teachers and provide the opportunity to widen the understanding of community members. This is particularly important where people are not aware of the benefits of upgrading measures, for instance the potential benefits to health of improved sanitation or solid waste collection facilities. Only when people perceive the benefits of a measure will they be prepared to contribute towards providing it.

Reductions in cost to government can be achieved either by involving community groups directly in the provision of facilities, as in Orangi, or through matching grant schemes which require a contribution from the community. Shifting the burdens of cost and administration from the government to the community should enable available resources to go further and thus allow an increased rate of implementation. Experience shows, however, that attempts to reduce costs and increase the implementation rate by using community members as cheap labour are unlikely to be successful.

Some strengthening in community organisation should result from any attempt to involve the community in upgrading works but better results are likely if this aim is explicit rather than implicit.

APPROACHES TO COMMUNITY INVOLVEMENT

There are two basic approaches to community involvement in upgrading work. These are:
Community participation; and
Community management.

Community participation is the term used when communities are involved in upgrading work but do not take the lead in managing it. Control remains with the government agency responsible for the work but the intention is that the community participation process ensures that the concerns of the community are taken into account in its planning and execution.

Perhaps the greatest danger with the community participation approach is that of agency short-circuiting. This happens when an agency promotes community participation in theory but in practice cuts out the sometimes lengthy processes of reaching community agreement.

Community management is the term used when the management of upgrading work and and subsequent operation and maintenance tasks is devolved to the community. The approach is particularly attractive where government lacks the resources to provide and maintain improved facilities on the scale required to eliminate deficiencies. In any event, experience suggests that effective management of facilities is more likely to be achieved if it is devolved to those who have a direct interest in their performance. The present situation in Pakistan, with many informal areas without basic services and the majority with inadequate provision for operation and maintenance, suggests that community management of facilities should be promoted.

The **matching grant** schemes at present implemented in rural areas in Pakistan are a compromise between the two approaches introduced above. Technical aspects of the schemes are the responsibility of local government engineers but a committee including representatives of the community is responsible for overall planning and financial management.

Figure 2.2 diagrammatically illustrates the long-term advantages of a community management approach in a situation where government resources are insufficient to operate and maintain the facilities provided.

An important point to note regarding community management is that it does not necessarily mean construction by the community. In many cases, small contractors will be used, as could be government resources on occasion. The important thing is that control remains with the community.

The community participation approach may be expected to achieve the basic objectives noted in the previous section. If second and third level objectives are to be achieved, it will normally be necessary to adopt a community management approach. The choice of approach will therefore depend on the objectives to be achieved but these in turn should be framed in relation to the preconditions for community involvement which will now be examined.

PREPARING FOR COMMUNITY INVOLVEMENT

Preconditions for community involvement

In order for the basic aims of community involvement to be achieved, the preconditions to be met are as follows:

◆ the government officers and institutions concerned must accept that the community has a role in decision making;

◆ there must be a community demand for the proposed works, in other words, people must want the problem to be solved;

◆ the information required to make informed decisions must be available to the community;

The community management approach with its more ambitious objectives will require that the following additional preconditions are met:

◆ there must be clear benefits to both community and government in the community management approach and both must perceive these benefits;

◆ available technologies must be within the community's capacity to finance, construct, manage and maintain;

◆ the community must understand its options and be willing to take responsibility for the system;

◆ the existing legisation and government policy framework must permit and support community management;

◆ the community must have the institutional capacity and personnel resources to manage the development and operation of the system;

◆ effective support services must be available to the community through either government or NGOs and the people must have faith in the individuals and organisations providing these services.

Initial investigation of community involvement options

Before embarking on a programme to involve the community in upgrading work, the existence or otherwise of these preconditions must be investigated. Where some or all do not exist, further investigations are required to determine the action that would be required to bring them about. These initial investigations should cover:

◆ existing legislation/government procedures; do they allow for the possibility of community involvement ?

◆ the attitudes of government officials at all levels to the idea of community involvement;

◆ the willingness of community members to become involved in upgrading schemes; and

◆ existing community organisations and their potential for involvement in upgrading work.

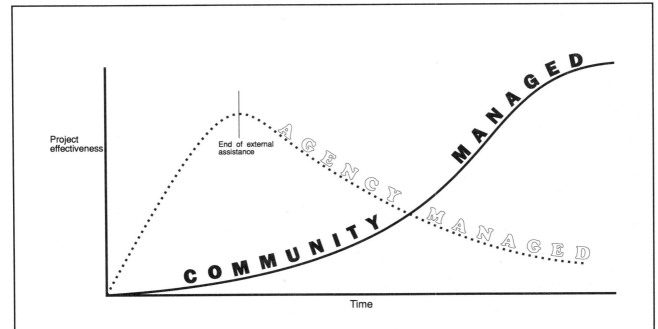

Figure 2.2. Possible long-term performance of agency and community managed projects

The investigation must be wide ranging as it is concerned with the overall potential for community involvement rather than local conditions. The social survey techniques described in Chapter 4 should be used for investigations in the community. In-depth interview techniques may also be used to obtain the views of government officials.

Preparation for a community involvement programme

In the likely event that all the preconditions for community involvement are not met, a preparation phase will be required before a programme can be introduced. This might involve:

◆ lectures, seminars and workshops for government officials designed to convince them of the need for community involvement and explain how they can act to promote it;

◆ similar consciousness-raising exercises in the communities which are targeted for early upgrading works. and

◆ action to ensure that the necessary amendments to existing legislation, by-laws and working practices are made.

An important example of the last concerns tariffs for water supply and sewerage connections. It is reasonable to assume that user charges should be reduced for community managed facilities but some charge will still be necessary to pay for the operation and maintenance of the higher order facilities to which community managed facilities are connected. Fair charging rates and mechanisms must be in operation from the outset if the community managed option is to work.

Limits of community management

When considering the community management approach, it is important to have an idea of the limits of its viability. An example can illustrate this point. Attempts to involve the community in the overall planning of water supply services are unlikely to be successful because community members will not have the necessary information and knowledge. This is not to say that community involvement is not possible and desirable. For example the views of community members on such topics as service levels should be obtained. Nevertheless, the main opportunities for community management will occur at the tertiary level. The situation with regard to individual services is as follows.

Street paving Community management of the paving of local lanes is possible although some technical assistance is required if falls are critical to drainage. (See Chapters 7 and 8)

Sewerage and sanitation Community construction and management of sewers is possible if agreement on procedures and tariff structures can be reached with the concerned authorities. Some technical assistance in planning and implementation will be required. (See Chapter 6). The organisation of individual householders to provide on-plot sanitation can be managed at the community level.

Water supply There is some scope for tertiary provision if above-ground galvanised steel GI mains are used. Further details are given in Chapter 5. The points made for sewers regarding procedures and tariff structures apply.

Solid waste collection Management of local collection services through the community is possible but successful operation will be dependent on the provision of district level services by the municipal authorities.

Successful efforts to promote community management will move the interface between privately managed and publicly managed facilities. Good planning can facilitate connections at this interface. For instance, laterals may be laid from main sewers to shallow connection chambers at the entrances of lanes and branches from water mains can be brought to the surface and plugged, in readiness for later connections of community or municipality-built surface GI mains.

Choice of approach

The choice of approach will be influenced by the findings of the initial investigation and the outcome of preliminary efforts to set the stage for community involvement. If it seems that the preconditions for community management are either present or attainable, the aim should be to provide an organisational and legislative framework that allows individual communities to provide and manage some of their own services. Communities and local groups can then consider the costs and benefits of a community management approach and make their own choice of approach. Where it is unlikely that the pre-conditions for community management can be achieved, a community participation approach should be adopted.

In theory, such an approach should guarantee a minimum level of service provision with higher levels being possible where the community takes responsibility for them. For instance, the government might provide water to a standpost at the end of a lane but the design might allow for individual connections, thus giving lane residents the option of organising themselves to provide a service line in the lane. In practice, there is little formal experience of such an incremental approach, at least in Pakistan. However, the fact that community management can offer the advantages of early service provision, guaranteed maintenance and some reduction in tariffs would possibly be enough to encourage people to adopt a community management approach.

Another point to consider when considering the choice of approach is the way in which the community managed option can be integrated into a conventional project approach. To some extent, the two are incompatable. Projects have set targets which normally must be achieved in a time frame of at most 5-6 years. In contrast, a community managed programme will tend to start slowly and build up momentum over a rather longer period. One way of overcoming this problem is to restrict project funding to primary and secondary level facilities and provide for those at the tertiary level under local and community funding. If this approach is to be adopted, is is important that adequate planning and support frameworks for local initiatives are available. Procedures for establishing the planning framework will be considered in Chapter 3.

IMPLEMENTATION STRATEGIES

(a) For a community managed programme

A programme giving the option of community management is possible if the necessary pre-conditions are present or attainable. This does not mean that it will automatically happen. Where there is no tradition of community management of services, it is advisable to demonstrate the viability of the approach before attempting to introduce it widely. This can be done by adopting a staged approach to the introduction of community management involving the following phases:

- **a demonstration phase** involving a pilot scheme or schemes designed to test out the community management approach and demonstrate its viability;

- **a consolidation phase** with an emphasis on developing and proving the institutional and support arrangements required to allow the approach to operate on a large scale; and

- **an expansion phase** aimed at the general introduction of the approach.

Each of these phases will now be briefly considered.

Demonstration phase

This phase may be used to demonstrate and test appropriate technologies as well as the community management option. It should follow on from the initial investigations of existing conditions, priorities, attitudes and levels of organisation already described. The area selected for a demonstration phase should fulfill the following conditions:

- it should be fairly typical of the areas to be upgraded but without any particularly difficult problems;

- there should be access to any off-site infrastructure required for the technologies likely to be preferred; and

- there should be evidence of a sense of community solidarity and willingness to become involved in a community managed scheme.

The third condition should ideally be demonstrated by the fact that the community asks to be included in the programme.

The demonstration schemes should be monitored to determine the cost of the facilities and the level of support services provided and any problems encountered in organisation, legislation and liaison with government authorities.

Opportunities must be given for government officials and representatives from other communities to see the demonstration schemes being implemented and operated. The communities selected for inclusion in the demonstration phase should be aware of this and must agree to receive visitors.

Consolidation phase

The emphasis in this phase switches from the individual scheme to the framework within which similar schemes can be implemented. Primary objectives of the phase must be to develop the suport structures and mechanisms which will allow the demonstration schemes to be widely replicated. Particular tasks required during this phase include:

- framing the changes in legislation, regulations and procedures necessary to facilitate a community managed approach;

- planning and development of the institutions necessary to provide support to community efforts. These might include government bodies, NGOs or a combination of the two;

- setting up of training procedures and facilities for support staff;

- setting up of training procedures and facilities for community members; and

- establishment of arrangements such as matching grant schemes, loan facilities and revolving funds to unlock community resources.

These tasks are essential. Without a workable institutional structure, the community managed approach cannot progress and experience suggests that initiatives which do not move towards a comprehensive development effort eventually wither and die.

During the consolidation phase, monitoring and evaluation of the pilot projects should continue and new projects should be started. Rapid development of ideas and responses can be expected and indeed is desirable at this stage. There is therefore particular need for regular review of the process and its achievements and this review should involve programme planners, community facilitators and community members.

Expansion phase

During the expansion phase, the emphasis moves to the promotion of upgrading through the community managed approach throughout the project area. (If the emphasis is on a programme rather than a project, the area to be considered may be a city, a province or even the whole country). The techniques used in promoting the approach may include:

◆ advertising through the media; and

◆ working through extension agents.

The former is likely to reach more people for a given expenditure but it has limitations in that it does not provide opportunities for in-depth discussions of the options and cannot take local conditions into account. The techniques should therefore be seen as complementary with the media being used to introduce concepts and extension agents deployed to follow them up.

In order to maximise the utility of extension agents, they should be based at well advertised local offices so that they are readily approachable by groups who want to implement a community managed approach.

(b) To achieve community participation

A degree of participation often exists in municipality-built schemes in that requests for improvements in services often originate in the community. The first priorities when promoting community participation should be to:

◆ formalise and standardise existing informal procedures;

◆ provide some means of programming the actions requested; and

◆ ensure that all are fairly represented in the process.

The action programming process described in Chapter 3 provides a possible framework within which to achieve these aims. As for the community management option, community participation procedures should be tested and demonstated on a small scale before they are intoduced generally. The best area for a demonstration project will be one in which the councillor or councillors are sympathetic to participation and the community shows that it wants to

be involved. The demonstration projects should therefore be selected after initial meetings with councillors, community representatives and ordinary community members. Preference should be given to areas which already show a degree of egalitarian community organisation.

Community participation is only meaningful if people are involved in the initial decisions as to what should be included in the upgrading programme. Social surveys and community meetings can be used to obtain information on what people want but **these must precede rather than follow decisions on programme content**. Ideally, decisions on programme content should be made at community meetings. These initial meetings should perhaps cover districts of 500-1000 houses. Subsequent meetings on the detailed implementation of the programme should be concerned with local neighbourhoods, typically comprising one or more streets and 15-50 households.

CHANNELS OF COMMUNICATION

The role of facilitators

Effective community involvement in upgrading is only possible if good channels of communication exist between communities and administrators. Facilitators help to provide this communication and thus overcome gaps in understanding between people and project planners. As Figure 2.3 suggests, they can have a particularly important role in ensuring that the needs of women, children and disadvantaged groups are taken into account.

During the planning phase of a project, the facilitators work with the community, helping the people to articulate their views and concerns and motivating them to become involved in actions to improve their living conditions. (In the OPP, they are in fact referred to as motivators rather than facilitators. They could also be described as extension agents). This phase should extend over several weeks during which one facilitator will normally be working with several groups. During this phase, each facilitator should take care to seek the views of disadvantaged or weaker groups within the community and should also look for any political or social factors which may infuence the way in which decisions are made. He or she should then guide the community in the choice of technologies and approaches and should finally give advice on how to plan for implementation.

For community managed schemes, the facilitator should provide guidance on construction supervision and the resolution of technical queries and problems. He or she should also act for the supporting authority in ensuring that minimum standards of workmanship are achieved, calling on the services of technical specialists as required.

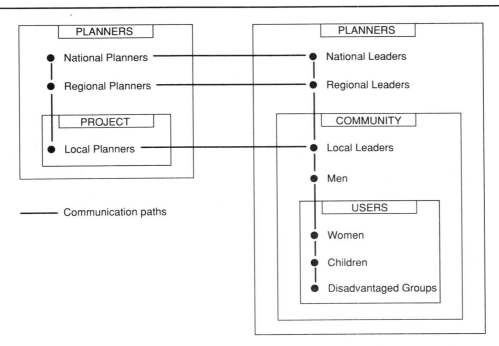

Project Planners normally speak with the community through Local Leaders who are assumed to represent the whole community.

(a) Communication paths without facilitators

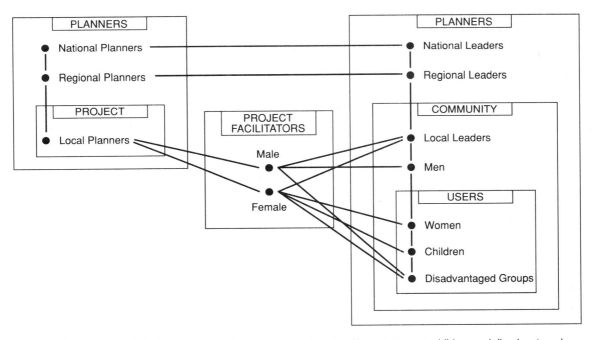

Male and Female facilitators can work on an individual basis with men, women, children and disadvantaged groups to bring them into the planning process and find out their needs.

(b) Improved communication paths with facilitators

(Based on Diagram in SEARO Regional Health Papers No 9, WHO, New Delhi 1985)

Figure 2.3. Role of facilitators in improving communication between project planners and communities

facilitator at this stage is to bring the concerns of the community to the notice of the project management.

Another important role of facilitators is to impress upon people the importance of correct operation and mainte-nance of facilities. In community managed schemes, they will have a direct role in introducing people to the required maintenance schedules and ensuring that the management structure required to undertake all the necessary tasks is in place. Even in schemes managed by the authorities, there will be a need to provide people with information on what to do in the event of problems.

It is preferable if facilitators are closely matched in back-ground and customs with groups that they are dealing with. There is much to be said for recruiting them from the communities with which they are working. A reasonable level of secondary schooling will normally be required but commitment and interest in the work are more important than formal qualifications.

Facilitators should be trained in social development skills but they should also have some understanding of the technologies that they are likely to be involved with. Male and female facilitators will be required in order that interviews can take place with men, women and children. In most cases, it will be appropriate for a team of one male and one female facilitator to work together.

It is sometimes argued that facilitators should be non-directive but a completely non-directive approach is im-possible and probably undesirable. What is important is that they should listen to the views of community mem-bers and allow a dialogue while emphasising the impor-tance of the key issues.

Community meetings

Ongoing informal communication between project plan-ners and the community is provided by facilitators. This should be supplemented at the appropriate times by meetings designed to provide an opportunity for discus-sion and agreement on key issues. Such meetings are required:

◆ when the possibility of upgrading is first mooted;

◆ in order to decide between the participatory and community management approaches; and

◆ at intervals during planning and implementation.

It is arguable, and is indeed strongly held by the OPP that the unit of organisation for community based work should be the lane. This corresponds with the experience in Sri Lanka where the size of CDCs seldom exceed 50 households. Meetings organised at the lane level can be attended by representatives of all the households in the lane plus the facilitators and technical personnel. Because of the importance of obtaining the views of women, they should be encouraged to attend or a separate meeting should be held if this proves impossible. At the first meeting a representative or representatives of the community should be elected. In the OPP model an organiser is chosen who is then responsible for ensuring that the community deliver their side of the agreement. The organisers handle all financial matters so that OPP itself does not become involved with finances. This is a principle which should be followed as far as is possible in all schemes. The CDC model differs slightly in that each CDC has a management committee.

Where the community participation approach is favoured, lane level meetings will provide an opportunity for site specific problems to be resolved. However, there will also be a need for meetings covering larger areas, possibly the mohalla or even the district, particularly at the beginning of a project. In the first instance, open meetings should be held, perhaps several meetings if the area is big. Later, it may be appropriate to hold regular meetings attended by representatives of the community. Representation might be on the basis of area or sections of the community but in general both will be required. Special efforts should be made to represent women adequately.

There is a danger that some sections of society will be inadequately represented at public meetings. Women are an example. It is important, therefore, that public meetings should be complemented by other means of assessing people's priorities and views. These may have to be small-scale and relatively private and could take the form of informal discussions between facilitators and community members. The facilitators may then bring the results of these discussions to community meetings.

Another danger is that committees may turn out to be self-serving and unrepresentative. This danger can be reduced if committee members have clear responsibilities and duties.

3.

PREPARATION OF ACTION PROGRAMMES

SUMMARY

The theme of this chapter is the need to provide a framework within which communities, political representatives, government officers and NGOs can act to improve conditions in informal areas. The suggestion is that this framework can be provided by local action programmes and the main concern of the chapter is with the procedures for developing such programmes. Local action programmes require data collection, presentation and analysis, development and evaluation of possible strategies for meeting needs, selection of a preferred strategy and conversion of this into an action programme, implementation of the programme components and continuing monitoring and evaluation of the success of the programme.

The key to the success of programmes will be the extent to which all those affected by them are involved in the decision making process. It is advisable that the decision on the programme to be adopted should be made at an open meeting or workshop attended by all those concerned with the programme. This will form the focal point but will be only one point in an ongoing process which emphasises community involvement.

KEY POINTS

◆

Action programmes provide a context within which the various initiatives in upgrading areas can be integrated.

◆

The boundaries of areas covered by action programmes should be fixed in the light of physical features and political/administrative divisions. Programmes will typically cover about 500 ha.

◆

Although superficially similar to conventional planning approaches, the action programme approach places much more emphasis on involving all those concerned with the outcome in the planning process.

◆

The institutional and financial capacities of municipalities and other organisations are explicitly considered in the approach.

◆

Key decisions are made at public meetings or workshops.

◆

Ongoing monitoring of implementation is essential. Regular updating of the programme must be carried out in the light of this monitoring.

BACKGROUND

By definition, informal areas are unplanned in any overall sense although it is true that there is a degree of planning in many individual residential subdivisions. The lack of overall planning gives rise to problems, for instance with drainage, which must be tackled at an overall level. The situation is made worse by the way in which local government funds are channelled through local councillors and other political representatives, with little attempt being made to ensure that actions are coordinated. The result is considerable wastage of valuable resources.

To date, the master plans and structure plans produced for Pakistani cities have had limited effects. This is partly due to a failure to develop and interpret city-wide plans and concepts at the local level. An attempt to introduce local plans was made in Peshawar in 1986-87 but this failed because there was no political will to enforce the development control procedures on which it was based. The lesson from this and other experiences is that successful local planning is dependent on involving the politicians, community organisations and institutions operating at the local level. The processes by which the plans are prepared are at least as important as their content in ensuring that they are followed.

The action programming concept proposed in this chapter provides a possible approach to planning at the local level. It provides a framework within which the various schemes and initiatives within an area can be integrated. It is based on the approach used in Peshawar but with the emphasis firmly placed on obtaining consensus on the required programmes rather than enforcing development patterns through development control.

THE ACTION PROGRAMME APPROACH

Scope and scale of action programmes

Action programmes must be concerned with services and infrastructure although the precise scope of any individual programme will depend on local conditions and priorities. Programmes should also provide a degree of guidance to the development of new built-up areas.

The area covered by programmes should be sufficient for the needs of the strategic infrastructure to be considered but small enough to allow a process in which local communities can be involved. In effect, this will mean that a single programme will suffice for a small town but separate programmes should be prepared for the various districts in larger cities. No hard and fast rules can be given but it is probable that individual action programmes should not cover areas greater than about 500 ha.

The action programme process

The steps involved in the action programme process are:

◆ collection of data on existing situation and identification of problems and needs;

◆ development of general strategies to deal with these problems and needs;

◆ agreement on action to be undertaken and responsibilities for action;

◆ preparation and implementation of individual plan components; and

◆ monitoring and evaluation.

In many cases, the first two can be based on the data collected for overall city plans. Certainly, the strategies for local areas must be compatible with these overall plans.

If it is to be successful, an action programme must not be a matter for the planning authority only, whether this be a development authority or a municipality. Rather, all those who will either be affected by the plans or will be concerned with implementing them must be represented in the planning process from the start. They will include among others:

local residents;
comunity based organisations (CBOs);
political representatives;
specialist infrastructure agencies and departments;
other service providers;
land-owners and commercial/industrial interests.

The challenge is to develop procedures which involve all these groups and persuade them of the need to work within mutually agreed guidelines. The need for consultation at all stages cannot be over-emphasised.

The ways in which local residents can be involved in local upgrading initiatives have been described in Chapter 2. The action programme approach has more widespread concerns but many of the points made in that chapter are also relevant at this broader level. The OPP experience has shown that it is possible for planning to develop upwards from the lane level to that at which local collector sewers and drains are provided. This suggests that there is a need to develop links between community action at the local level and community involvement in planning at the district level. This might be done by providing places for representatives of CBOs on a district planning committee charged with the implementation of the action programme.

Another point to be emphasised is the need to involve local political representatives in developing and implementing the action programmes. It must be recognised that planning is fundamentally a political process. This is particularly important in view of the large degree of control that local coucillors and elected representatives have over development funds.

Bearing these points in mind, the steps in the process will now be examined in more detail.

THE STAGES IN THE PROCESS

Data collection

The data collected should cover physical conditions, existing infrastructure and services, planned programmes, institutional arrangements and the attitudes and priorities of residents. Each of these is briefly examined below.

Physical conditions and existing services

Information on physical conditions and existing services can be collected from existing records, by site visits and by talking to residents and employees of the concerned organisations who have knowledge of local facilities. This information should then be shown on a series of plans which should include:

◆ a base plan showing physical features, roads, streets, lanes and any other rights of way, developed and undeveloped areas, and any other important features. This plan should ideally be at a scale of 1:2500, 1:5000 or their imperial equivalents. Where resources are limited, the techniques described in Chapter 4 may be used to develop adequate base plans.

◆ a land-use plan, developed from the base plan. This should show types of development, ie. formally sanctioned housing, un-authorised land subdivisions, katchi abadis etc. Any industrial and commercial areas, land used by or allotted for public facilities such as schools and land which is currently undeveloped should also be shown.

◆ a plan showing land ownership. It is not necessary that this plan should show all land holdings but only publicly owned land, for instance any owned by the Auqaf, and perhaps major private land holdings.

◆ plans for the major infrastructure components. These should include plans for water supply, sewerage, drainage, electricity supply, street lighting and street surfacing. The street lighting and surfacing information may be presented in the form of inventories with streets numbered on the base plan.

◆ A plan showing the political and administrative boundaries.

All these plans should be prepared in the first instance to show the existing situation. They can then be used as the basis upon which to develop proposals for new development and provision of new facilities.

Proposed schemes

It is important that the Action Programme takes into account all existing proposals. Information should therefore be obtained from all the relevant government departments and agencies about their future plans for the area. These can then be shown on the base plans, distinguishing between those schemes that are firmly committed and those that are tentative. The former should definitely be included in the action programme but the opportunity may be taken to review the latter during the preparation of the programme.

Institutional arrangements

Information on institutional structures and capabilities will be required in order to determine how action programme proposals can be implemented. Points to be investigated include:

◆ whether local offices of municipalities, government departments and infrastructure agencies exist and, if so, what powers are devolved to them;

◆ the size of the capital budgets of the various departments and agencies, the ways in which these budgets are used and whether they are sufficient to implement the options examined.

◆ the manning levels, both theoretical and actual, of the concerned departments and agencies, together with present staff capabilities;

◆ the present budgets, availability of skills and potential capabilities of the organisations and departments responsible for maintenance;

◆ the present activities and potential for involvement in development work of NGOs and CBOs.

It may be difficult to obtain precise information on some of these subjects. Even where this is the case, it should be possible to obtain some basic qualitative information which will be useful in planning. For instance, where it is found that the existing solid waste collection service is inadequate, the reason may be that staffing levels, operational budgets or both are deficient. In such a situation, it is doubtful whether the running costs of major initiatives to improve the service will be affordable unless they include measures to improve cost recovery and devolve some responsibility for collection to local communities.

Attitudes and priorities of residents

Valuable information on the attitudes and priorities of residents can be obtained by the initial site appraisal and social survey techniques described in Chapter 4. However, the best guarantee that action programmes address the needs of residents will be provided by ensuring first that community involvement at the local level is effective and second that the programme takes full account of the schemes at that level. Indeed, it may prove that the programme is largely driven by the need to accommodate and coordinate local schemes.

Development of a planning/upgrading strategy

The development of a planning and upgrading strategy involves data analysis, the assessment of the various development options and finally the decision on the preferred option. The way in which these tasks are carried out is crucial to the success of the whole Action Programme process. In the past, formal planning exercises have had little effect on the way in which development occurs in informal areas. It is arguable that plans have failed because they have been developed by professionals in the light of the apparently best available information with little reference to either those who will be involved in implementing the proposals or those who will be affected by them. This is true as much for theoretically flexible structure plans as it is for the more deterministic master plan approach. There is thus a need to ensure that the various interested groups are involved at all stages of the development of the strategy. This applies particularly to the decisions on the preferred development option. Brief notes are given below on the tasks required to develop the strategy.

Data analysis

Analysis of the data collected is required in order that problems and needs can be identified. This will include analysis of social, institutional and physical data. The important thing to remember when analysing data is the use to which the analysis results are to be put. With this in mind, data analysis should aim to do the following:

◆ assess present levels of service and identify areas with serious deficiencies;

◆ assess the potential for new development within the programme area;

◆ in the light of the first two, determine the likely demands for services in the area covered by the programme;

◆ estimate the financial and institutional capacity of existing organisations to meet these demands;

◆ analyse existing and programmed primary and secondary facilities in order to determine whether they have any spare capacity to service tertiary upgrading;

Assessment of development options

Development options should be assessed in terms of:

◆ what development actions are required;

◆ who should be responsible for them; and

◆ how they can be financed.

In effect this task requires that a series of scenarios is presented, each starting from the existing situation and projecting forward an approach to upgrading and development. The capital costs to government of each scenario should be assessed, as should its maintenance costs and institutional requirements. It is anticipated that this exercise will often show the clear benefits of community involvement in the financing and management of schemes.

Data collection and development of possible strategies may be expected to take between 4 and 6 months, depending on the professional skills available. Where existing planning skills are limited, as for example in smaller municipalities, there is much to be said for providing some outside input at this stage, possibly from consultants but preferably from a specialist planning unit based in an appropriate ministry, for instance Housing and Physical Planning or Local Government. However, it will be unwise to rely entirely on outside input and the ultimate aim must be to develop local programme planning skills.

Agreement on plan and action programme

Once the various scenarios have been prepared, brief reports highlighting their main features should be circulated to all concerned for information and comment. Representatives of all concerned organisations and groups should then be invited to a meeting or workshop at which the options should be discussed with the intention of reaching agreement on the strategy to be adopted. Sufficient information on costs and financial capabilities should be available to this meeting to enable the broad financial implications of decisions to be assessed.

A planning team or committee, including representatives of all the main interest groups should then be appointed and charged with the task of producing a document outlining the main conclusions reached at the action programme workshop. (In practice, the documents will usually be produced by professionals and approved after scrutiny by committee members).

The main feature of these documents will be the proposed action programme itself but supporting information should also be included so that the finished document presents a complete justification of the proposed programme. This should then be circulated and ratified at another meeting or workshop.

The end result of the process should be an agreed action programme with implementation targets specified for a 5 year period.

Implementation, monitoring and evaluation

Implementation of individual plan components

This should be the responsibility of the concerned organisations and agencies. Where necessary, the intended actions should be included in future budgets and programmes. Some dialogue may be necessary where the action programming process results in major changes in an agencies plans. The planning authority or unit should keep a record of the progress with implementation.

Monitoring and evaluation of progress

The one thing that can be guaranteed is that there will be changes in the programme over the period in which it is implemented. It is therefore important that progress in programme implementation is monitored and that changes are made as necessary to ensure that the programme remains realistic and implementable. Failure to do this will mean that the programme becomes meaningless and the whole process will then collapse. Plans and programmes are only useful when they exist on the ground. The most beautiful and well thought out plan is no use if it remains as a drawing on a wall.

The planning team will have a continuing role in coordinating actions and monitoring the implementation of the plan. A forum for continued public involvement with the plan is also required. This could perhaps take the form of public meetings at intervals of perhaps 6 months at which the progress of the programme could be reviewed and any necessary changes could be approved. The actual requirements may vary from place to place and need to be worked out in practice.

A formal review of progress and updating of the programme should take place at intervals. Comprehensive review at intervals of say every 5 years is one option. A better alternative may be to develop a continuous updating process so that new schemes are introduced to the programme as old ones are implemented.

PRECONDITIONS FOR SUCCESS OF THE APPROACH

In order for the approach to be successful, it must be accepted by all concerned, in particular government officials and politicians. Any attempt to introduce participatory local planning procedures must therefore be preceded by efforts to introduce and explain the approach to politicians and officials. A related point is that the approach must be fully integrated into government procedures, otherwise it will have no influence and will be disregarded by all concerned. Before its introduction, it will therefore be advisable to carry out a study to determine what changes in current government rules and procedures will be required to implement the approach. Action must then be taken to ensure that these changes can be achieved.

The introduction of the approach on a pilot scale in a particular area or areas will provide an opportunity to show politicians and officials how the approach will work. However, it is important that the pilot project is sanctioned at a high level in government and that all concerned are committed to the general adoption of the approach if the pilot scheme proves to be successful.

4.

SITE APPRAISAL AND SURVEY

SUMMARY

This chapter deals with the gathering and organisation of the information required to plan and design upgrading schemes. It covers the initial site appraisal, physical surveys, and social surveys.

The introduction explains the place of each of the above activities in the upgrading process and the reasons why it is required. A section is then devoted to each.

Procedures for initial site inspection are given and a check list of things to look for during this inspection is provided. The collection and analysis of data from existing records is also covered in the section on initial site appraisal.

Survey scales are discussed and a brief introduction to appropriate survey techniques is given. The emphasis is on techniques that can be used to obtain reasonably accurate results quickly.

The section on social surveys covers both qualitative and quantitative surveys. For the latter, a step by step introduction to the planning and implementation of a questionnaire survey is given.

KEY POINTS

◆

It is preferable if preliminary site inspection is undertaken by a mixed team of professionals and community representatives.

◆

Suitable scales for district level plans are 1:2500, 1:5000 and their imperial equivalents.

◆

Suitable scales for detailed planning and design of upgrading schemes are 1:500, 1:1000 and their imperial equivalents.

◆

For small schemes, reasonably accurate plans can be produced by simple plane table and tape survey methods. Extension of these methods to serve larger areas is possible if there is a framework within which the survey can be fitted.

◆

The socio-economic information provided by social surveys helps to ensure that schemes are appropriate and affordable.

◆

Qualitative survey techniques such as in-depth interviews and group discussions should be used to explore people's priorities and the options for upgrading.

◆

Structured questionnaire surveys are an important source of statistically significant information for use in project design.

INTRODUCTION

The first part of this chapter deals with initial site appraisal. This is needed to obtain a preliminary view of problems in order to be able to assess where efforts need to be directed. A physical appraisal on site should preferably be undertaken by a mixed team of professionals and community representatives. It should be supplemented by meetings with infrastructure agencies and inspection of infrastructure plans which will provide information to put its findings into context.

A physical survey of the project area is required if schemes for upgrading infrastructure are to be properly planned and documented. The second part of this chapter is devoted to physical surveys. It considers the scales for survey drawings, the level of detail required and the possibilities for simplifying survey procedures. A brief introduction to survey procedures is also given.

Social surveys are commonly used to obtain information on such factors as household size and income, existing facilities and present practices, preferences etc. It is arguable that not all this information is required for a community based approach but some will be required in all cases. The third part of this chapter provides an introduction to social survey theory and techniques.

INITIAL APPRAISAL

The aim of initial site appraisal is to get a rough qualitative impression of an area and its problems. Information should be gathered on both topographical and physical features and the extent, condition and performance of existing facilities. Initial appraisal should include:

- ◆ site inspection;
- ◆ discussions with community members; and
- ◆ collection of data on existing and proposed services.

Site inspection

Preliminary site inspection may be undertaken by professionals acting alone or by a mixed team of professionals and community representatives. The latter is preferable since it helps to ensure that any action proposed is in accordance with the wishes and perceived needs of residents. Inspection teams should not exceed 4 in number and should include at least one professional, usually an engineer, and one community representative. When there are several teams, as for instance at an action planning workshop, they should pool their findings at the end of the inspection. This will enable dominant themes to be identified and a consensus to be reached on the priorities for action.

There is a danger that the presence of a site inspection team may raise the expectations of community members either too early or in the wrong way. This danger is obviously much reduced if members of the community are involved in the survey. In any event, the survey team should be made aware of the sensitivity of their work and instructed to comply with local customs and practices and avoid making specific promises as to the work to be undertaken. Site inspections should be avoided where there is no intention of implementing improvements.

By their very nature, preliminary site inspections should be open ended and so should not follow a rigid pattern. Nevertheless, a check list of the things to investigate and the actions to take during an inspection will provide a useful framework around which to conduct the inspection. A typical check list is given in Annex 1 at the end of this chapter.

Informal discussions with community members in the course of site appraisal will provide an initial idea of what their problems are and how they view these problems. It will be seen from the checklist at the end of the chapter that some information, for instance that relating to flooding levels and on-plot facilities, can be obtained or checked by talking to local people.

Collection and analysis of existing records

The information gathered by site inspection must be supplemented by that obtained from existing records. Such records will include some or all of the following:

Government survey plans. These will often be out of date but may serve as a basis on which approximate initial site plans can be based. The most useful scale will probably be around 1:2400 - 1:2500 but some useful information may be obtained from smaller scales.

Utilities plans. These will not always be accurate, particularly with regard to tertiary facilities. They should be checked on site, preferably with an operative of the appropriate agency who can confirm or amend what they contain.

The results of any social surveys. These will be particularly useful if they provide information on existing facilities (sanitation facilities etc.).

PHYSICAL SURVEY

As was indicated in the introduction to this chapter, survey plans are essential if upgrading schemes are to be properly planned, designed and documented. There is thus no doubt that survey plans are required but there is a need to decide on appropriate scales and the levels of detail and accuracy that are required for upgrading work.

Survey scales

For district-level planning, the most suitable scale is 1:2500 or its imperial equivalent (1:2400). At these scales, it is possible to show every street and lane, indicate levels and plot water supply mains, sewers, collector drains and catchment boundaries and electricity supply facilities. The type, extent and condition of existing surfacing can be recorded if streets and lanes are numbered and an inventory is prepared. The boundaries of existing development, open space, public facilities, physical features and any standing water can also be shown. The scales are suitable for preliminary planning of infrastructure extensions and improvements.

For detailed design of upgrading schemes, larger scales are required. Normal practice is to use a scale of 1:500 or 1:480 but a scale of 1:1000 will often be adequate, particularly in areas where the majority of plots are larger than about 100m^2 in area. One 1:1000 plan covers the same area as four 1:500 plans and use of the smaller scale can considerably reduce the number of plans needed for larger schemes. On the other hand, 1:1000 plans can become rather congested with information when project proposals are added to them. This problem can be overcome if:

◆ Each service is shown on a different copy of the plan; and

◆ Some information is shown on a separate schedule.

There will sometimes be a need to draw up plans of typical plots. A scale of 1:100 will normally be suitable for this purpose.

Appropriate survey techniques

Plane surveys

The most appropriate survey technique for a given job will depend on the size of the area to be surveyed and the accuracy and level of detail required. Higher order techniques are usually required for larger areas. The options for fixing locations and measuring in plan are as follows:

Tape survey For small sites, it will usually be adequate to measure distances by tape. In built-up areas, it will not always be possible to measure the angles between streets accurately using this method but it should nevertheless be adequate for most upgrading tasks. Tape surveys are relatively easy to carry out and reasonable results should be obtainable by non-specialists after a limited amount of training.

Plane table survey Plane table surveys are extensively used in Pakistan. They have two advantages over tape surveys, the first that the survey can be plotted on the plane table on-site and the second that angles can be measured. It will be advisable to use trained survey technicians for plane table surveys although there is no reason why these technicians should not be trained specially for work on upgrading projects.

Triangulated survey using a theodolite. A theodolite survey is normally used for plans of areas greater than 15-20 ha. The technique is to fix a series of points throughout the area by theodolite traverse and to fill in the detail around these points by plane table and/or tape surveys. A trained surveyor is required for this type of survey.

Given the nature of upgrading, the high degree of accuracy present in triangulated surveys is not strictly required. In the right circumstances reasonably accurate plans can be produced using lower order techniques. The important thing is to have a framework or reference points to which plane table or tape surveys can be tied. The former might be provided by blowing up a smaller scale plan, for instance the 1:20,000 or 1:25,000 survey plans which are available for the larger cities in Pakistan. The stages in production are as follows:

◆ Divide the small-scale map into squares, each typically representing 100m x 100m.

◆ Produce a grid of the squares representing the same area at the larger scale on a plain sheet of paper.

◆ Transfer the centrelines of identifiable features such as main roads, drains and railway lines from the smaller scale to the larger scale using the grid squares as a reference.

◆ Fill in the detail using tape and measure or plane table techniques. Minor discrepancies between the site survey and the positions of features transferred from the smaller scale plan can be accommodated by adjusting lengths on the plan while keeping within the overall framework. This should give a plan which is accurate to within 5% which should be adequate for preliminary planning and for the design and measurement of minor upgrading works.

This process is illustrated in Figure 4.1.

A similar approach can be used to make, extend and update old survey plans.

Level surveys

Level surveys should be carried out using a surveyors level and staff. Levels should be read and computed to the nearest millimetre (or 1/8", 0.01ft for imperial staffs) but will not normally need to be plotted to more accuracy than the nearest centimetre. Level surveys should normally be carried out by a trained surveyor or survey technician.

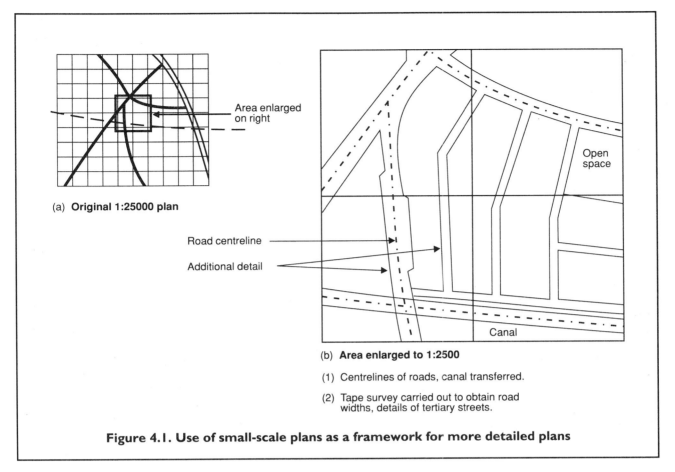

(a) **Original 1:25000 plan**

Area enlarged
on right

Open
space

Road centreline

Additional detail

Canal

(b) **Area enlarged to 1:2500**

(1) Centrelines of roads, canal transferred.

(2) Tape survey carried out to obtain road
widths, details of tertiary streets.

Figure 4.1. Use of small-scale plans as a framework for more detailed plans

It is **very important** that all level surveys are closed,ie. they should start and finish with a reading on a position whose level is known. This point cannot be emphasised too much. If a survey is not closed, there is no way of knowing whether a mistake has been made, either in the readings taken or in the computation. When the levels are computed for a closed survey, any mistakes will show up because of a discrepancy at the closing point. The surveyor can then check his work, first the computation and, if necessary, the survey itself. Engineers responsible for supervising survey work should check the surveyors survey book to ensure that the survey has been properly closed.

Surveys should be recorded in proper level books which are available in specialist survey equipment shops in Lahore and Karachi. Odd scraps of paper should never be used. The best practice is to record the survey neatly at the time that it is done, clearly indicating the purpose, location and date of the survey.

For large schemes and when possible for smaller schemes, surveys should be tied in to the Survey of Pakistan datum. In order to do this, it will be necessary to find the nearest point to the survey area at which there is a known level tied to the datum. The surveyor should then run a line of levels from the known point to a fixed benchmark within or adjacent to the project area. Bearing in mind what has

already been said, it is very important to close this survey back to the original point.

For small schemes, it will often be sufficient to work to a local arbitrary datum, provided that either:

◆ drain and sewer levels are not critical (as would be the case where there are good falls so that minimum sewer/drain depths can be maintained). or

◆ it is possible to include the invert levels of the trunk sewers and/or drains with which the sewers/drains provided under the scheme may be connected.

When surveying anything other than the smallest area, it is useful to fix a number of temporary benchmarks from which levels can be taken. These should be easily identifiable, firmly fixed so that there is no chance that they will move and placed so that they will not be disturbed during implementation. Examples include the corners of steps and tharas, tops of walls, corners of manhole frames etc. Broad expanses of concrete or road should not be used as it will be difficult to decide on subsequent visits the exact spot which was previously used for the benchmark. The location of the benchmark should be clearly described in the surveyors level book and, where possible, it should be identified on site by a painted marker. Once temporary benchmarks have been established, they can later be used as the base for surveys to provide level information in the areas around them. It is advisable to recheck their levels if they are used again after being left unused for months or years.

SOCIAL SURVEYS

Social survey techniques are covered here in rather more detail than those for physical surveys because they are less likely to be familiar to engineers and others working on upgrading schemes

Objectives

Social surveys may be used to obtain information on the following:

◆ existing on-plot facilities;

◆ socio-economic indicators;

◆ the attitudes and priorities of residents;

◆ the adequacy or otherwise of existing services; and

◆ the habits and practices of residents.

At the planning stage of an upgrading scheme, social surveys can provide reliable knowledge about the area to be upgraded and its residents. Later, surveys may be used to provide feedback on the work undertaken and the performance of the facilities provided. They may also be used to monitor the changes that occur in an area as the result of an upgrading programme.

A good social survey provides information which enhances project design, ensuring that the facilities provided are appropriate and affordable. Community meetings and in-depth interviews, both of which will be described shortly, provide a degree of community involvement at the beginning of a project.

Social survey techniques

The social survey techniques most likely to be used in upgrading programmes are individual in-depth interviews, group discussions and sampling surveys. The first two provide qualitative information about an area and the people living in it. Sample surveys can provide quantitative information provided that they are correctly carried out. The difference between qualitative and quantitative surveys can be illustrated by an example. In depth interviews with a small number of people can suggest that there is a lack of adequate sanitation in an area but a sample survey can reveal the percentage of houses without a flush toilet. Both types of survey have their place. Quantitative surveys can provide hard data upon which to base project decisions and costings but qualitative surveys are more flexible and can be used to explore issues in detail.

Social surveys will usually start with an exploratory qualitative stage, aimed at determining the key issues, and will then move on to a sample survey. The techniques used in qualitative work are briefly described below and the remainder of the chapter will then provide an introduction to those used in quantitative sample surveys.

Qualitative surveys

As indicated above, there are two basic qualitative survey techniques, individual in-depth interviews and group discussions. In this section, the semi-structured interview which is a development of the basic in-depth interview approach will also be considered.

The aim of qualitative studies is to discover the range of behaviour and attitudes that exist within the community. It is therefore important that the sample should be representative of the groups found in the community. Sample sizes for qualitative studies are necessarily small but must be big enough to enable reasonable coverage to be given to the main groups within the community. Surveys are not random so the accuracy with which they reflect the actual situation is dependent on the surveyor's skill in selecting participants who are representative of these groups. It is rare to conduct more than 50 in-depth interviews or more than 12 group discussions in any one study.

In-depth interviews

In these, key informants are selected and interviewed. The interviewers have a list of topics for discussion but no formal questionnaire. Each interviewer formulates his or her own questions, based on the topic list and encourages the respondents to talk freely on and around the topics, guiding the talk to new topics as and when necessary. Clearly, some skill is needed to structure interviews in a way that provides useful information and it is important that the interviewers used for in-depth interviews are given training in the technique.

Key informants may be religious leaders, teachers or other professionals living in or working closely with the community. Articulate community members and representatives of specific community groups may also be interviewed. For instance, it will be useful to interview representatives of the sweepers (garbage collectors) if the aim is to gather information related to solid waste collection. When talking to informants, it is important to remember the perspective from which they approach the subject under discussion and the section of the population for whom they can speak.

Interviewers should have had experience in survey research, be able to communicate easily and perceptively with a wide range of people and able to conceal strong personal beliefs. They need thorough briefing on the background and objectives of the project, provided in a way that does not develop preconceptions as to what they are going to find. Interviews should be carried out in a place where the respondent feels able to talk at ease, usually the home or the workplace.

Group discussions

In these, the interviewer guides the conversation of a small group of respondents (typically about eight) through a list of topics. As with in-depth interviews, this technique allows respondents to talk at length in their own words and at their own level of understanding and allows linkages between topics, attitudes etc. to emerge. Discussion can range freely to include topics which were not anticipated beforehand. The interviewer or group leader can also clarify issues or investigate further as seems appropriate. Group discussions can be used to define areas of interest and help in the planning of more formal sample surveys. The interviewer can decide on who should be included in the group, making sure that the members are representative of all the concerned interests. The workshop approach to action planning described in Chapter 3 is a development of the group discussion concept.

It will often be advisable to hold group discussions on a regular basis, forming a panel for this purpose. This will be particularly useful for obtaining feedback for use in an ongoing review of the aims and procedures of an upgrading project.

A disadvantage of group discussions is that certain types of people, for instance the old, the disabled and the socially disadvantaged will tend not to attend them. However, they will provide information about the dominant concerns and attitudes within the community. In-depth discussions are more suited to studies of individual motivation and needs where the psychology and circumstances of the respondent need to be related. Their disadvantages are in the extra time and cost required to conduct interviews and analyse data.

Group discussions may be followed by specifically targeted in-depth interviews in order to follow up on important points and opinions.

The leaders of group discussions have to ensure that all participants speak early in the discussion, if necessary by asking direct questions. Apart from this, he or she should keep in the background as far as is possible, intervening only to ensure that the discussion moves forward, to seek clarification on specific points and to draw out the views of the less forceful members of the group. The last task may be related to efforts to ensure that one person does not dominate the discussion.

The leader of the discussion will be responsible for distilling the results of the discussion into a useable form in order to present the main conclusions as accurately as possible. Qualities of receptiveness, objectivity and creativity are required for this task and group discussion leaders should therefore be chosen carefully.

Semi-structured interviews

These represent a half-way stage between in-depth interviews and sampling surveys. They use forms with questions asked in precise terms and in a specific order but with the answers left open rather than pre-coded. Such interviews are cheaper than in-depth interviews because they require less rigorously trained personnel and are easier to analyse. At the same time, they provide more in-depth coverage of issues than conventional sample surveys. They are most appropriate for sample sizes between 100 and 200 people, sufficient to allow broad quantification across the sample but not for detailed analysis of sub-groups. For larger samples, the time required to conduct a survey and analyse its content will tend to make the approach too expensive.

Quantitative surveys

There are two main types of quantitative survey, formal interviews and postal surveys. Only the first type is considered here. The data collected in formal interviews is designed to have statistical validity and to provide a database, accurate to within declared parameters, on which to make planning decisions. The process followed in preparing a sample survey normally includes the following:

- ◆ preliminary planning;
- ◆ reconnaissance visit to community to be studied;
- ◆ preliminary discussions with community;
- ◆ identification of interviewers;
- ◆ outline design of questionnaire and survey structure;
- ◆ recruitment and training of interviewers;
- ◆ pilot survey;
- ◆ refinement of questionnaire design, procedures;
- ◆ main survey;
- ◆ collation and analysis of data; and
- ◆ reporting and presentation of findings.

Each of these stages will now be considered briefly.

Preliminary planning.

The aim of this is to decide the scope and objectives of the survey. There may be a case for expanding the scope to include questions on subjects which are not of immediate concern but which are felt to require investigation. However, the questionnaire needs to be kept to a manageable length and the temptation to try to find out everything about everyone in the community should be resisted.

The other important planning decision to be made is whether a longitudinal survey, including a repeat survey or surveys at some time in the future is required. One-off 'cross-sectional' surveys are cheaper but provide no information on the effects of upgrading. In some cases, there is a case for an initial comprehensive survey followed by more limited interviews at later dates.

For small areas, it will be possible to survey every household. For larger areas, a sample, typically including 5-20% of households, should be surveyed. In order to ensure that the survey is representative, the sample should be distributed evenly throughout the survey area. For instance, to obtain a 20% sample, every fifth house should be sampled.

Reconnaissance visit

This has already been covered in the section on rapid site appraisal. It will usually be followed by qualitative investigations of the type already described.

Preliminary discussions with the community

These may take the form of a public meeting at which the approach to upgrading and the broad limits of what is possible can be discussed. The action planning workshop described in Chapter 3 represents a logical development of the public meeting approach.

The preliminary discussions will help to clarify any issues which may be problematical, for instance the need to allow for different sorts of tenancy in different parts of the proposed project area. Another important task at this stage is to determine whether it is feasible to employ interviewers from the community being surveyed. Frequently, the involvement of the community in putting forward potential interviewers has an overall beneficial effect but the final decision must depend on the circumstances.

Questionnaire design

A good questionnaire will be designed specifically to suit the situation being investigated. It should be clear and unambiguous with questions that are easy to administer and understand. The questions should have a clear purpose and should not be included just for the sake of doing so. For sensitive issues, such as income, it is useful to approach the same subject from two different angles. For instance, a direct question on income might be supplemented by one on the jobs done by wage earners in the household, thus allowing the income data to be confirmed from knowledge of prevailing wage rates.

Recruitment and training of interviewers

For all but the smallest surveys a team of interviewers will be required. Team members should be able to communi-

cate and to record their discussions appropriately. This suggests that they should have some educational qualifications, typically a school certificate. However, it is certainly not true that interviewers need to be highly qualified. Familiarity with the area and an ability to relate to people are more important than formal qualifications. Where interviewers are new to the work, it is important that they are provided with training which should include practical experience with the questionnaire itself.

Piloting

The questionnaire and interviewers should be tested in the field before the start of the main survey. The purpose of this pilot phase is to identify holes in the survey framework and to expose parts of the survey which do not work well. This allows for redesign of the questionnaire before high levels of resources are committed.

Piloting also reveals the extent to which the interviewers have been trained and are carrying out their task correctly. At this stage, those interviewers who are clearly unsuited to the work can be removed and training/briefing can be provided for the rest to rectify any deficiencies in their approach which have emerged during the pilot survey.

Refinement of questionnaire

The questionnaire should be redrawn as necessary in the light of the pilot survey. The refinement should not be confined to the content of the questions but should extend to the way in which they are organised and structured. After this, the final questionnaire can be printed, numbered and distributed.

Survey monitoring and administration

It is important to establish procedures for running the survey and storing the completed questionnaires. Each questionnaire should have a unique reference number and there must be a system which shows which questionnaire is from which individual house. Records should be kept of the questionnaires issued, the interviews attempted, the dates on which they were conducted and whether they were successful or not.

An important task is the repeat interviewing of a small proportion of the interviewees. This monitoring process allows checking of the accuracy of an interviewers work and an assessment to be made of the consistency of answering between interviews. In this way, unsatisfactory interviewing can be eliminated and interviewers retrained as necessary.

Each interviewer needs a flipboard and pen, an identification document stating for whom he or she is working and a briefing sheet giving an introduction and notes on how to operate the questionnaire. This should give notes on how to decide on what to do when uncertainties arise during the interview. This sheet should be prepared in the light of the experience gained during the pilot interview.

The survey manager must spend some time on the site during the survey, particularly at the start. He or she should talk to each interviewer at the end of each session in order to receive feedback from them. Any problems that arise should be dealt with immediately and decisions communicated to all other interviewers in order to ensure that the survey is uniformly administered.

Collation and analysis of data

Small numbers of questionnaires can be analysed by hand, using a calculator as required. The technique commonly used is to prepare a large spreadsheet with individual interviews represented by rows and questions by columns. The answers to questions are entered in the spreadsheet and the overall situation obtained by summing the results in each column. For larger surveys, it is advisable to use a computer to analyse data.

In either event, a coding format is required for recording data. A typical question with coding format might read as follows:

Q5: What form of sanitation is present in the house?

Cistern flush latrine	1
Pour-flush latrine	2
Concrete slab flushed to drain	3
Dry latrine with container	4
Dry latrine without container	5
No latrine	6
Other	7

For 7 please specify _____

When conducting an interview, the interviewer will ring the appropriate code number when he/she obtains an answer to a question. Note that provision is made for an answer outside the range of those explicitly specified on the questionnaire.

The degree of analysis of data required will depend on the amount and type of data collected and the use to which it will be put. The simplest tabulations and calculations consistent with the aims of the survey should be used. Specialist advice should be taken if it is desired to consider

the statistical significance of results but this will not normally be necessary for surveys associated with upgrading.

Reporting and presentation of findings

Survey results should be available for use as soon as possible after completion of the survey. A draft report with preliminary results should therefore always be produced and circulated at the earliest opportunity. A final report should follow, illustrating the findings graphically through graphs, pie-charts and bar-charts whenever possible. Interesting information gained during the survey should be included in the report. For instance, some interesting or unusual methods of dealing with solid waste may have been noted during the survey and these can be described in the report.

It may be useful to hold a seminar of the concerned professionals to present the material using visual aids and encouraging debate on the relevance of the results.

A presentation should be made to the community from which the data was collected, preferably to a community meeting but failing that to community leaders. Not only is this a matter of courtesy, but it is also a major step in ensuring the future cooperation of the community in the upgrading process. Where appropriate, this presentation should be included in the action planning process described in Chapter 3.

Participatory survey techniques

In recent years, there has been considerable interest in the use of participatory techniques to gather and analyse information. These techniques are commonly referred to as PRA (Participatory Rural Appraisal) techniques. Despite their name, they can be applied in both rural and urban areas, although most applications to date have been in rural areas. The PRA approach starts from the recognition that:

◆ community members have considerable knowledge about their situation;

◆ conventional quantitative survey techniques can make considerable demands on scarce resources;

◆ conventional quantitative survey techniques are not well suited to obtaining information about differences rather than means;

Full consideration of PRA techniques is beyond the scope of this manual, but further information is available within Pakistan.

ANNEX I

CHECK LIST FOR PRELIMINARY SITE INSPECTION

Water supply

Where do people obtain water from ?
Are there problems due to poor pressures, intermittent supply, or poor quality of supply ?
Is waste water from standposts causing a nuisance?
Are overhead storage tanks present and used ?
What water supply arrangements are typically present on-plot ?

System pressures can be tested by turning on taps. Note the time of day since pressures are usually lower during the morning than at other times. **Also, check that the area is being supplied at the time that discharge from taps is tested.**

Information on supply times can be obtained from residents and checked against information supplied by water authorities.

Visual inspection will reveal if the water supply is turbid. Excessive salinity can be detected by taste. Laboratory tests are required to determine chemical and bacteriological quality but inspection on site can reveal the existence of features such as water mains passing through foul drains which increase the probability of pollution.

Information on on-plot water supply facilities can be obtained from inspection of typical plots. Where there are house connections, check the number of taps and whether there is a bathroom and/or WC. Otherwise check whether there are shallow tubewells on-plot

Sanitation

Look for evidence of flush toilets (septic tanks in streets and lanes, faeces in drains, connections to sewers). Confirm impressions with inspections of representative houses and eventually by formal surveys. Note other sanitation arrangements that may be present. Note the location, condition and use of any communal facilities that exist in the area.

Sewerage

Look for evidence of sewers, in particular for manhole covers. (Later compare information gathered on site with that obtained from official records and arrive at best estimate of situation.) Lift manhole covers and inspect the condition of sewers, noting particularly whether they are running freely.

Street surfacing

Obtain a rough idea of the extent, type and condition of existing surfacing, distinguishing between through streets and those which serve only to provide access.

Note any encroachments or aspects of the street layout which inhibit access.

Note any industries or businesses which generate high traffic volumes or loadings.

Drainage

Note the approximate coverage of existing lined and unlined drains.

Note any obvious drainage problems, for instance ponds of sullage in low lying areas, poorly maintained drains, restrictions on drainage paths (including encroachments) etc.

Check the availability of main drains or other suitable disposal points in the area.

Ideally, an inspection should be carried out during or after heavy rain so that any drainage problems can be clearly identified. This will not always be possible and local residents should be asked about the extent and frequency of drainage problems.

Solid waste disposal

Note the location and condition of any solid waste bins in the area. Where formal facilities do not exist, note the location of informal solid waste dumping points. By talking to residents and observation on site, obtain preliminary information on the frequency and quality (in terms of the amount of solid waste removed) of the collection service. If possible, note the equipment available for collection.

Street lighting

Note the presence or otherwise of street lights. Where street lights exist, roughly ascertain the percentage that are working either by questioning residents or by visiting the area at night.

Other points

Note the general condition of housing, regularity of plot layout, rough size of plots, building materials used etc.

Note the presence of open space and community facilities. Ask local people whether there is any publicly owned land in the area, for instance that owned by the Auqaf.

5.

WATER SUPPLY

SUMMARY

This chapter deals only with piped water systems because they are by far the most common form of supply in urban areas. Other systems, such as on-plot and local supplies, are not considered.

In order to put upgrading works into context, the first part of the chapter provides background information on the components of water supply systems. The need to ensure that all these components are in balance is emphasised. The objectives of water supply improvements are then explained with special reference to health. A section on overall planning follows, giving simple methods for the assessment of the adequacy of existing supply facilities. Guidelines are then given for the estimation of supply and storage requirements and the planning of distribution system layouts. A general approach to the design of distribution systems is recommended and this is followed by simple guidelines for sizing tertiary mains and standpost supplies. An introduction to primary/secondary system design is then given and this is followed by a section on the location and spacing of sluice valves, fire hydrants, wash-outs and air-valves. The final part of the chapter deals with construction, in particular pipe materials and methods of laying and testing pipes. Additional information for the design of primary and secondary facilities is given in Annex 1.

KEY POINTS

A water consumption of at least 30 lpd is necessary if the levels of hygiene necessary for good health are to be achieved.

◆

Standpost supplies should be designed for a per-capita consumption of about 40 lpd and those to house connections for 100-150 lpd (litres per person per day), depending on circumstances.

◆

The maximum distance from any house to a standpost should not exceed 100m.

◆

Most water supply systems are arranged in a hierarchical system. Action at one level within the supply hierarchy will not have significant effects if serious deficiencies remain at another level. The first task in planning to upgrade supplies is therefore to identify deficiencies.

◆

Tertiary mains may be smaller than the normal minimum standard of 75mm in certain circumstances. Guidelines on the provision of small diameter mains are given.

◆

Where a 24hr/day continuous supply is not possible, designs should ensure that water mains do not pass through drains and other sources of contaminated water.

◆

Systems served by a single tubewell should be avoided since they will fail completely in the event of a pump breakdown.

◆

Provision of elevated storage will provide benefits where the supply capacity is equal to or greater than the peak daily demand. Otherwise, the first priority should be to increase supply capacity.

◆

Primary and secondary distribution systems should be loops. The number of sluice valves required to subdivide the system can be reduced if tertiary mains are branches.

◆

Sluice valves and fire hydrants should not be provided if they cannot be maintained. In practical terms, this means that it should be possible to isolate areas of 5-10 ha rather than every branch main.

BACKGROUND

Piped water supply systems are present in most urban areas in Pakistan. The basic components of these systems, not all of which will be present in every case, are as follows:

Production facilities. Intakes, water treatment works, tubewells, etc.

Bulk supply mains. These carry water from production facilities to service reservoirs. They are only required where the source is remote from the supply area, as in Karachi and Faisalabad.

Storage facilities These allow variations in demand over the day to be balanced and may also provide some back-up capacity in the event of a break in supply.

Primary or trunk mains. These are intended to convey water in bulk from one part of the network to another. They will not normally be required where supply is from tubewells located at intervals throughout the supply area.

Secondary mains. These link tubewells, service reservoirs and trunk mains with service mains. They normally have diameters of 150mm or greater and are laid to form loops.

Tertiary or service mains. These are mains of 100mm dia. or less that distribute water locally. They are often branches rather than loops. (See Figure 5.1)

House and standpost connections. Typically 12-25mm diameter.

Where production is concentrated at a limited number of locations, these components are usually combined in a hierarchical system. Water is transported through reducing sizes of distribution main until it finally reaches the consumer through the house and standpost connections. Where supply is via tubewells from an aquifer, a more decentralised system will often be possible. In Peshawar, for instance, there are over 100 tubewells located throughout the city. Nevertheless, some centralisation of supply will simplify operations such as chlorination.

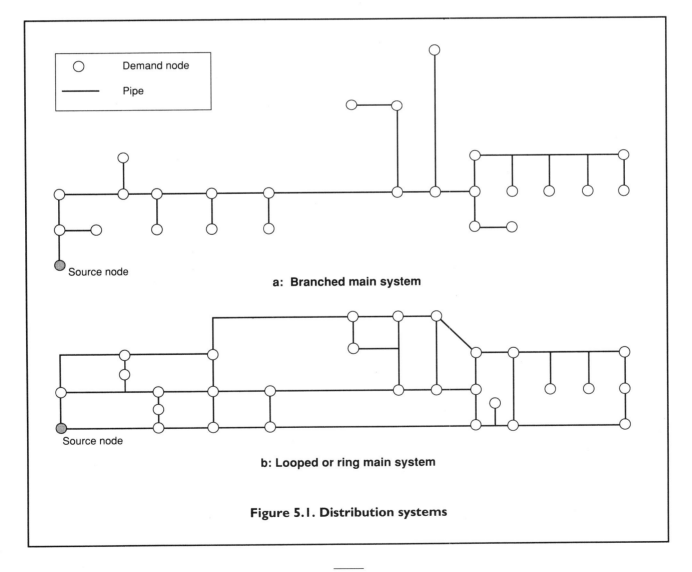

a: Branched main system

b: Looped or ring main system

Figure 5.1. Distribution systems

Upgrading schemes impinge directly upon tertiary level facilities, house connections and perhaps secondary distribution mains. However, for the system to perform satisfactorily, it is important that all its components are adequately sized. No amount of increase in the size of tertiary mains will result in an improved service if the supply to the area is inadequate. Conversely, the full benefits of improvements in supply capacity will not be realised if adequate tertiary mains are not present.

There is thus a need to ensure that actions at the various levels are coordinated and to check the adequacy of higher order facilities when preparing a programme for action.

OBJECTIVES

The basic objectives of water supply improvements relate to health and the convenience of users. However, health and convenience objectives cannot be achieved unless the cost of constructing and operating facilities can be afforded. A further objective is therefore that the facilities provided are affordable both to the operating authority and the consumers.

Water and health

Good access to clean water is a prerequisite for good health. A prime objective of water supply improvements, therefore, is to provide an accessible supply of water in sufficient quantity and of adequate quality to prevent the spread of diseases associated with poor water supplies.

The availability of a good quality water supply reduces the likelihood that faecal-oral diseases, including a wide range of diarrhoeal diseases, cholera and typhoid, will be contracted through drinking polluted water.

The incidence of many common illnesses, such as diarrhoeas, enteric fevers, infectious skin and eye diseases and certain louse-borne infections can be reduced by improvements in personal and domestic hygiene. These, in turn, are dependent on the amount of water available.

From a public health point of view, it is more important to provide an adequate quantity of water than to ensure its quality. A minimum per-capita supply of about 30 litres per person per day (lpd) is required to achieve satisfactory levels of hygiene.

Convenience

Improving the ease with which users obtain water is an important objective where existing sources are remote, unreliable, available at unsocial times or otherwise inconvenient. Improvements in convenience will have particular benefits for the women who are usually responsible for water collection.

Affordability

Where water supplies are poor, people often have to pay high prices for water obtained from vendors. Upgrading projects must aim to provide water supplies which, while adequate in relation to health and convenience, are also affordable to consumers. At the same time, the charges made for water should be sufficient for the supply authority to recover its capital costs and operate and maintain the system. In order to achieve these objectives, the levels of service provided must be considered when improvements are planned. The minimum service levels required to achieve health and convenience objectives are listed below and further information on the selection of appropriate service levels is given in the section on planning.

Minimum service levels

Accessibility Water should be available either on-plot or at public standposts within 100 metres of all plots.

Continuity Where possible, the supply should be continuous. This will not be possible in many upgrading areas and designs should therefore ensure that water mains do not come into contact with contaminated water.

Reliability In order to reduce the possibility of complete breakdown in supply, systems should not be served from single tubewells, treatment facilities should have parallel units and bulk supply mains should be duplicated.

Minimum pressure Designs should allow for a minimum pressure head at the tap of 4 metres. This means, in the majority of cases in which all taps are at ground level, that the minimum head above ground level at the plot should be 5 metres. The implications for pressures at other points in the distribution system will be considered later in this chapter.

PLANNING

Overall planning provides the framework within which individual water supply improvement schemes can be incorporated. The first step in the planning process is to investigate the existing situation in order to establish where deficiencies lie. After this, the levels of service which it is reasonable to aim for and the broad actions required to achieve them should be determined. The planning process for upgrading schemes will have to cover some or all of the following:

- the tertiary facilities in the area to be upgraded;
- the secondary distribution system serving the area; and
- the supply to the overall supply zone of which the area to be upgraded forms a part.

Tertiary facilities

The presence or otherwise of branch distribution mains and, where appropriate, public standpost facilities should be established from official records and from surveys on site. (Note that official records are not always accurate and should always be cross-checked). In general, any mains of 75mm and greater serving single streets and lanes can be assumed to be adequate. Similarly, a 100mm main serving up to about 100 houses should be adequate. Replacement will only be necessary if there is strong evidence that such mains are in poor condition. The presence of long house connections along the sides of a street is a good indication that no main runs along it.

Existing mains should be plotted on a plan at a scale of 1:2500 or greater. The routes of proposed mains can be shown on the same plan once it has been decided whether the supply is to be to standposts or house connections. They will usually be predetermined by existing rights of way and the location of the nearest secondary mains.

Primary and secondary mains

The initial concern with regard to primary and secondary mains is to:

◆ determine the location of the nearest mains to the area to be upgraded;

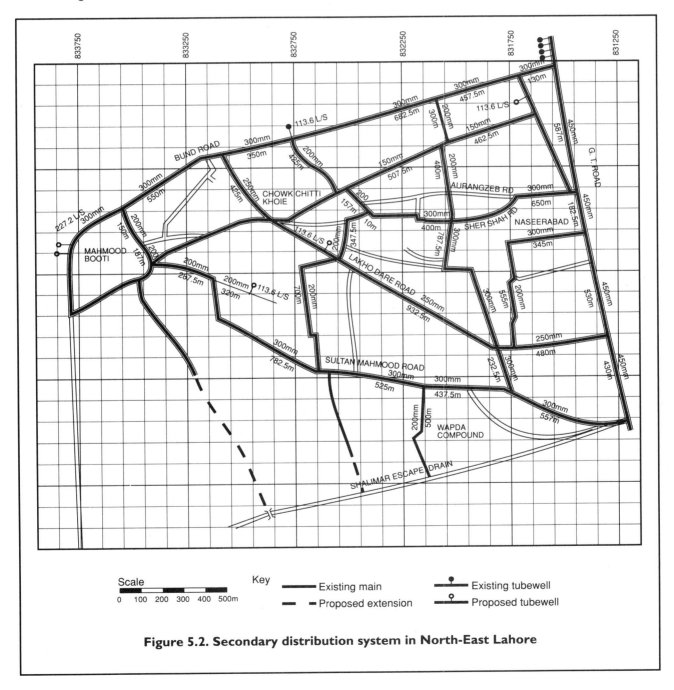

Figure 5.2. Secondary distribution system in North-East Lahore

◆ establish whether they have sufficient capacity to serve the proposed scheme.

The primary/secondary system includes all mains of 150mm diameter and greater, In small systems, some 100mm mains may be included in the secondary network. The system should form a looped grid with mains spaced at intervals of about 500m. Looped systems are more flexible because they allow water to take alternative routes through the system. This means that operating pressures throughout the system are kept at a more constant level and at least a partial supply can be maintained in the event of a pipe failure.

For small schemes, which are close to an existing secondary main, the adequacy of supply can be checked by measuring the pressure of supply in the main at the point where the connection to the new scheme will be made. The pressure measurement should be made at a time of maximum demand, normally around 0800 hours. The supply can be assumed to be adequate if the pressure head in the main is at least 10 metres above the highest point in the area to be served by the proposed scheme. If this is the case, detailed design of the scheme may commence without further consideration of overall planning issues.

For larger schemes and where pressure in the mains indicates problems with the supply, analysis of the primary/secondary distribution system will usually be required. The sizes and locations of existing primary/secondary mains should be established and plotted at a scale of between 1:2000 and 1:5000 so that any missing links in the system can be identified. Where there is no existing system, it will be necessary to decide the routes to be followed by the primary/secondary mains. As far as is possible, these mains should follow through roads and it should be recognised that the irregular layouts of many informal areas will mean that the grid will not be particularly regular. Figure 5.2 shows the main grid for the North East Lahore Upgrading Area.

The proposed primary/secondary grid must be analysed to confirm that it is adequate to serve its supply area. An introduction to analysis methods is given later in the section on detailed design.

Adequacy of existing supply

In order to assess the adequacy of the existing supply it is necessary to have information on the extent of the supply area, the availability of water to supply that area, the design

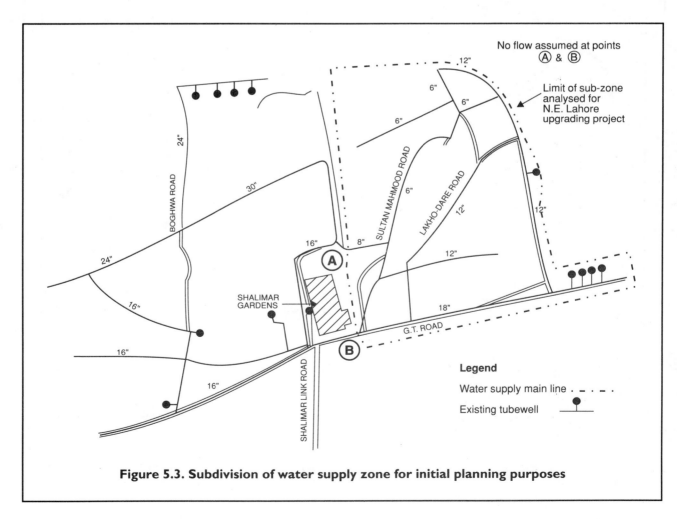

Figure 5.3. Subdivision of water supply zone for initial planning purposes

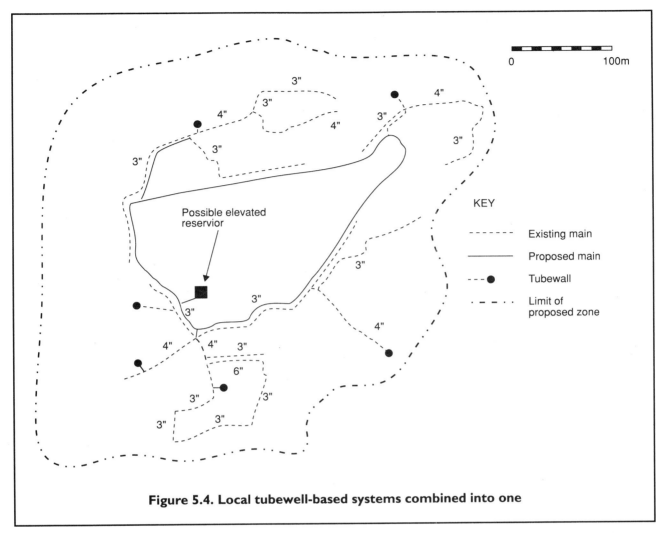

Figure 5.4. Local tubewell-based systems combined into one

KEY

- - - - - - - Existing main

———————— Proposed main

- - ● - - Tubewall

· — · — · — Limit of
proposed zone

0   100m

population and any industrial, commercial or institutional demands for water in the area.

Extent of supply area to be considered

For centralised systems, the supply area considered should be that covered by one supply zone or easily isolated sub-zone as shown in Figure 5.3. Information on the extent of supply zones can be obtained from the operating authority. Where the existing supply is from a number of tubewells, each serving its own distribution system, it is possible to consider each system separately. However, it is preferable to consider the possibility of combining several such systems together so that there is the option of providing back-up supply when one tubewell is not operating. As a general rule, there should be at least three tubewells per supply zone. On the other hand, there is little point in excessive centralisation of systems which rely on separate tubewell sources. Figure 5.4 gives an example of a system supplied by local tubewells.

There may be operational advantages in delivering water from tubewells direct to an elevated reservoir from which water can gravitate into supply. This will allow water to be

chlorinated at a single point for each zone rather than at individual tubewells and will thus allow much greater control over the chlorination process. The possibility of providing such a system should be considered at the planning stage, even though it may not be possible to implement it in the short term, and may affect the extent of the supply area to be considered.

Existing supply capacity

Estimates of the amount of water supplied should ideally be based on the results of metering, either at the point at which the water enters a zone from the larger system or of the discharges from individual tubewells. Unfortunately, there are few bulk meters on water supplies in Pakistan at present and rough estimates may be all that is possible. The introduction of bulk metering should be a priority wherever it is not already present. Where there are no bulk meters, approximate supply estimates may be obtained from information on the rated capacity of tubewells and water treatment facilities. However, such information should be treated with caution as the actual capacity will not always be the same as the rated capacity.

Population

Information on the present and future population of the supply area and the per-capita water demand are required to calculate the domestic demand for water. In developed areas, the population can be obtained by multiplying the number of housing units by the average household size. The former can be obtained from physical surveys and the latter from social surveys. Further information on calculating populations is given in Annex I.

Industrial, commercial and institutional demands

At the planning stage, information should be obtained on the water demand from any large industrial, commercial or institutional premises within the supply area. It will not normally be necessary to make specific allowance for the demand from small workshops, shops and local primary schools. Further information on industrial, commercial and institutional demands is given in Annex I.

Assessment of existing per-capita supply

In predominantly residential areas, the average amount of water provided per-capita in a day is given by q_d where:

$$q_d = Q_d \times 1000/P$$

in which q_d is in litres, Q_d is the total amount of water supplied per day in m^3 and P is the population. Where the supply is from tubewells or other sources that do not operate full time, it may also be useful to work out the maximum rate of per-capita supply, given by q_h where:

$$q_h = Q_h \times 1000/P$$

in which Q_h is the maximum rate of supply in m^3/hr. If the ratio $24Q_h/Q_d$ is much greater than 1, it suggests that there is scope for increasing the level of service by increasing the periods of supply.

Where there are significant industrial, commercial or institutional demands, the per-capita demand should be based on a modified supply figure from which these non-domestic demands have been deducted.

Decisions on levels of service

Type of connections

The existing average daily per-capita supply provides a guide to the type of connections to be provided in an upgrading scheme. In general, house connections will be preferable to standposts where q_d is 100 lpd or more. Where it is less than about 50 lpd, extensions to the system should probably be to standposts in the first instance. The choice will also be affected by the expectations of the beneficiaries which will in their turn be influenced by the existing situation. For instance, it is unlikely that public standposts alone will be appropriate where many plots already have handpumps drawing palatable groundwater from a shallow aquifer. However, there will be many situations in which it will be necessary to provide some public standposts to supply water to those people who cannot afford house connections. In recently developed areas, the best strategy may be to provide public standposts in the first instance while recognising that increasing numbers of house connections will be made over time. In such areas, it may be advisable to design primary and secondary mains for the demand from house connections even though standposts are provided in the first instance.

Continuity of supply

Where the existing supply is provided for very limited periods, it will be unrealistic to expect a continuous supply in the near future. Where the existing supply is provided for more than about 15 hours per day, the possibilities for providing a continuous supply should be investigated.

Where separate supply systems are served by single tubewells, the possibility of combining the systems and staggering the shut down periods for tubewells should be considered. This should reduce the periods when there is no supply although problems of low pressure will still occur if the combined supply capacity is inadequate. In the longer term, there could be operational advantages in linking the tubewells via separate supply mains to a central elevated tank from which water would gravitate to supply. This would allow water to be chlorinated at a single point for each system rather than at individual tubewells.

Design per-capita consumption

The design per-capita consumption should be decided in the light of the intended levels of service. Typical values will be:

◆ 30-50 lpd for standpost supplies;
◆ 100-150 lpd for house connections with a near continuous supply.

Where possible, the figures should be based on metered consumptions for an area similar in character to the project area but with a good water supply.

Where the supply is only provided for limited periods, a figure of less than 100 lpd may have to be assumed for house connections, at least in the short term.

Additional bulk supply and storage facilities

The design consumption figures are used to calculate the bulk supply and storage capacities required. The maximum amount of water required in a day is given by Q where:

$$Q = P\{c \times f_d + w\}/1000$$

where Q is in cubic metres per day;
P is the design population;
c is the per-capita water consumption in litres per day;
f_d is the peak day factor, ie the peak daily demand divided by the average daily demand;
w is the per-capita allowance for leakage in litres per day.

In most informal areas, it will not be necessary to make additional allowance for industrial, commercial and institutional demands.

The value of f_d will typically be around 1.1 while **w** can be taken to be 25-40% of **c**, depending on the expected level of maintenance. An additional allowance for wastage at the tap, equal to about 25% of **c** should be made for supplies from standposts.

For systems with limited amounts of high level storage, water must be supplied to the system at rather higher rates to cater for variations in demand over the day. The relationship between supply capacity, the peak daily requirement for water (Q) and the storage capacity is shown in Figure 5.5. The peak daily water requirement figure used should include allowance for leakage and wastage.

The priorities for action will depend on the capacity of production facilities relative to demands, the level of provision of storage facilities and the operating regime.

These factors are inter-dependent and their combined effect must be analysed. However, the following basic rules can be used to make preliminary decisions;

◆ Where water is provided for less than about 6 hours in a day, the priority should be to extend the period of supply;

◆ Where no elevated storage is available, little is to be gained by pumping into supply during night-time periods of low demand.

◆ Where the supply capacity is less than about 75% of Q, the priority should be to increase supply.

◆ In other cases, the ratios of existing supply capacity to Q and available storage capacity should be calculated and plotted on Figure 5.5. If the point is below the line, possible upgrading strategies are represented graphically by the range of projections to between points (a) and (b) on the line.

Storage may be provided either in centralised elevated reservoirs or in small tanks located on-plot. Small on-plot tanks can be constructed by individuals and community initiatives should therefore seek to encourage their use where preliminary analysis has shown that provision of storage will bring benefits. Tanks may be located on roofs and should typically have capacities in the range 500-1000 litres. (As a rough guide allow 100 litres per person).

Where centralised elevated reservoirs or storage tanks are to be provided, their location will be influenced by topography. In general the best locations will be at the highest points within their supply areas. However, all other things being equal, they should be located as close to the centre of their supply areas as possible. Analysis of capital and running costs is required to determine the most economic combination of increased production capacity and storage. Such analysis is beyond the scope of the present manual.

Water may be delivered to elevated reservoirs via supply mains that are completely separate from the distribution system or through mains that form part of the distribution system. The former system is more expensive but allows greater control over the quality of water delivered to the consumer. This is because all water has to pass through the reservoir and so there will not be large variations in the length of time that the water is in the system. This means that chlorination levels are relatively easy to control. Where water is supplied to the reservoir via the distribution system, some areas will be served from the reservoir at times and directly from the source at other times. This means that the length of time that the water is in the system will vary and this in turn will affect the residual chlorine concentration. Despite this disadvantage, a combined supply/distribution system will often be the only option in the short term where funds are limited.

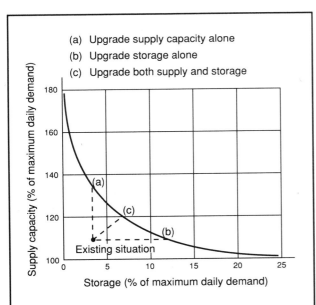

Figure 5.5. Relationship between required supply and storage capacities

DESIGN

General approach to distribution system design

When water flows through distribution mains, pressure head is lost because of friction. The object of design is to distribute head-losses between primary, secondary and tertiary mains and house connections so that the pressure at taps never falls below a minimum level. In practice, this is done by:

◆ specifying a minimum allowable head in the primary/ secondary distribution system; and

◆ specifying maximum allowable head-losses in tertiary mains and connections.

For low-rise areas where there are few if any taps above ground floor level, the minimum head allowed in the primary/secondary system should be 10m. Where there are houses with taps at higher levels, an additional 3m should be allowed for each floor to which water has to be supplied. Note that these figures are in relation to the highest ground levels in the served by mains and not to the ground levels along the mains themselves.

Suitable maximum head-loss values in tertiary mains and connections are 3m and 2m respectively, leaving a minimum of 5m head above ground level available at the tap.

Details of design methods and rules for tertiary mains, house connections and standposts are given in the following section. An introduction is then given to the analysis and design of primary/secondary systems.

Design of tertiary mains

The routing of tertiary mains has already been covered in the section on planning. Tertiary mains may run through from one part of the main grid to another or they may be dead ends. Although the latter will provide marginally lower pressures, it reduces the number of valves necessary to subdivide the system and therefore has some operational advantages

Many water supply agencies specify a minimum main diameter of 75mm but this is larger than required for hydraulic purposes for tertiary mains. Pipes in conventional materials such as asbestos cement and ductile iron are not manufactured in sizes smaller than 75mm but it is possible to use smaller diameter plastic and galvanised steel (GI) pipes for tertiary mains. The required diameter can be related to the number of houses served in accordance with the following guidelines:

1. For mains supplying house connections

No. of houses	Diameter (mm)
<12	38
12-20	50
21-40	75
41-100	100
101-200	150

2. For mains supplying standposts

Flow (litres per sec)	No. of taps served	Diameter (mm)
1	3	38
2	6	50
5	15	75

For larger systems which serve only standposts, the mains should be designed on the assumption that all taps are open.

House connections

Assuming an allowable head-loss in the connection of 2m, a 12mm pipe is adequate for house connections up to about 10m in length. A 20mm pipe will be adequate for connections up to 100m in length. These figures are for single connections. 20mm pipes should be used for connections serving two houses.

Public standposts

The basic decisions to be made when designing for supply from public standposts are:

◆ how many taps are required; and
◆ where should these taps be located.

Number of taps required

The number of taps required is influenced by the flow rate from the tap, the time for which standposts operate each day, the population served and the per-capita water consumption. These factors may be overruled by the need to maintain maximum spacing standards. We will see how these factors are inter-related in the following paragraphs.

The flow rate of water delivered by the tap depends upon both the size and make of the tap and the available head, (that is, the water pressure in the distribution pipe immediately upstream of the tap). The flow rates delivered by the most common types of tap for different values of available head are shown in Figure 5.6. A reasonable first estimate is to assume a minimum available head of 5 metres at the standpost. Standard half-inch and three-quarter inch taps deliver about 600 and 1000 litres per hour (0.17 and 0.27 litres per second) respectively at this

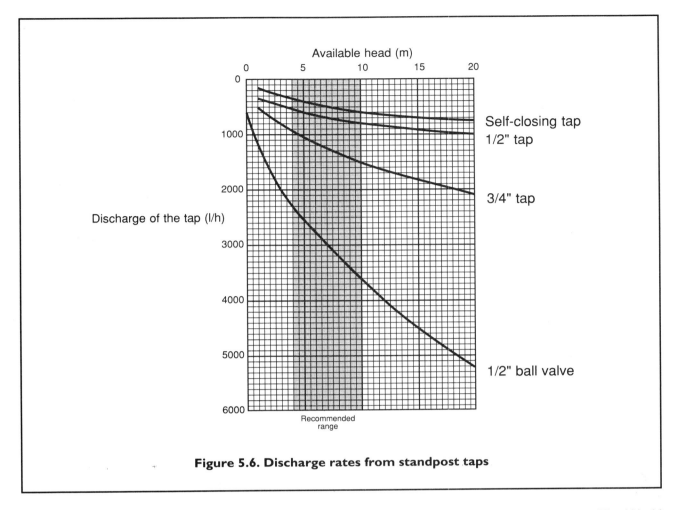

Figure 5.6. Discharge rates from standpost taps

pressure. In general, it is preferable to use three-quarter inch taps for standposts. For continuous use and allowing 25% wastage at the tap, the flow from a three-quarter inch tap will be sufficient to fill about 40 containers, each having a volume of 20 litres, in one hour.

Assuming a per-capita water consumption of 40 lpd, a single three-quarter inch tap would supply enough water for 240 people if operated continuously for 12 hours each day. In fact, the tap will only be used continuously at periods of peak demand and the number of people served by a single tap should be limited to 125. Where water is supplied to the standpost for 6 hours or less during the day, the number of people served by a single tap can be calculated from the formula:

$$N = T \times D/(1.25 \times c)$$

where N is the number of people served by a single tap;
T is the number of hours during which water is supplied each day;
D is the tap discharge in litres per hour;
c is the per-capita consumption in litres per day.

More than one tap should be provided at each standpost as the additional cost is negligible compared with the benefits from reducing the queuing time. The World Health Organisation recommends that there should not be more than 250 people served by several taps on a single standpost. The area in hectares which can be served by one standpost is equal to (nN/P) where n is the number of taps on the standpost and P is the population per hectare.

In less densely populated communities, the distance from the household to the standpost is likely to limit water use. All houses should be within 200 metres of a standpost. However, if plot sizes are very large and the housing density is correspondingly low, a standpost system may be grossly inefficient and it might be cheaper to provide house connections and meter the water consumption.

At public water supply points, considerable quantities of wastewater result from spillage and leakage; the standpost or handpump should be provided with an apron as shown on Figure 5.7, draining to a soakaway or drain in order to prevent insanitary conditions from developing. The design should be carried out with the aid of the community; their customs and habits in respect of water collection and use must be accommodated. For example, if people wish to bathe at the standpost, then a large paved and drained apron should be provided to enable them to do so.

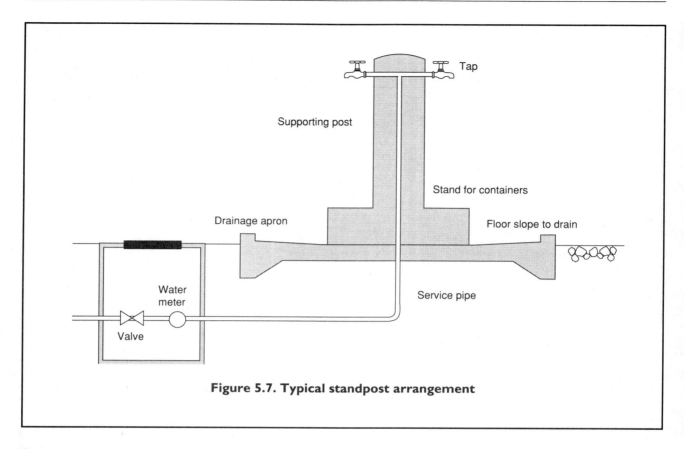

Figure 5.7. Typical standpost arrangement

Primary/secondary system design

Full consideration of the design of main reticulation systems is beyond the scope of this manual and only the main steps in design are listed below. These steps are:

◆ Decide the system layout; (see planning section above);

◆ Produce a simplified version of the system, removing smaller mains and any short lengths of main between junctions which are close to each other.

◆ Define the pressures and supply rates at supply points (service reservoirs, tubewells and take-off points from trunk mains.)

◆ Define nodes at all supply points and at intervals throughout the system, including all junctions between mains.

◆ Divide the area served by the system into sub-areas centred on these nodes and calculate the peak water requirement for each area, including allowance for leakage.

◆ Define the maximum ground level in each sub-area together with ground levels and heads at supply points and minimum water levels in reservoirs.

◆ Assign sizes to mains and analyse the system using an appropriate method. (Hardy-cross or a computer programme such as the LOOP programme distributed by the World Bank). Head-losses may

be calculated from design charts and nomograms or by the expression, adapted from the Hazen Williams formula:

$$h_f = 10.9(Q/C)^{1.85}L/D^{4.87}$$

where h_f is the head-loss in length L;
C is Hazen Williams coefficient; and
D is the pipe diameter.

Typical values of C for various pipe materials are as follows:

asbestos cement	140
uPVC	140-150
new cast-iron	130
old cast-iron	80

◆ Add additional mains and/or alter the main sizes as necessary to obtain at least the minimum allowable pressure head at all points in the system.

Further details of the method outlined above can be found in standard text-books. It involves fairly difficult calculations if a computer is not available. The following procedure can be adopted to give a rough approximation for fairly simple systems.

◆ Sketch a plan of system, showing the location of water demands.

◆ Assume breaks in mains to eliminate loops and convert the system to a series of branches. The breaks should be located so that demands are roughly divided in relation to the capacity of mains.

◆ Assign demands at nodes and proceed to analyse the system.

A simple example of the method is illustrated in Figure 5.8.

The elimination of loops means that flows and hence head-losses in all pipes can be calculated directly, removing the need for complex iterative calculations. The calculation process is thus greatly simplified. The procedure will tend to overestimate flows in some mains and should be used with caution.

OPERATIONAL FEATURES

Sluice valves

Sluice valves are used to subdivide the distribution system, allowing operators to allocate water between areas and to shut down sections of the system to facilitate maintenance or effect repairs.

Valves on mains which connect supply zones are normally kept shut. The purpose of these valves is to allow water to be transferred into a zone in the event of a supply failure in that zone. Such valves are referred to as shut valves. Engineers involved in upgrading projects should not normally be required to install shut valves but should be aware of the limits of supply zones and the location of shut valves.

A variation on the shut valve principle is used in areas, such as some parts of Karachi, which have a poor bulk water supply. Because of the shortage of water, supply is provided to various zones or sub-zones in rotation. In such cases, valves must be provided on the supply mains to isolate the various zones and allow the required rotation of supply.

All other valves will normally be kept open. Their purpose is to enable parts of the system to be isolated for repair and maintenance purposes while supply is continued to the rest of the system. As a general rule, valves should be provided so that areas of between 10 and 25 hectares can be isolated. The number of valves required can be reduced if the number of through tertiary mains is kept to a minimum. Figure 5.9 illustrates what this might mean in practice.

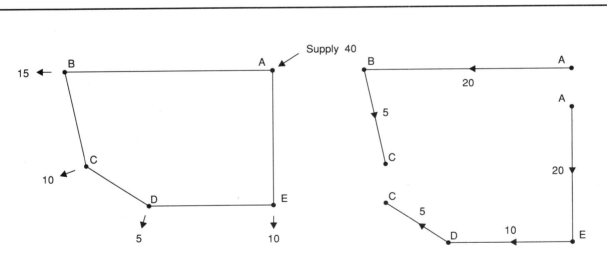

(a) Nodes, showing supply/demand in litres per second

(b) Network split down, showing assumed flows in each pipe

(c) Analyse as two branched systems as follows:

- Assume pipe diameters
- Calculate h_f in each pipe from Hazen Williams
- Check : i) $h_{f_{AB}} + h_{f_{BC}} = h_{f_{AE}} + h_{f_{ED}} + h_{f_{DC}}$

  ii) Residual heads at all nodes are within the range specified

- If these checks are not satisfied, alter the pipe diameters and recalculate h_f

Figure 5.8. Simplification of looped system for calculation purposes

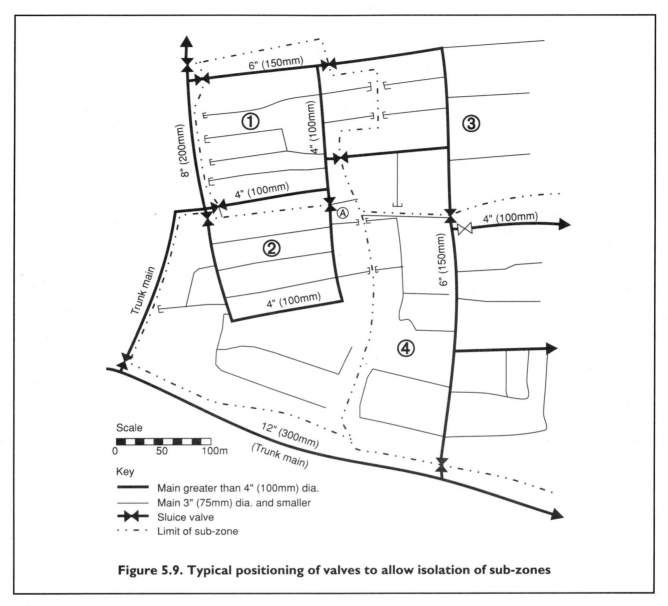

Figure 5.9. Typical positioning of valves to allow isolation of sub-zones

Scale

0   50   100m

Key

——— Main greater than 4" (100mm) dia.
——— Main 3" (75mm) dia. and smaller
►◄ Sluice valve
·—·— Limit of sub-zone

Fire hydrants

Conventional practice is to provide fire hydrants at intervals determined by the longest hose that is available on the fire appliances used in the area. Typically, this will mean that hydrants are spaced at about 200m intervals along primary and secondary mains.

An initial investigation is advisable, however, to determine whether existing hydrants are adequately maintained. Where either adequate maintenance cannot be guaranteed or the water supply is intermittent, there is a case for providing 75mm dia. standpipes at intervals of perhaps 1-2 km throughout the area. These should be high enough to discharge into fire tenders and water bowsers. Where the water supply is intermittent, a tank should be provided adjacent to the standpipe and this should be kept full at all times. The capacity of the tank should normally be about 10m³. The arrangement is shown in Figure 5.10.

Washouts

Washouts should be provided at low points in the distribution system to enable mains to be drained for maintenance and repair. Typical washout arrangements are shown in Figure 5.11

Air-valves

Air valves should not normally be required in upgrading schemes because any air that collects in mains will be vented through house connections.

CONSTRUCTION DETAILS

Pipe materials

For mains of 75mm diameter and greater, the commonly used pipe materials are ductile iron, asbestos cement (AC)

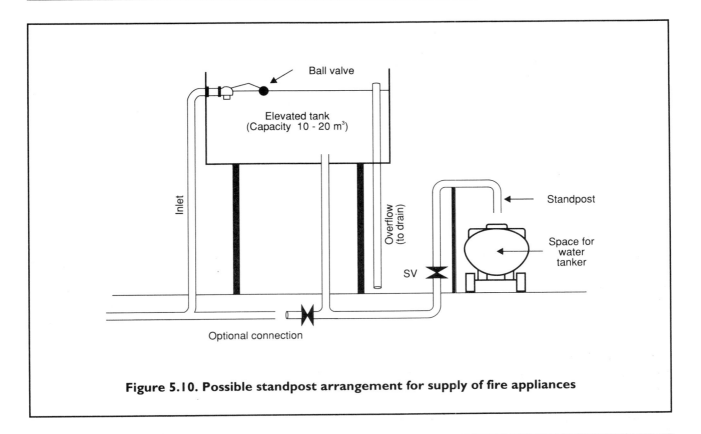

Figure 5.10. Possible standpost arrangement for supply of fire appliances

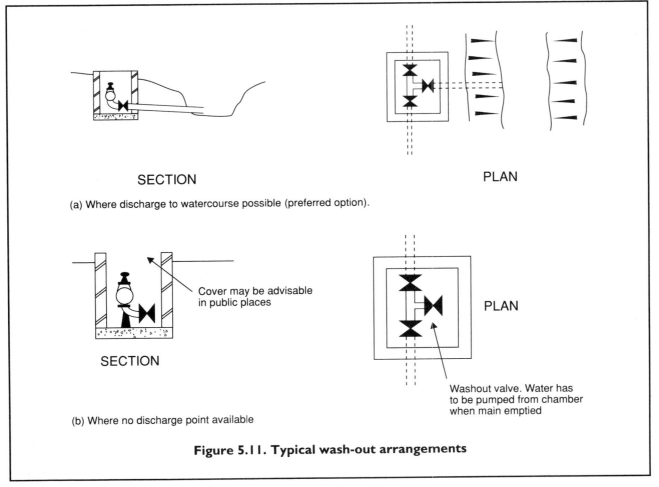

Figure 5.11. Typical wash-out arrangements

and uPVC. Some old established mains may be cast iron. For the smaller diameter mains that will be required in most upgrading schemes, the normal options for new mains will be asbestos cement and uPVC. Both of these materials are manufactured in Pakistan and they are considerably cheaper than ductile iron. However, most fittings for uPVC have to be imported and the non-availability of fittings can lead to problems with maintenance and in making house connections. For these reasons, AC will generally be the preferred option.

Two types of coupling are available for AC mains. Both rely on a lubricated rubber ring to ensure water-tightness. Comete couplings manufactured from asbestos cement are used on new mains. Where connections have to be made into existing mains or a gap has to be closed, cast iron gibault couplings should be used. PVC pipes are of the spigot and socket type, the spigot of one pipe pushing into the socket of the next to make a tight joint. Water-tightness is ensured by a rubber ring.

Galvanised steel (GI) mains are sometimes used in sizes greater than 75mm. Their threaded joints are easy to make and GI pipes are therefore more suitable for use in community managed schemes than other types. Against this must be set the fact that they are liable to rust and therefore have a much shorter life than other types of pipe. Some increase in life can be achieved by protecting the outer face of the pipe from corrosion by painting it with bitumen and then wrapping it in bitumen-soaked jute sacking. However, the length of GI main laid below ground should be minimised.

As already indicated in the section on the design of tertiary mains, diameters of less than 75mm can be used for these

mains. The options in these diameters are galvanised steel (GI) and medium density polyethylene (MDP).

At present MDP has to be imported into Pakistan. The smaller diameters are provided in rolls that can be unwound on site, reducing the need for connections to a minimum. Where connections are required, they are made by fusion welding using special equipment. MDP pipes are commonly used in rural water supply schemes and have recently been introduced to Pakistan for use in gas mains. Technically, they provide an attractive option but at present they are rather more expensive that GI pipes.

Galvanised steel pipes are commonly used for house connections. To protect against corrosion, the lengths of house connection which run underground should be protected with bitumen and jute sacking in the same way as distribution mains. Given its long life and good hydraulic properties, MDP may be an attractive option for house connections in the future.

Pipe laying and testing

Minimum cover

In streets subject to traffic loads, the cover over water mains should be at least 900mm or greater if recommended by the pipe manufacturer. Lanes less than about 3m wide cannot carry heavy traffic and some reduction in minimum cover is justified. The suggested minimum cover in such lanes is 600mm. Again, the pipe manufacturer should be consulted.

GI mains may be laid above ground in upgrading schemes, providing care is taken to ensure that they do not cause obstructions across doorways and rights of way. In general, they should only be used in pedestrian lanes and sizes should not normally exceed 50mm. Figure 5.12 shows a typical detail for an above ground GI main.

Trench widths

Pipe trenches should not be wider than necessary. Suggested widths are as follows:

PIPE DIA	TRENCH WIDTH
mm	mm
<80	500
80-200	600
250-400	800

Bedding

In good ground most pipes can be laid directly on to the trimmed and compacted trench bottom. Where ground conditions are poor, as is the case in many informal areas, pipes should be bedded and surrounded in sand or gravel.

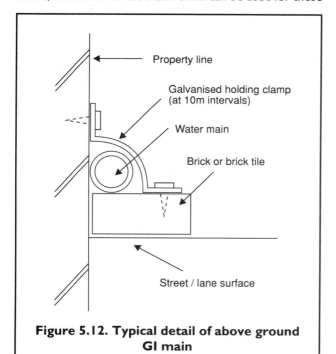

Figure 5.12. Typical detail of above ground GI main

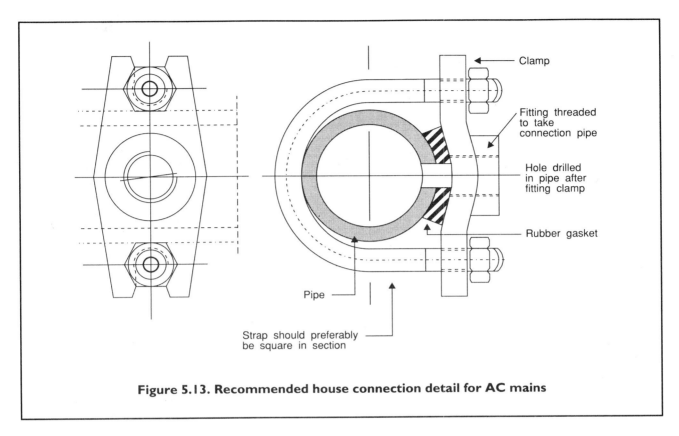

Figure 5.13. Recommended house connection detail for AC mains

Local specifications may require a bed and surround in any case. The bedding should be compacted to a thickness of 150mm for pipes of 150mm diameter and above. This thickness may be reduced to 100mm for smaller pipes. The provision of a stone-free bedding is especially important in the case of uPVC pipes which have an increased tendency to fail if they are in contact with hard objects. Holes should be scooped in the bedding to accommodate couplings. **Under no circumstances should pipes be supported by objects such as bricks.**

Thrust blocks

Concrete thrust blocks should be provided at all bends and tees to resist the force produced by the pressure in mains.

Pressure testing

Water mains should be pressure tested after they are laid to ensure that there are no defective pipes and that the joints are sound. The length of the test section should normally be about 500m. Full details of testing techniques

can be obtained from pipe manufacturers and specialist water supply agencies. Where tertiary mains are laid by municipalities and community groups who do not have the necessary skills or equipment for testing, they should wherever possible request a specialist organisation to carry out the testing.

House connections

Poorly made house connections are probably the main cause of leakage from water mains. Attention paid to ensuring good connections will therefore be rewarded. Connections should be made by drilling a hole at the top of the distribution main and inserting a ferrule. This should be held in place by a standard saddle clamp to a design approved by the pipe manufacturer. Figure 5.13 shows the clamp recommended for AC pipes manufactured in Pakistan.

Most house connections will require a 12mm or smaller ferrule. The same technique can be used for 20mm, 25mm, 32mm and 38mm connections but a tee should be used for 50mm connections.

ANNEX I

INFORMATION REQUIRED FOR OVERALL PLANNING AND DESIGN

Population

An estimate of the existing population in an area can often be obtained from census data ,which will normally be available for individual wards. For the detailed calculation of future population, population densities can be obtained by multiplying the average housing density in different areas by an estimate of the average household size. Calculations for the former should allow for development of presently undeveloped plots. The best procedure will be to calculate densities in representative fully developed areas and apply the figures thus obtained to all similar areas within the supply area. The present average household size can be obtained from analysis of social survey results. Some increase with time will be appropriate, typically 10-20% over a 30 year design period.

Per-capita consumption

Typical per-capita consumption figures have already been given in the main text. Per capita demands in areas with house connections vary widely, depending on the continuity and pressure of the supply and the opportunities for using water on-plot. Demands tend to be much higher where houses have gardens which require watering. The maximum average per-capita demand in informal areas is unlikely to exceed about 200 lpd and may be much lower where supply is intermittent. If possible, design figures should be based on the results of metering studies on houses already receiving a good water supply. Some care is required when conducting such studies since water meters tend to over-record when there is air in the system due to a discontinuous supply.

Industrial, commercial and institutional demands

Most areas to be upgraded contain small businesses, shops and facilities such as schools and health centres. In some places, industries will be situated within or adjacent to upgrading areas. Allowance must be made in design for the water demand from such premises.

In general, small workshops and commercial premises do not use a lot of water and can be treated as standard housing units for design purposes. Typical standard allowances for the demand from schools and clinics are 45 lpd and 350-500 l per bed per day respectively but the actual figures in most informal areas are likely to be lower. Where possible, information should be obtained from metered records for similar facilities in areas with good water supplies. However, it will usually be necessary to make assumptions. Reasonable figures might be 20 lpd for schools and 200 l per bed per day for small hospitals and health centres.

Where large factories are present within the design area, their water use should be considered individually. Bear in mind that some factories will have their own sources of water and will not draw large quantities from the public system. Large users will usually be metered and historic information on their consumption should be available from metered records. This information should be used in design, adjusted as necessary to accommodate plans for increased consumption in the future.

Fire demands

Separate allowance for fire fighting demands is not required in most low income areas. Any fire hydrants should be on primary and secondary mains, ideally of 150mm dia. and over, which should normally be capable of carrying the required flow of 15 litres per second to any fire hydrant at a residual pressure head of 4 metres.

The total daily water demand is the sum of the domestic, commercial and institutional demands. Provision for fire demand should not be included in the total.

Peak demands

Demand for water varies through the year, reaching a peak during hot dry periods. A daily variation is superimposed on this gradual variation as water demand peaks in the morning and falls to a minimum at night. The normal design procedure is to apply peak factors to the average demands in order to determine maximum demands.

The peak day factor, defined as the ratio of the maximum daily demand to the average daily demand, is used in the design of production and storage facilities and bulk supply mains. When unconstrained, its magnitude depends on climatic factors and the requirement for seasonal uses such as garden watering. However, peak consumption is often constrained by the capacity of the supply system. In the absence of site specific information, a value of 1.1 may be taken for typical informal areas.

The peak hour factor is used in the design of primary and secondary distribution mains. It may be defined as the ratio of the maximum hourly demand to either the maximum or average daily demand. In this manual, it is related to the average daily demand. Its magnitude depends on a number of factors, including the number of houses served, the relative number of house connections and standposts, and the extent to which houses, commercial and industrial premises have their own water storage facilities. For the design of a primary/secondary distribution system with a continuous or near continuous supply, a factor of 2.5 should be taken if local data is not available.

Where water is supplied for less than about 12 hours per day, peak factors are likely to be higher. Where local data is not available, the peak hour factor in such situations may be taken as 30/N where N is the number of hours supply during the day.

The peak hour factors given above apply to areas with house connections. People who rely on standposts have to queue for their water and at peak times all standposts are in continuous use. The capacity of the distribution system for a standpost supply can therefore be calculated if the number of standposts and the quantity of water discharging from each standpost are known.

Peak hour factors vary with the population served, the smaller the supply area, the larger is the peak factor. For this reason factors for tertiary mains are much higher than those given above for primary/secondary systems. In practice, it is better to calculate the peak flows in tertiary mains directly using probability theory. Suggested figures for design obtained from probability based analysis have been given in the section on the design of tertiary mains.

Leakage and wastage

Leakage from the distribution system must be allowed for when calculating flows. Even in well maintained systems, it is likely to be 15-20% of the total supply. In the absence of local data, the figure used for design should be realistic, bearing in mind the age of existing elements of the system and the likely level of maintenance. Typical allowances for leakage will be in the range 25-40% of the average daily demand.

The term wastage is used here to refer to water wasted within the consumer's premises. Causes of wastage include leaking pipes and broken taps. If there is significant wastage, the apparent per-capita consumption will be increased. The application of peak factors to this apparent average per-capita consumption will lead to over-design since wastage is more or less continuous and does not peak with peak demand. Where high levels of wastage are suspected, either the design per-capita consumption figure should be adjusted downward or the peak hour factor should be reduced.

6.

SANITATION AND SEWERAGE

SUMMARY

This chapter deals mainly with the disposal of human faecal wastes. A variety of on-plot and off-plot options are introduced but the main emphasis is on leach-pit and sewerage systems. The former deal with WC wastes while the latter also deal with sullage, ie. waste water produced in kitchens and bathrooms. Sewers invariably also carry some stormwater and allowance for this is made in the design procedures described.

The chapter is divided into three main sections. The first covers the background, the objectives of sanitation improvements, with particular emphasis placed on potential health benefits, the available sanitation options and the choice between those options. The second section deals with the design of leach-pit systems, the preferred option for on-plot facilities. The third section deals at some length with the planning, design and construction of the various sewerage-based options. The emphasis in this section is on tertiary systems since these will usually be the main concern of those involved with upgrading. However, an introduction to the planning and design of primary/secondary level systems is also given, emphasising the way in which these systems affect local upgrading decisions. Wherever possible, design information is given in the form of graphs and tables.

KEY POINTS

◆

Improved sanitation should result in reductions in diarrhoeal disease and worm infestation if it is accompanied by improvements in hygiene.

◆

Pour flush latrines are the preferred sanitation option for low-income urban areas in Pakistan, discharging to leach pits, or sewers.

◆

Solids accumulate in leach pits and septic tanks at a rate of about 40 litres per person per year.

◆

There will normally be a need for sullage drains when WC wastes are disposed of on-plot.

◆

An allowance for storm flow should be made when designing nominally separate sewers.

◆

Where the available fall or water use is limited, adequate solid waste collection cannot be guaranteed or the majority of houses already have septic tanks on their WC outlets, a sewered interceptor tank system may be appropriate.

◆

The minimum cover on sewers in narrow lanes that carry no heavy traffic may be reduced from that allowed by conventional standards. This, in turn allows inspection chambers rather than manholes to be used in such lanes.

◆

The minimum diameter for conventional sewers will normally be 150mm except where local standards require a 225mm minimum diameter. Sewers down to 75mm diameter can be used in sewered interceptor tank systems, provided that tanks are regularly desludged. Where regular desludging cannot be guaranteed, the minimum diameter used in such systems should be at least 100mm.

◆

The sewer gradient adopted should normally be the greater of the minimum allowable gradient and the ground slope. Guidelines for minimum gradients, related to design flows are given in the main text.

BACKGROUND

Until recently, most latrines in informal areas of Pakistan were of the dry type, often nothing more than a concrete slab but sometimes incorporating a small container which was emptied daily by a sweeper or house member. This state of affairs was unpleasant and unsatisfactory. Over the last 10 years or so, many such crude latrines have been replaced by 'eastern' squat type pour-flush latrines with the result that more than 50 % of the houses in many informal areas now have flush latrines. While improving conditions inside houses, this process has often adversely affected conditions outside them. Few informal areas are served with sewers so that latrine effluents are discharged to existing open drains, sometimes but not always after passing through a small septic tank.

Efforts to improve the situation by providing sewers in informal areas have met with mixed success. Even where it is possible to provide sewers, pollution of rivers will occur in the absence of adequate sewage treatment. Alternatives to sewerage are offered by various on-plot sanitation systems but these do not deal with sullage water. Most also require that faecal solids are removed from plots from time to time and this is an important factor to consider when choosing the most appropriate sanitation option. The present chapter accordingly includes information on how to choose the appropriate system for any situation, together with data on the planning, design and construction of sanitation systems.

OBJECTIVES

There are three basic reasons for improving sanitation facilities. These are:

◆ to improve the health of the users;

◆ to improve the environment; and

◆ to provide greater convenience for the users.

While all these are important, the first should always be a prime objective. Good sanitation breaks some of the routes by which the disease organisms or pathogens which are present in the excreta of an infected person are transmitted to other people. Thus improved sanitation is essential if the incidence of faecally transmitted diseases in the community is to be reduced. Such diseases include cholera and typhoid but the potential for reducing the incidence of common diarrhoeal complaints and worm infestation is equally important.

It must be recognised, however, that sanitation on its own will not bring the desired health benefits. It must always be accompanied by efforts to improve hygiene since some transmission routes are broken by good hygiene rather than sanitation. This point is illustrated by Figure 6.1, which shows the various transmission routes and the place of sanitation in breaking them.

OPTIONS AND CHOICES

Technical options

The available sanitation options may be divided into broad categories for preliminary planning purposes. The underlying choices are between wet and dry systems and between those which retain faecal material on plot and those which remove it from the plot. The options can be summarised as shown in Table 6.1.

Dry systems

On-plot systems

Almost all on-plot systems comprise some form of pit latrine, consisting basically of a hole in the ground, covered by a slab. Excreta and anal cleansing materials are deposited directly into the pit through a hole in the slab. Pit latrines are rarely used in urban areas in Pakistan, wet systems being preferred partly because water is generally available and partly because people use water for anal cleansing. In view of this, they are not considered in detail in this manual. A range of pit latrine types is shown in Figure 6.2 and this may be used for technology selection in situations in which pit latrines are the best sanitation option.

	Dry systems	Wet systems
On-plot	Pit latrines	WCs connected to leach pits and via septic tanks to soakaway.
Off-plot	Bucket latrines and their variations. (Unacceptable)	WCs connected to sewers. WCs connected via septic tanks to drains and sewers.

Table 6.1. Summary of sanitation options

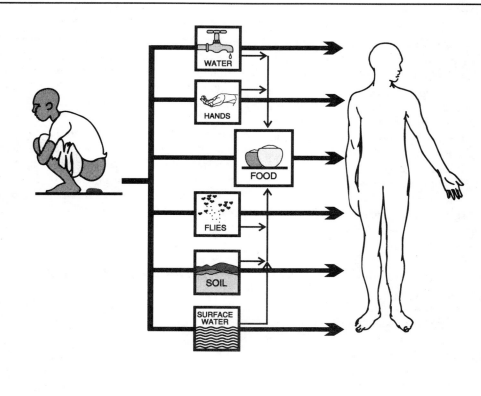

a: Faecal-oral transmission route of disease

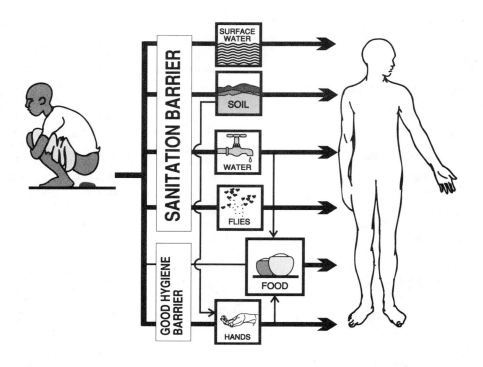

b: The sanitation and hygiene barrier

Figure 6.1. The importance of sanitation

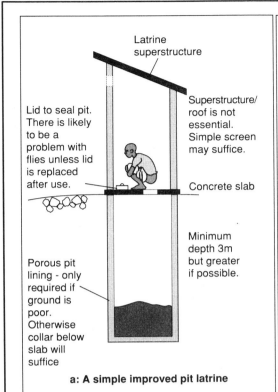

Latrine superstructure

Lid to seal pit. There is likely to be a problem with flies unless lid is replaced after use.

Superstructure/ roof is not essential. Simple screen may suffice.

Concrete slab

Minimum depth 3m but greater if possible.

Porous pit lining - only required if ground is poor. Otherwise collar below slab will suffice

a: A simple improved pit latrine

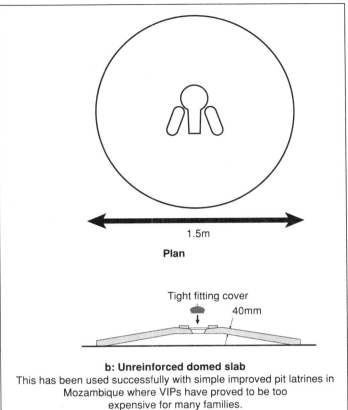

Plan

1.5m

Tight fitting cover

40mm

b: Unreinforced domed slab
This has been used successfully with simple improved pit latrines in Mozambique where VIPs have proved to be too expensive for many families.

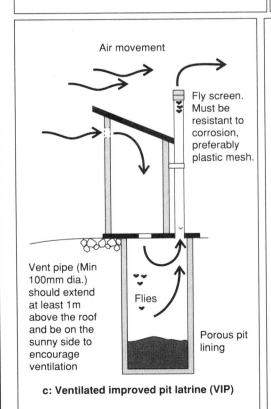

Air movement

Fly screen. Must be resistant to corrosion, preferably plastic mesh.

Vent pipe (Min 100mm dia.) should extend at least 1m above the roof and be on the sunny side to encourage ventilation

Flies

Porous pit lining

c: Ventilated improved pit latrine (VIP)

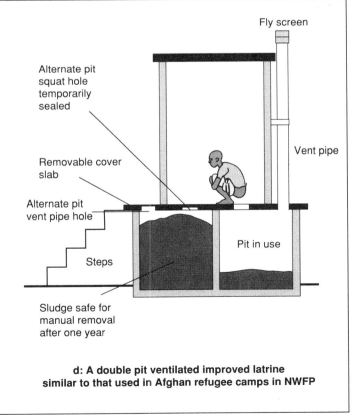

Fly screen

Alternate pit squat hole temporarily sealed

Removable cover slab

Alternate pit vent pipe hole

Vent pipe

Pit in use

Steps

Sludge safe for manual removal after one year

d: A double pit ventilated improved latrine similar to that used in Afghan refugee camps in NWFP

Figure 6.2. Typical pit latrine arrangements

Off-plot systems

Bucket latrine systems are unacceptable since they require handling of fresh faecal material and allow flies and other insects access to faeces in close proximity to food. The 'dry' latrines already referred to in the background section are a crude form of bucket latrine and their replacement should be a priority in upgrading programmes.

Wet systems

The preferred sanitation system in urban areas in Pakistan will almost always be some form of wet system. All wet systems incorporate a WC which may be flushed from a cistern (cistern flush) or by pouring water from a suitable container, typically a bucket or bowl (pour flush). Pour flush systems are cheaper, use less water (typically 3-6 litres per flush compared with 9-19 litres per flush for cistern flush WCs) and are less complex than cistern flush systems. The majority of WCs in low income areas are of the pour flush type and their use should be encouraged.

However, the main choices to be made with wet systems concern the means used to dispose of the effluent (water, faecal solids and anal cleansing materials) flushed from the pan. The available options can be categorised as follows:

- **Wholly on-plot:** single leach pit; twin leach pits; septic tank discharging to soakaway;
- **Partially on-plot:** septic tank discharging to sewer or drain;
- **Wholly off-plot:** conventional sewers.

The term on-plot signifies that effluent is disposed of either on the plot or immediately adjacent to it. On-plot options generally deal only with WC effluents and will require separate arrangements for the disposal of sullage water. Partially on-plot systems retain solids on or near the plot but remove waste water. They can be used either for WC wastes alone or for all waste flows. In general, it is preferable that sullage flows by-pass septic tanks providing that sullage connections are adequately trapped.

Factors affecting choice of system

In the first instance the choice will be between on-plot and sewered options. The factors which will effect the choice made include:

- **Cost**. Cost comparisons should include all costs, including those of off-site sewers, sewage treatment and maintenance where appropriate.

- **The availability of technical knowledge and skills** If these are limited, simple technologies should be preferred although there is of course the option of providing training in the more complex technologies.

- **The impact of the various available options on health and the environment.** All properly designed sanitation systems prevent household members coming into contact with infective faecal material and thus reduce direct health risks. However, they may have other effects which give rise to health risks elsewhere or adversely affect the environment, for instance those which arise from discharging untreated sewage to water-courses.

- **the operation and maintenance requirements of the various options.** These must be considered in relation to the capabilities of the individual householders, community groups or government departments that will be responsible for operation and maintenance. For instance, the arrangements for periodically removing solids will need to be considered for many on-plot options. When considering these options, it is necessary to determine who will be responsible for solids removal and how they will carry out the task in a hygienic way.

Bearing the above points in mind, Table 6.2 compares the main features of on-plot and sewered systems.

Sewers will probably be the best option where all of the following apply:

- trunk sewers are available close to the site;
- the housing density is high (>40-50 per ha.);
- there is or will be a good on-plot water supply.

On-plot sanitation will definitely be preferable where densities are low, there are no trunk sewers and the water supply is limited. There will many situations in which the choice will not be clear. In such situations the decisive factor may be the preference of the people living in the area to be upgraded.

Where a system requires that ongoing operation and maintenance tasks are devolved to individual householders or community groups, it is essential that responsibilities are clearly explained at the outset. Wherever possible, and certainly where new technologies are being introduced to an area, some form of technical back-up should be available to ensure that people are able to cope with tasks such as pit-emptying when they arise.

SEWERED SYSTEMS

Water use should be at least 60 litres/person/day for conventional sewers. Sewered septic tank systems can work with water use down to about 30 litres/person/day.

Remove all waste water from plot.

Wastewater not treated in any way.
Will pollute water courses if not treated.

Require some specialist skills in design and construction.

Require cooperation between community members to ensure that all connect to the sewer.

Cost increases with increasing average plot size

Minimal maintenance required if used correctly.
In practice, many sewers in informal areas require frequent cleaning.

Possible problems with final disposal in flat areas. These may be reduced by using a sewered septic tank system.

Sewer construction difficult if there is a very high water table.

ON-PLOT LEACH PIT SYSTEMS

Minimum water use required about 20 litres/person/day.

Separate arrangements required for water from bathrooms, kitchens etc.if water use above about 30 litres/person/day.

Faecal material decomposes in pits.

Require only basic building skills.

Can be constructed by individual householders independently of neighbours

Require space to provide leach-pit or pits on or next to plot

Periodic pit emptying required.

Can be used in flat areas.

Aquifer may be polluted if the water table is within about 4 metres of the surface

Table 6.2. Comparison of on-plot and sewered systems

ON-PLOT LEACH-PIT SYSTEMS

Design

The theory of leach pit design is very simple. It is necessary to know the following:

◆ *The rate at which solids will accumulate.* Allow a rate of 40 litres/person/year if local information is not available.

◆ *The highest level of the groundwater table.* Where the unconfined aquifer is a water source, the distance between the bottom of the pit and this level must be sufficient to prevent contamination of the groundwater. For the fine soils found beneath most Pakistani cities, this distance should be at least 2m and preferably 4m.

◆ *The rate at which water will percolate into the ground.* This is only required if it is intended to discharge sullage water to the leach pit.

For a solids accumulation rate of 40 litres/person/year, the required pit volume V is given by the equation:

$$V = 0.04 \times P \times T$$

where V is in cubic metres, P is the number of people regularly using the latrine and T is the interval in years at which the pit is desludged.

A large single pit as shown in Figure 6.3(a) will often be the best option where the groundwater table is low, particularly where ground conditions are good so that only the top part of the pit has to be lined. (A 1.5m diameter by 4m deep pit should last a family of 6 for about 30 years and even a 1m diameter by 3m deep pit would last the same family for around 10 years).

Where the depth of pit is limited, either by a high water table or because of the danger of undermining existing buildings, pits will have to be desludged at relatively frequent intervals. Any person handling raw faecal material runs a risk of infection. This danger can be overcome by using the double pit system illustrated in Figure 6.3(b). In this system, the first pit is used until it is full and the flow is then directed into the second pit. When this is nearly full, the contents of the first pit are removed and flow is diverted back to it. The process is repeated every time a pit is almost full. The interval between the time when the pit is full and that when it is emptied must be long enough to ensure that the contents have decomposed into an odourless, pathogen-free material which can be removed without any danger to public health. In view of Pakistan's pronounced cold season, it is advisable that pits should be designed to take at least 2 years to fill. For a family of 8, this requires a volume of about 0.64m³ which can be provided by a 0.9m diameter by 1m deep pit.

Design and construction details

The connection pipes between WCs and leach pits may be PVC, clay or concrete. In Pakistan, locally produced 90mm diameter PVC pipes will often be the best option because of their smoothness. These pipes just fit inside standard 100mm diameter concrete pipes and the latter may be used where external loads are expected.

The slope of connection pipes should be at least 1 in 40 and preferably 1 in 20. The former slope requires 1.8 inches (46mm) fall on a standard 6 ft (1.83m) pipe.

In poor ground, leach-pits should be lined with 112mm (4.5") brickwork laid with spaces of about 100mm (4") between adjacent bricks. In firm ground, it may only be necessary to line the top 0.5m of the pit.

SEWERAGE - PLANNING

Two tasks are involved in the planning of a sewerage system:

◆ Decide the type of system to be adopted;
◆ Select a suitable sewer layout.

Type of system

The main types of sewer system are as follows.

Separate system

This is designed to carry foul flows only, ie. flows from toilet, kitchen and bathroom areas. Storm run-off is excluded. In practice, it is extremely difficult to exclude all storm flows, particularly when sewers are installed after houses have been built. For this reason, separate systems should always be designed with some allowance for these flows. Information on the allowance that should be made will be given in the section on design flows.

Combined system

This is designed to carry both foul and storm flows and thus removes the need for a separate storm drainage system. Except where rainfall is very light, storm flows will tend to be very much greater than foul flows. This leads to two problems. First, sewers will carry relatively small foul flows for most of the time and there may be problems with deposition of solids. Second, there will be a need to cope with large storm flows at treatment works and pumping stations. For these reasons, combined systems are rarely used in normal practice nowadays. Nevertheless, they may be an option in upgrading areas where limited space precludes the provision of separate foul and storm systems. In such cases, provision must be made for separating foul and storm flows before treatment.

Interceptor tank system

In this, solids are removed in interceptor tanks located on house connections, normally on the WC connection only. It has the advantage that sewer sizes can be reduced and flatter gradients can be used because there is no need to transport solids. Against this must be set the need to arrange for tanks to be desludged at regular intervals. Protagonists of interceptor tank systems claim that they are cheaper than conventional sewers but experience suggests that this will not always be the case. Where there is any doubt about costs, both the conventional approach and that using interceptor tanks should be costed.

A variation on the basic interceptor tank system is to provide shared septic tanks serving 5-20 houses from which the effluent is discharged to the sewers. In this system, the connections from houses to septic tanks are designed as conventional sewers and the sewers downstream from the septic tanks to sewered interceptor tank system standards. Interceptor tanks at the ends of community-built systems will protect the main sewers from any solid materials carried in the branch systems and the system may therefore be attractive to sewerage authorities which are concerned by the prospect of direct discharges from community built sewers to their own sewers.

Figure 6.4 shows typical layouts for two branch sewers, the first discharging to a single shared septic tank and the second preceded by interceptor tanks on every connection

Choice of system

A combined system may be considered where:

◆ sewage does not have to be pumped and storm flows can be separated downstream; and
◆ rights of way are limited in width and separate storm facilities will be difficult to install.

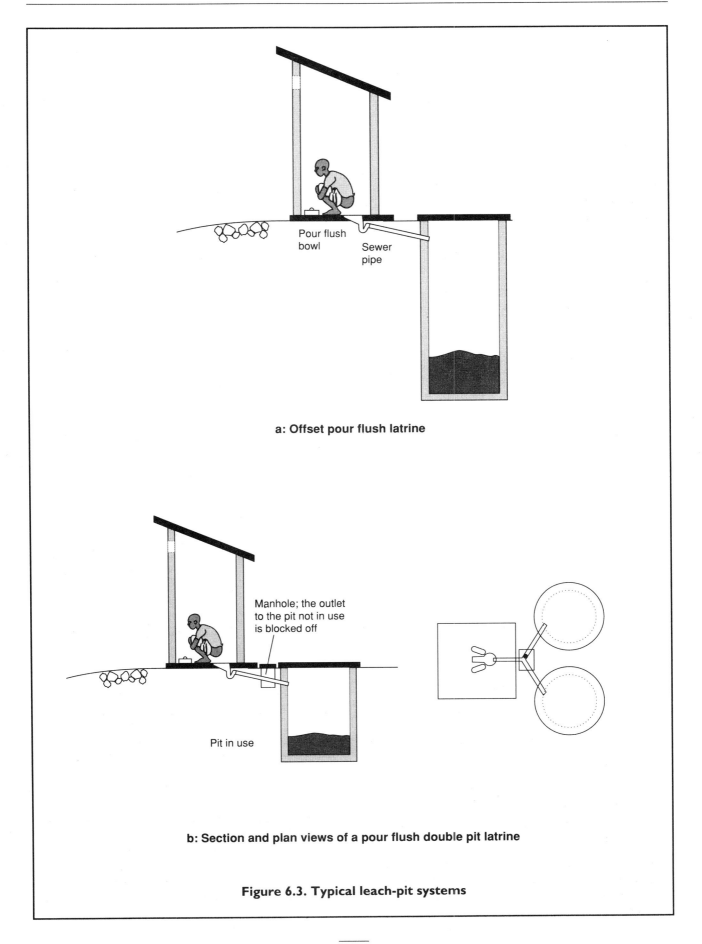

a: Offset pour flush latrine

b: Section and plan views of a pour flush double pit latrine

Figure 6.3. Typical leach-pit systems

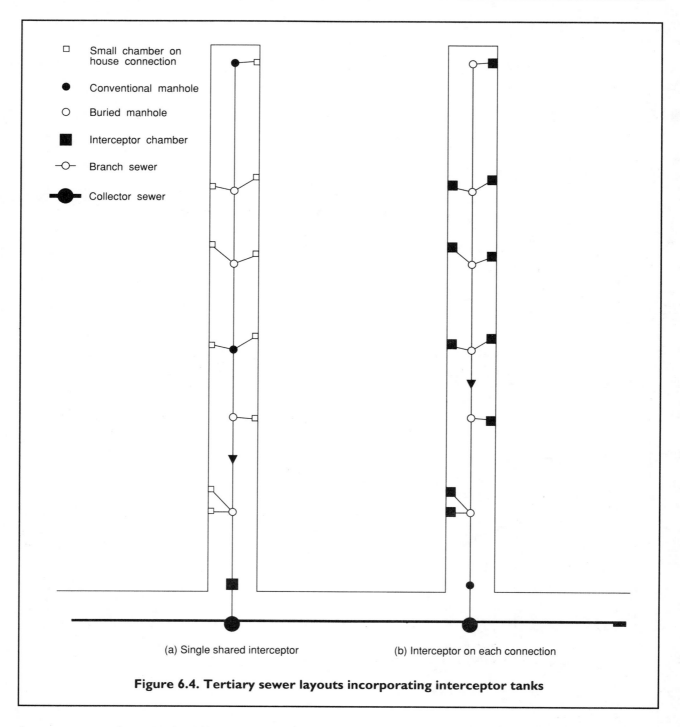

□	Small chamber on house connection
●	Conventional manhole
○	Buried manhole
■	Interceptor chamber
─○─	Branch sewer
─●─	Collector sewer

(a) Single shared interceptor   (b) Interceptor on each connection

Figure 6.4. Tertiary sewer layouts incorporating interceptor tanks

An interceptor tank system should be considered where:

◆ the available fall is limited, for instance by a high water table or the relatively high level of existing collector sewers;

◆ the majority of houses already have septic tanks on WC outlets;

◆ solid waste collection services are poor and there is evidence of frequent blockages in conventional systems in similar areas. (This will often be the case).

Otherwise, a nominally separate system should be used with some allowance included for storm flows.

Sewer layout

The cost of sewerage depends on the length of the system and the depth of the sewers. In general, layouts should aim to minimise sewer lengths, providing that this does not result in increased depths. In practice, this means that sewers will normally follow topography as closely as possible with trunk and collector sewers laid along natural drainage routes.

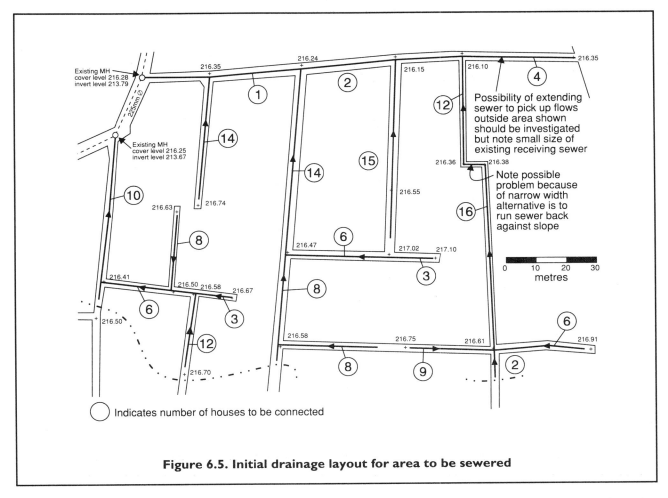

Indicates number of houses to be connected

Figure 6.5. Initial drainage layout for area to be sewered

Local (tertiary) sewers

In order to determine the best layout, a plan of the area to be sewered is required. If a survey is not available, a simple plan of the area should be prepared at a scale of 1:500, 1:1000 or their imperial equivalents as explained in Chapter 4. The route and levels of the nearest sewers to which sewers can be discharged (or drains if sewers are not available and temporary discharge to an existing drain is acceptable as in Orangi) should be shown. Levels should be provided at intersections, changes in slope and at any points that are obviously low-lying relative to surrounding areas.

Once the plan has been prepared, the layout can be drawn on it. The best layout for local sewerage schemes connecting to existing collector sewers or drains will usually be fairly obvious with sewer routes following streets and lanes in most cases. In theory, there is the possibility of laying branch sewers serving a few houses through or behind plots but this is rarely an option in Pakistan. (Some informal schemes in Karachi do provide narrow service lanes at the rear of plots). The selected routes should follow the fall of the land except where there is little fall and a saving in overall length can be achieved by laying a sewer against the natural fall. Figure 6.5 shows a typical plan with

sewer routes marked. Figure 6.6 shows how this basic plan can be developed to show the location of manholes. Figure 11.4 shows how this can be developed into a finished sewerage layout drawing.

Collector (primary and secondary) sewers

For overall system design, the basic procedure is similar except that a plan scale of 1:2500 or even 1:5000 will be more appropriate. It will often be helpful to plot the routes of existing main drains and catchment area boundaries on the plan since it is likely that sewerage systems will have similar routes and catchment boundaries. Figures 6.10(a) and (b) show the stages in developing the overall plan for a secondary sewerage system, starting with the plotting of all drains and moving on to the identification of secondary sewer routes.

Pumping of sewage should be avoided wherever possible because it will increase running costs and the system will be liable to failure in the event of plant breakdown or power cuts. Where it is unavoidable, pumping facilities should be centralised as far as possible. **Designers should avoid providing pumping stations in upgrading schemes unless the organisation to operate and maintain them exists.**

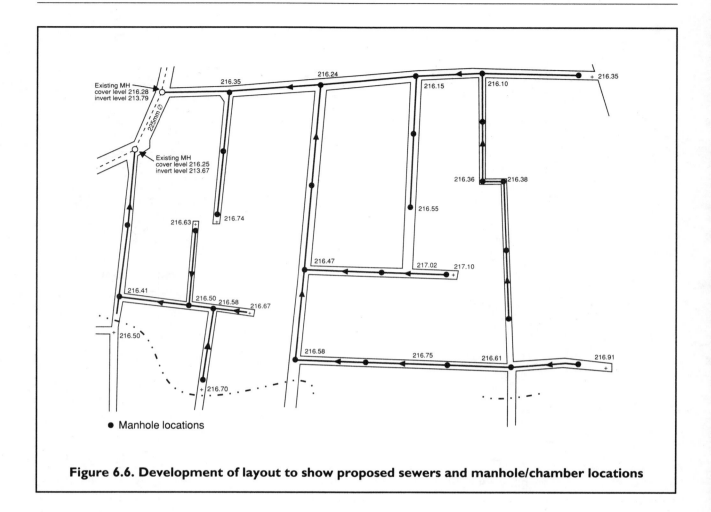

Figure 6.6. Development of layout to show proposed sewers and manhole/chamber locations

SEWERAGE - DETAILED DESIGN

The initial objectives of sewer design are to determine the size of sewer required and the gradient at which it should be laid. In conventional design, both are related to the peak flow in the sewer. For tertiary sewers, the design process is often simplified because the size of the sewer is governed by the minimum allowable diameter rather than the capacity required to carry the peak flow. The procedures for determining sewer gradients and sizes will be considered first for tertiary sewers in both conventional and interceptor tank systems and then in outline for trunk/secondary sewers.

Conventional tertiary sewers

Number of houses served

The calculation of peak flows in tertiary sewers requires information on the number of houses served rather than the contributing population. The number of houses contributing to each sewer length should be added to a copy of the layout plan as shown in Figure 6.5. The cumulative number of houses contributing at any point on the sewer can then determined. All plots should be included, including those which are undeveloped.

Design flow

For all sewers, the design flow is the peak foul flow plus any allowance that is to be made for infiltration of groundwater and ingress of stormwater. Once the number of houses contibuting to a sewer has been decided, the peak foul flow in the sewer can be calculated directly from an analysis of the probable frequencies and rates of discharge from WCs, washing areas, showers etc. converted into standard load units. The analysis is complicated and the results are normally presented in graph form. Figure 6.7 may be used to determine the likely peak flow for a sewer serving up to about 300 houses. It assumes a fairly high water use and the maximum level of on-plot facilities that will normally be found in low-income areas and is thus conservative.

Since almost all tertiary sewers will be laid above the water table, groundwater infiltration can usually be discounted. The allowance for storm water in nominally separate tertiary sewers can be taken to be equal to the peak foul flow, ie. the sewer should not run more than half full at the peak foul flow.

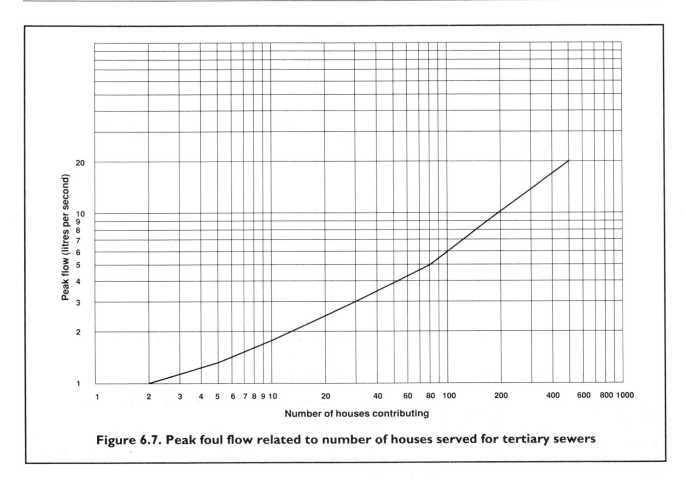

Figure 6.7. Peak foul flow related to number of houses served for tertiary sewers

Determination of sewer diameter

Using the maximum peak foul flow values given in Figure 6.7, assuming an equal allowance for storm water and using appropriate minimum sewer gradients, the following conclusions can be reached for nominally separate systems.

- a 100mm sewer at a gradient of 1:150 will serve up to about 15 houses;

- a 150mm sewer at a gradient of 1:175 will serve up to about 60 houses

- a 225mm sewer at a gradient of 1:210 will serve up to about 260 houses.

These figures assume that the sewers run freely without blockages. In practice, most sewerage authorities specify that the minimum diameter of public sewers should be either 150mm or 225mm. Many authorities in Pakistan required the larger diameter, arguing that smaller sizes will suffer frequently from blockages and are therefore unacceptable. While inspection confirms that sewers in low-income areas are often partially blocked by silt and solid waste, there is no real evidence that 150mm diameter sewers require more maintenance than those of 225mm diameter. Indeed, research suggests that a smaller diameter sewer is more efficient hydraulically for flows within its capacity. More research is needed on this topic but the following minimum standards are suggested for places where there is an existing 225mm minimum diameter standard:

- Single branch sewer serving up to 25 houses 150mm dia.

- All other sewers 225mm dia.

If these standards are adopted, the sizes of the vast majority of tertiary sewers can be determined on the basis of minimum diameter standards rather than the peak design flow.

The procedure for combined sewers is first to determine the gradient as for a nominally separate sewer and then to calculate the size of sewer required to carry the combined flow at this gradient.

Sewer gradient

The sewer gradient should be the greater of:

- the minimum allowable gradient; and

- the slope available to maintain minimum cover. This will usually approximate to the ground slope but may sometimes be influenced by the minimum allowable cover over the sewer.

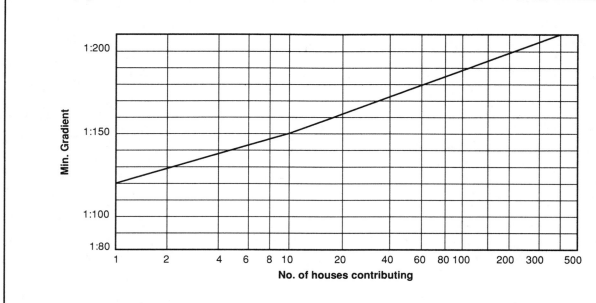

Figure 6.8. Relationship between minimum sewer slope and number of houses served for tertiary sewers

In steeply sloping areas, it may also be appropriate to specify a maximum sewer gradient and provide drop manholes where this is less than the ground slope. For drops up to about 1m, it is probably unnecessary to provide a piped drop, particularly when the only materials available with which to construct the drop are expensive cast-iron pipes.

Minimum gradients The gradients of conventional separate and combined sewers must be sufficient to ensure that solids do not settle permanently. Figure 6.8 gives the suggested relationship between sewer slope and number of houses contributing for tertiary sewers. Once the layout has been decided and the number of houses on each sewer leg counted, as previously described, the minimum allowable gradient for each sewer length can be obtained from this figure.

Maximum gradients It has been traditionally assumed that flow velocities in sewers should be limited in order to prevent wear of the sewer invert. Recent research suggests that such restrictions are not necessary but this may not be true in informal areas where large quantities of grit are carried in sewers. It is therefore advisable to restrict maximum velocities in sewers to 2.5 m/sec, giving the following maximum gradients for the sizes commonly used for tertiary sewers:

Sewer diameter	Gradient
100mm	1:5
150mm	1:9
225mm	1:15

Sewered interceptor tank systems

Interceptor tanks on house connections have two important consequences for the sewers to which they connect. These are that:

◆ peak flows are attenuated (spread and reduced) in the interceptor tanks so that sewers can be smaller; and

◆ gross solids are removed, greatly reducing the probability of blockages and allowing flatter slopes to be used.

The greater the number of house connections contributing to the flow, the smaller will be the flow attenuation. This implies that the greatest reductions in size over conventional systems will occur for tertiary sewers. Size reductions should also be significant for some secondary sewers. All sewers in the system, including trunk sewers, should operate satisfactorily at flatter gradients than conventional sewers, provided that interceptor tanks are regularly desludged.

Sewer diameter

Research is needed into the design of sewered interceptor tank systems and the guidelines given here are based on observation of the performance of existing systems. There are examples, including some in Peshawar, of 75mm dia. uPVC sewers serving up to 15 houses and operating satisfactorily. Allowing for flow attenuation, the following design guidelines are recommended where regular desludging of interceptor tanks can be guaranteed:

75mm dia. sewer to serve up to 15 houses;
100mm dia. sewer to serve up to 30 houses;
150mm dia. sewer to serve up to 75 houses;
225mm dia. sewer to serve up to 260 houses;

Where regular desludging cannot be guaranteed, there may still be a benefit in providing interceptor tanks since they should retain gross solids that would otherwise block the sewer, even when full of sludge. However, the minimum diameter allowed should be increased to 100mm.

Sewer gradients

As already indicated, minimum gradients for sewered interceptor tank systems can be less than those for conventional sewers. The following figures, which result in pipe full velocities of 0.4-0.45 m/sec, are suggested for use where regular desludging of interceptor tanks can be expected:

Sewer diameter	Gradient
75mm	1:150
100mm	1:200
150mm	1:275
225mm	1:450

Where regular desludging cannot be guaranteed, gradients should be as for conventional sewers.

Size and dimensions of interceptor tanks

More research is required on the subject of the size and dimensions of interceptor tanks. Some authorities advise that the tanks should be designed in accordance with conventional septic tank theory, typically giving about 24 hours retention at average flows. However, there are examples of smaller tanks performing satisfactorily and a minimum retention of 12 hours at the average flow should be satisfactory. This will require that the tank is desludged at intervals of 1-2 years rather than the 3-4 years that would be normal for conventional septic tanks. Tanks should consist of a single chamber and do not need a baffle pipe on the outlet since there should be no objection to floating solids being carried out into the sewer. The plan dimensions of tanks on individual connections should not need to exceed about 1m x 0.75m.

Primary/secondary systems

The procedure for the design of primary and secondary sewers is briefly described here with attention focussed on those aspects which assume particular importance in informal areas.

Determination of catchment areas

The catchment areas for primary/secondary sewers can be determined in the light of the sewer routes, the topography and the planned extent of the tertiary sewers draining to the system.

Subdivision of system for calculation purposes

Once the catchment boundaries have been fixed, nodes should be located on a plan of the system at all junctions between primary/secondary sewers and at further intervals as required to ensure that sewer legs between nodes drain between 3 and 10ha. The areas of these sub-catchments are then calculated and the sewer legs are numbered, starting at the head of the longest sewer run, as shown on Figure 6.9. Figure 6.10 shows the stages in determining main sewer routes, catchment boundaries, node locations and catchment subdivisions for an area in North-East Lahore.

Calculation of design populations

The population of each sub-catchment must now be calculated. For areas which are already substantially developed, this should be based on average population density figures. These are obtained by multiplying housing densities for typical areas obtained from analysis of plans by average household sizes based on the analysis of social surveys. Calculations for the former should include presently undeveloped plots while some increase in the latter with time may be assumed. An allowance of 10-20% growth in average household size over a 30 year design period will usually be appropriate.

For urban fringe areas and others in which development is still occurring rapidly, it may be appropriate to estimate future design populations by projecting forward existing population figures, using the expected annual percentage rate of growth. However, care should be taken to ensure that this procedure does not give future population densities that are unrealistically high.

Calculation of design flow

The design flow for conventional separate systems is obtained by calculating the average dry weather flow

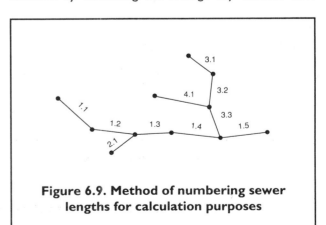

Figure 6.9. Method of numbering sewer lengths for calculation purposes

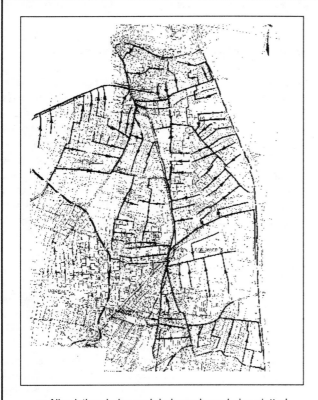

a: All existing drains and drainage boundaries plotted

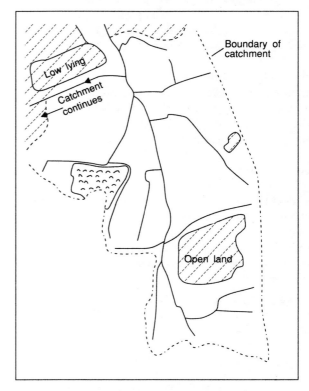

b: Main sewer routes identified

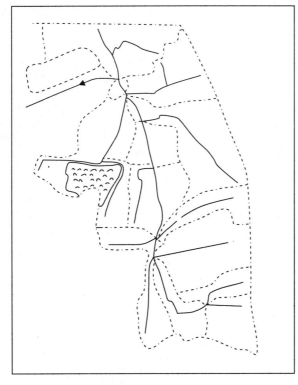

c: Catchment area sub-divided

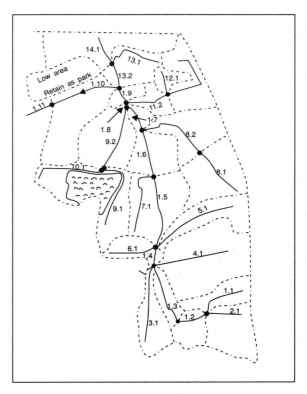

d: Sewer legs numbered

Figure 6.10. Development of secondary sewer scheme for typical area

(DWF) and then applying a factor, typically 6, to obtain the design flow. The factor allows for both peaks in the DWF and some ingress of stormwater. Because of the allowance made for storm water, there is no need to allow an additional air space above the flow at the design flow. Thus, the sewer capacity can be related directly to the design flow. The DWF in residential areas is related to:

◆ the design population; and

◆ the per-capita water consumption;

The calculation of design populations has already been covered in the previous section. For informal housing areas, where per-capita water consumptions in areas with house connections will usually be in the range 75-150 lpd, the average sewage flow can be taken as 80% of the average water consumption. (The water supply figure should exclude leakage but include on-plot wastage). Conventional sewers will not normally be appropriate for areas served by public standposts.

Additional allowance will have to be made for any industrial and institutional flows but these will not normally be significant in residential areas. Where relatively large industries or institutional discharges occur within the design area, specific allowance for them should be made in calculations.

For combined sewers, storm flows should be calculated using the methods given in Chapter 8 and added to the peak foul flow in order to obtain the design flow. The minimum sewer slope, however, should be calculated on the basis of the peak foul flow. Suitable peak factors for calculating peak foul flows for larger sewers can be obtained from Figure 6.11

Determination of sewer gradients

As for tertiary sewers, the sewer gradients adopted for primary/ secondary sewers will normally be the greater of the ground slope and the minimum gradient required to prevent settlement of solids.

Figure 6.12 should be used to obtain a preliminary estimate of minimum slopes for primary and secondary sewers. It relates design flow to sewer slope and also indicates the maximum flows that can be carried by different sewer diameters at the given minimum slopes.

Sewer gradients should not exceed the following values:

Diameter	Gradient
225mm	1:15
300mm	1:22
375mm	1:30
450mm	1:39
525mm	1:47
600mm	1:57

Gradients may also be influenced by the minimum allowable cover over the sewer which will be considered later in the section on standards.

Determination of sewer diameter

The sewer diameter must be sufficient to provide enough capacity for the design flow at the design gradient. The simplest method for calculating sewer capacities is based on Mannings formula which states that:

$$V = R^{2/3}s^{1/2}/n$$

where **V** is the flow velocity;
R is the hydraulic radius (**d/4**);
s is the hydraulic gradient; and
n is Mannings roughness coefficient.

The value of **n** is usually taken as 0.013. However, recent research suggests that the value for slimed sewers should be higher. The need for a higher value is confirmed by observations in informal areas which reveal that few sewers run completely freely. A value of 0.015 has therefore been adopted in this manual.

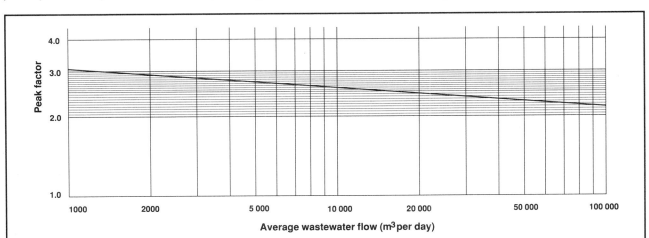

Figure 6.11. Relationship between peak foul flow factor and flow for primary and secondary sewers

For primary/secondary sewers, V should not be less than 0.7m/sec if "**n**" is taken as 0.015. (This is roughly the equivalent of the conventional standard of 0.75m/sec for an "**n**" value of 0.013).

For primary and secondary sewers, Figure 6.12 may be used to obtain an initial estimate of the required sewer diameter. Detailed calculations should follow using standard calculation sheets similar to that for stormwater drainage calculations given in Figure 8.4.

Invert levels and manhole types.

Sewer sizes and gradients are normally calculated between points at which manholes will be located. Invert levels at these points are calculated in the course of the detailed design and entered on to standard calculation sheets. The invert levels at intermediate manholes can then be worked out by interpolation but the depth should be checked in each case to ensure that minimum depth standards are not being broken. Once the invert levels and manhole depths have been obtained, the appropriate manhole design can be chosen using the criteria given later in this chapter. Figure 11.4 gives details of the way in which cover and invert levels, sewer diameters and gradients can be presented for tertiary sewers. For primary and secondary sewers, the information will normally be provided as a plan and section in the form shown in Figure 11.3.

Design standards and details

Minimum cover

The minimum permissible cover is an important factor in determining the depth of sewers throughout their lengths. Reduced sewer depths mean lower costs, partly because of reduced excavation but, perhaps more importantly, because of the smaller manholes that can be used on shallow sewers. Design criteria for manholes on shallow sewers will be given later.

Minimum cover standards should take into account both the traffic loading and the strength of the pipe. For local streets, the likely traffic loading can be related to the width of the street. Bearing these points in mind, Table 6.3 gives recommended minimum cover standards for the concrete sewer pipes commonly used in Pakistan.

The above figures are based on extensive field experience in Lahore and Peshawar. It should be noted that rights of way are invariably less than street widths because of obstructions such as house access steps and electricity poles. The covers provided over clay and plastic sewer pipes should be at least 500mm unless some protection, in the form of a concrete bed and surround, is provided to the pipe.

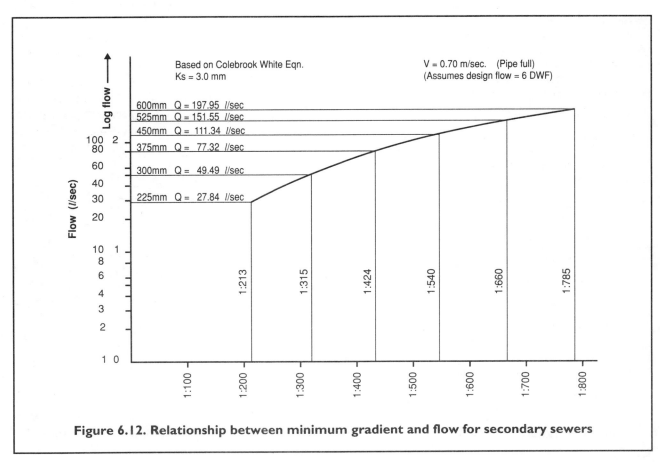

Figure 6.12. Relationship between minimum gradient and flow for secondary sewers

Street width	Heaviest vehicle	Recommended minimum cover
>3m	Motorcycle	250mm
3 - 4.5m	Suzuki car or van	350mm
4.5 - 6m	Cars, horse drawn carts etc.	400mm
>6 residential	Occasional trucks	500mm
Main roads	Heavy goods vehicles	800mm

Table 6.3. Minimum cover standards for 150mm and 225mm dia. concrete sewers

The standards given in Table 6.3 are those required for structural purposes. Sewers must also be deep enough to allow house connections to be made. As a general rule, the minimum depth to sewer invert for connections of 5 metres length and less should be 500mm with an additional 100mm allowed for every additional 5 metres length of connection.

Cover over 100mm concrete pipes can be less. In non-vehicular streets, house connections are often laid with virtually no cover. As a general rule, the covers allowed on 100mm concrete pipes should not be less than two-thirds of those given in Table 6.3.

Some reduction in cover is possible if a sewer is bedded and surrounded with concrete. This will normally only be economic for short lengths at the heads of those sewers whose levels have an effect on levels throughout the whole system.

Manhole and chamber dimensions

Manholes and chambers are intended :

◆ to allow drainage rods to be pushed into the sewer to clear blockages: and

◆ to allow access to the sewer so that unwanted material can be removed.

Manholes are designed to be entered to achieve these tasks. Inspection chambers are used on sewers which are shallow enough for the invert to be reached without entering the chamber. Suggested minimum plan dimensions for manholes and chambers are given in Table 6.4. The term 'partial entry' used in the table means that a man will have to stand on the benching in the manhole with his upper body above ground level.

Some typical details for small manholes are given in Figure 6.13

Manhole location and spacing

Accepted standards require that manholes are placed at all junctions, and changes in direction, gradient and size and at intervals that allow the sewer to be rodded or otherwise cleaned. For primary and secondary sewers, manhole spacing should not exceed about 90 metres and for tertiary sewers, 50 metres. Even this may be too great if proper drain rods with screw-in connections are not available. (The common practice in Pakistan at present is to tie bamboo rods together with wire. Such rods have been tested between manholes spaced 25 metres apart).

There is an argument for reducing the number of manholes or even eliminating them since observation suggests that most blockages are caused by material which enters sewers through missing or broken manhole covers. Given existing codes and standards and the probability that some connections will not be adequately trapped, it is unlikely that this approach will be widely adopted for conventional systems. However, it should be applicable for sewered septic tank systems since the septic tanks will retain large solids and greatly reduce the likelihood of sewer blockages.

A compromise approach, which would also be possible for conventional systems, would be to provide manholes with covers below ground level as shown in Figure 6.14. This would enable access to be gained in the event of problems but would prevent it under normal conditions. It would seem to be particularly applicable with surfacing materials such as bricks and blocks which can be removed and then reinstated. This approach should only be used on tertiary sewers

House connections

The standards recommended below for house connections apply to both conventional and sewered septic tank systems, except where variations are indicated.

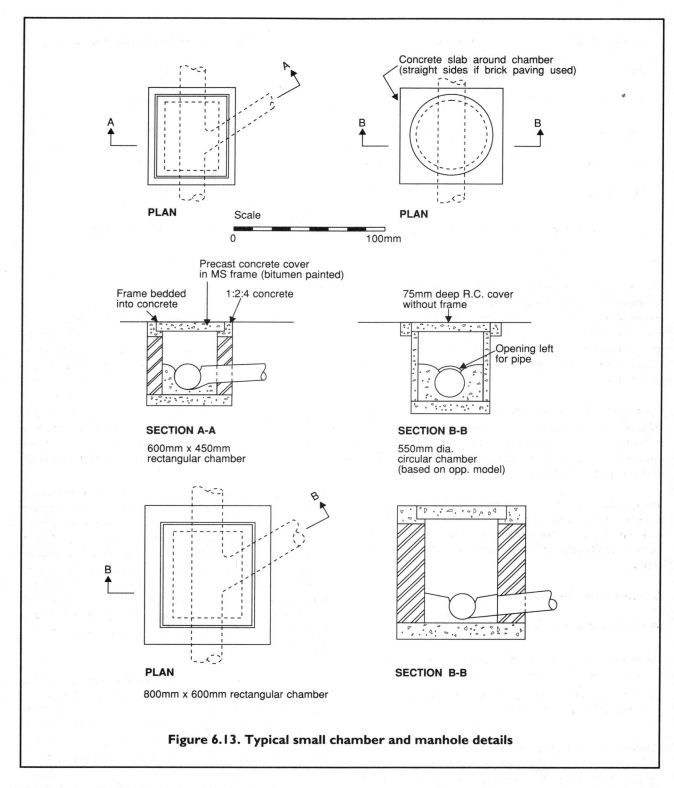

Figure 6.13. Typical small chamber and manhole details

Minimum pipe diameter This should be 100mm for concrete and clayware connections from WCs. 90mm uPVC pipes may be used for lengths up to 5m downstream of WCs. Underground connections carrying sullage only should normally be 75mm diameter but a reduction to 50mm may be appropriate for individual connections preceded by a grit/grease trap. Connections downstream of interceptor tanks may be 50mm diameter.

Minimum gradient For connections from WCs this should be 1:50. A gradient of 1:100 will be acceptable for a connection carrying sullage water only, provided that it is preceded by a grit/grease trap. The slope downstream of an interceptor tank may be reduced to 1:150

Cover See the section on cover to sewers.

Depth to sewer invert (mm)	Entry required	Size of rectangular manhole/ chamber (mm)	Diameter of circular chamber (mm)	Step irons required
<800	no	600 x 450	550	no
800-1000	partial	800 x 600	700	no
1000-1350	partial	1000 x 600	800	yes
1350-2000	yes	1200 x 750	1050	yes

Table 6.4. Recommended minimum plan dimensions for manholes and chambers

On-plot layout

Where possible, on-plot drains should all be directed to one point on the plot or immediately outside it in order to allow one connection from the plot to the sewer. A small inspection chamber should be built at this point and ideally the connection to the sewer should be trapped. For sewered interceptor tank systems, this chamber can be replaced by the interceptor tank. Where the connection is to a conventional sewer, it is advisable to have a grit/ grease trap on the sullage drains above the point where they connect to the drain from the WC.

Where existing arrangements are such that all on-plot drains cannot be brought together into one sewer connection, no inspection chamber is necessary on connections less than about 5 metres in length, providing that they can be rodded back from a manhole at the junction with the sewer.

Location of WCs

Given the range of possible on-plot arrangements, there are many possible locations for WCs. In the last instance, the choice of WC location must rest with household members but the following guidelines are intended to help technical advisers and community organisers to guide that choice.

Ideally, WCs to be connected to sewers should be located near the front of plots so as to minimise the length of connections. In many cases, it will be possible to convert an existing dry latrine. Where floor space at the front of the plot is not available, the possibility of situating the WC at first or even second floor level should be examined. This will probably be cheaper and easier than providing a WC near the back of the plot and running the discharge pipework under existing buildings.

Where disposal of effluent is to be to a leach pit or pits, the location of the WC must be reasonably close to open space where the pit or pits can be sited. This may be available in a courtyard or, where siting of pits under public rights of way is acceptable, in front of the plot.

CONSTRUCTION AND IMPLEMENTATION

These notes on construction and implementation cover only some of the main points. More detailed information is contained in standard specifications and guidelines for site supervisors. Implementation procedures are covered first, followed by notes on particular materials and system components.

Implementation procedures

The aim should always be to complete work as quickly as possible once it has begun. For safety reasons, trenches should not be left open for longer than is necessary. Similarly, delays in placing manhole and chamber covers should be avoided so as to reduce the time during which solid waste might be thrown into the sewer. Ideally, sewage flows should not be allowed into sewers until manholes have been completed and covers are available. Before this, sewers should be plugged at manholes, preferably using specially made wooden plugs.

It is important to lay sewers to level and some means of accurately measuring levels and falls is essential. The best method is to use profiles and a traveller, also known as 'boning rods'. A surveyors level and staff are required to fix the levels of the profiles but these will not always be available. Two other methods of measuring relative levels, a spirit level and straight-edge and a transparent tube filled with water, may be appropriate for tertiary sewers. The former method is preferable since a water level can give inaccurate results if not used carefully. The spirit level should be used with a straight edge to measure the fall on each sewer pipe. The required fall on a standard 6ft (1.83m) pipe for a gradient of 1:150 would be 1/2 inch or 12.2mm.

In good ground, sewers may be laid directly on the prepared trench bottom with a small hole dug at each joint to take the collar and so allow the whole of the pipe to be in contact with the trench bottom. Under no circumstances should bricks or stones be placed under the pipe to support it.

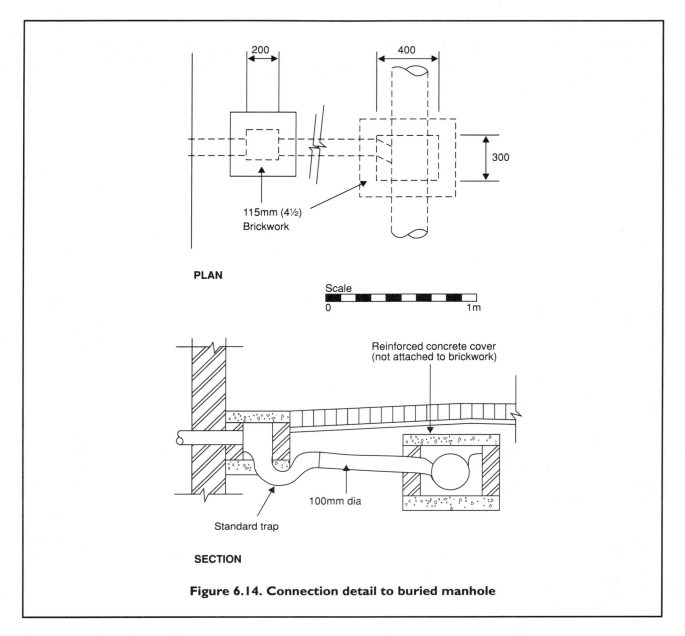

Figure 6.14. Connection detail to buried manhole

In poor ground, sewers may be laid on a bed of gravel, sand or broken bricks. If gravel or broken bricks are used, the size of the pieces should not be greater than 20mm. The depth of bedding should normally be 75mm for 100mm diameter sewers and 100mm for larger sewers. (For sewers greater than 600mm increased bedding depths will be required).

Materials

Pipes

Most government departments specify that spigot and socket joints must be used for public sewers. The wall thickness, concrete mix and reinforcement should be in accordance with the relevant specifications, the American Standard ASTM Designation C76 and British Standard BS5911. Many pipe manufacturers in Pakistan already

manufacture to these standards. For the smaller pipe sizes, reinforcement is not necessary although most manufacturers provide nominal light reinforcement. For such pipes, which may be manufactured in small local factories, the most important points to check are that the concrete mix is adequate (at least 1:1.5:3) and that the concrete is cured after the pipe is cast. This is done by submerging the pipe in water for several days after it has been cast.

Most spigot and socket pipes manufactured in Pakistan are nominally intended to have flexible rubber ring joints but the grooves and rubber rings are rarely of adequate quality. It is therefore better in most cases to make a rigid joint using cement mortar and omitting the rubber ring. Plain ended pipes with should be considered for tertiary sewers. The normal jointing procedure for such pipes is to push jute soaked in cement slurry into the joint and then to cast 1:3 concrete around the joint.

Manholes

The main points about manholes concern benching, the relative levels of pipes and covers. Benching should be brought up to above the soffit (crown) level of the main sewer. In general, the soffits of branch sewers should not be lower than that of the main sewer. Where the diameter of the main sewer changes at the manhole, the invert level of the outgoing sewer should be dropped by an amount equal to the difference in diameter between the outgoing and incoming sewers. In other words, sewers of different diameters should be laid soffit to soffit rather than invert to invert.

Manhole covers may be cast iron or reinforced concrete with or without a cast iron or mild steel frame. There is a danger that cast iron covers will be stolen for their scrap value and they should not normally be used in upgrading schemes. Standard framed circular covers should be used for conventional manholes. (At present, many of these have a 550mm clear opening but an increase to 600mm is desirable). For shallow manholes, it is desirable that the cover extends over the plan area of the manhole.

The most expensive part of the cover, indeed of the whole manhole is the frame and considerable cost savings can be made if it is omitted. This should be considered for covers which are not in vehicular streets and are not therefore expected to take heavy traffic loading. Unframed covers should be circular since rectangular unframed covers tend to break at the corners. Unframed circular covers have been used successfully by the Orangi Pilot Project.

WC details

'Eastern' style squatting latrines are the type most commonly used in Pakistan. Most WC pans available in the market are ceramic with costs (1991) ranging from about Rs120 upwards. They have a connection for a pipe from a cistern but are commonly used in a pour-flush mode. Cement mortar pans are also available at a cost of about Rs 80 per unit. These are less satisfactory than ceramic pans since the faeces are more likely to become attached to the sides of the pan. In view of the small price difference and the low cost of the pan as a percentage of that of the complete installation, ceramic pans should normally be used. The 'P' traps available in the market are ceramic and locally manufactured.

WC pans which require minimal amounts of water for flushing have been developed for use in pour-flush toilets. The use of such pans is advantageous where the discharge is to leach pits in poorly draining ground and where the water supply is poor. The reduction in flushing volume is achieved by some remodelling of the pan but mainly by reducing the depth of the water seal to 20-30mm. The standard 'P' traps available in the market in Pakistan have a water seal depth of 25mm and are thus suitable for pour-flush toilets.

7.

STREET AND LANE PAVING

SUMMARY

This chapter is concerned with the planning of paving schemes, their structural design the materials used in them and good design and construction details and practices. It should be read in conjunction with Chapter 8 which deals with the role of street surfacing as part of the drainage scheme for an area. Wider issues concerning minimum desirable access requirements and rights of way are not considered in detail since there is rarely scope to alter those that already exist, given the permanent nature of building construction in informal areas in Pakistan.

The chapter begins by examining the reasons for paving, and then provides an introduction to the main types of paving available. This leads in to a section on planning which covers the choice of pavement type, pavement width standards and overall decisions on pavement levels. The development of standard design details for street cross-sections, pavement structure and edge details is considered next. A short section on the application of these standard designs in particular upgrading schemes is followed by an introduction to construction details and good construction practice. Annexes provide additional information on the range of pavement options available and the design approach used to calculate the pavement depth required.

KEY POINTS

◆

The main functions of paving in upgrading areas are to provide a hard dry access and to improve drainage. Skid resistance is less important because of the low speeds possible in most streets in informal areas.

◆

Gravel, hardcore and waterbound macadam provide relatively cheap short-term surfacing options but are likely to deteriorate quickly, particularly where there are periods of heavy rainfall. For this reason, they will not normally be an option for long-term surfacing.

◆

The preferred options for surfacing through routes are bituminous carpets, surface dressing and possibly unreinforced concrete. Brick and unreinforced concrete will generally be the best materials for surfacing access streets and lanes.

◆

Conventional structural design methods are based on the number of standard 8.2 tonne standard axle loads to be carried. Such methods are inappropriate for access streets in informal areas where traffic loads will generally be light. An alternative design method which allows for variations in design load is presented.

◆

Brick pavements should be sand grouted and laid with no cross-fall in streets where the available longitudinal fall is less than about 1 in 300. Sand grouting may also be used where the objective is to minimise the amount of storm run-off. Otherwise, bricks grouted in cement mortar should normally be used.

◆

The key to good construction is the preparation of the subgrade. Provision should be made in contract documents for replacing poor quality subgrade material with compacted sand or selected fill material but this action will not always be necessary for lightly loaded pavements.

INTRODUCTION

Background

As already indicated in Chapter 1, few streets or lanes in informal areas are paved at the time at which plots are first sold. Some form of hard paving is usually provided eventually by municipalities. However, a long period often passes between the original development and the provision of paving and so a high percentage of streets and lanes are without paving at any given time. The quality of paving that is provided is very variable. In some cases, it consists of nothing more than sand grouted bricks laid directly onto the subgrade while in other similar streets the total pavement depth exceeds 300mm. Paving is usually provided in a piecemeal manner with no overall planning. The result is that the full benefits are often not obtained from the work that is carried out. Failure to consider the drainage implications of street paving work may lead to rapid deterioration of the surface.

A rational approach to the planning and design of paving schemes is required if these problems are to be overcome. Such an approach has to answer the following questions:

◆ what is the purpose of the paving?

◆ how can local paving initiatives be integrated into overall plans?

◆ what methods and materials should be used?

◆ what details and construction standards are appropriate to achieve the required purpose?

The appropriateness of methods, materials, details and construction standards will be dependent on the purpose of the paving which, in turn, will depend on the location. This chapter begins, therefore with a review of the reasons for paving. It then moves on to look at types of paving, the choice of surfacing materials, structural design of pavements, typical street cross-sections for a range of conditions and situations and important construction details.

Reasons for paving

Street paving has three basic functions. These are:

◆ to provide a hard, dry access to residential, commercial and industrial areas;

◆ to provide a smooth running surface with adequate skid resistance for vehicles;

◆ to improve the drainage of built up areas.

The relative importance of these three functions depends on the situation in which the paving is to be provided. The provision of a smooth, skid resistant running surface is a high priority for roads carrying fast moving traffic. In upgrading areas, where conditions rarely allow traffic to move quickly, the existence of a hard durable surface, graded to carry water away from houses and other premises, will be the main priority. Smoothness and skid resistance will be relatively unimportant.

In order to fulfil its basic functions, paving must have sufficient strength to resist the loads which are imposed on it and transmit them to the underlying ground (known as the subgrade). Thus, an important attribute of paving is structural strength which depends upon the materials used and the pavement thickness.

Types of paving

Conventional road pavements can be divided into two categories. These are:

◆ flexible pavements (bituminous);

◆ rigid pavements (concrete)

Flexible pavements consist of a top layer, known as a wearing course, of stones bound in bitumen supported by one or more layers of base material. The base layers may consist of cement or bitumen bound material but unbound base layers will usually be sufficient in upgrading schemes. The lower levels of the base are commonly referred to as the sub-base. Conventional rigid pavements consist of a concrete slab, laid over a base course where necessary. Flexible pavements have little or no strength in tension. They deform slightly under load and transmit the load directly to the subgrade. Rigid pavements are designed to act as concrete slabs and must therefore be able to resist tension. Figures 7.1 and 7.2 show the main features of flexible and rigid pavements respectively.

Two other possibilities are available for pedestrian and lightly trafficked areas. These are:

◆ brick and block pavements;

◆ unbound pavements.

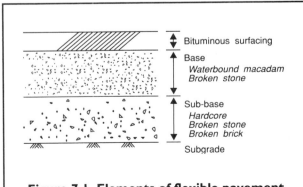

Figure 7.1. Elements of flexible pavement

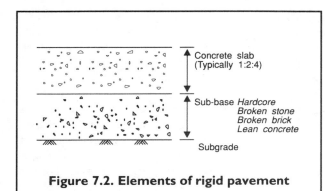

Figure 7.2. Elements of rigid pavement

An unbound pavement, for instance broken brick or graded hardcore rolled well and perhaps blinded with sand, might have a life of up to about 5 years provided that it was regularly maintained, there was adequate provision for drainage and traffic was limited to light cars. In practice, it is unlikely to be an option except in areas with little rainfall or as a temporary measure to be upgraded with a hard surface within 1-2 years.

Brick and block pavements will often be the appropriate option for upgrading access streets and lanes. They may be laid on a bed of either sand or cement mortar and can be supported by a sub-base where required. The bricks or blocks may be grouted with either sand or cement mortar, the former providing the advantage that the paving can be lifted and then relaid to allow the installation of services. Some typical brick pavement details are given in Figure 7.5.

Further details of the various paving options are given in Annex 1.

PLANNING

At the planning stage, decisions have to be made about the type and width of paving, the methods and materials to be used and the role that the paving is to play as part of the drainage system. These decisions are to some extent inter-related. In particular, the materials to be used and the pavement levels adopted will be influenced by the way in which the paving is to be incorporated into the drainage system.

Choice of pavement type

Cost is the basic factor determining the type of pavement to be used. This, in its turn, is influenced by the location, the expected traffic, the ground conditions and the durability of the various options. Where stormwater run-off is to be carried on the pavement surface, its effect on the durability of the construction must be considered. Other factors to be considered include the availability of equipment and skills and the accessibility of the area to be paved. There is no point in specifying surfacing methods which

require equipment which is either not available or cannot work effectively in the area to be surfaced. In general, the options to be considered are as follows:

Pedestrian and lightly trafficked areas (i.e. those carrying some cars but few if any commercial vehicles):-

◆ hardcore/murrum/granular fill;
◆ sand grouted bricks/concrete blocks;
◆ cement grouted bricks/concrete blocks;
◆ in-situ unreinforced concrete;
◆ hand-laid asphalt;

Through routes carrying commercial traffic

◆ surface treatment;
◆ bituminous carpet;
◆ unreinforced concrete;

The final choice of paving type should be made only after typical designs have been prepared and costed for the various options available. The costing should, as far as is possible, take into account the design lives of the options considered and their requirement for maintenance. A gravel or hardcore surface will be much cheaper in capital cost but will have higher maintenance costs and require a greater maintenance effort than other options. Bituminous carpet and surface treatment surfaces are more susceptible than concrete and brick surfaces to damage by stormwater. They may thus have higher maintenance costs if used in situations where storm water is to be allowed to run on the road surface. Ideally, a discounted cash flow should be prepared; some information on the calculation of construction and maintenance costs and the way in which these costs are analysed and compared is given in Chapter 12.

Pavement width

The pavement width required depends on the width of the street and the traffic to be carried by the street. For streets up to about 5m in width, it will usually be advisable to pave the whole width, other than that required for any drains. For wider streets, paving should usually be provided only to accommodate access needs. In other words, the width of paving should reflect the traffic which will use the street or lane. Suggested standards are shown in Table 7.1.

Pavement levels

Pavement levels should always be taken into account when planning and executing upgrading schemes. At the very least, the relationship between the proposed pavement levels and those of adjacent plots should be considered.

Type of traffic	Paved width
Pedestrians only	2 metres
Light local traffic	3.5 metres
Tonga/minibus routes	6 metres
Routes for commercial/public transport vehicles	7.2 metres

Table 7.1. Minimum paved width standards

Upgrading works should avoid raising pavement levels to a point where water can flow from the pavement onto adjacent plots. There will be instances where levels will have to be raised above the levels of some low lying plots, for instance where subsequent development has been raised to a level which makes it impractical to work from the levels of the lowest plots. However, the decision to accept levels above those of the lowest plot levels should only be taken after searching for alternatives and discussing the options with community members. Often, the owners of low lying plots will say that they are willing to raise levels on-plot.

The detailed determination of levels is a design task but the overall scheme for street levels should be considered at the planning stage in conjunction with drainage proposals. In general, the levels of main through streets should be established first, wherever possible in relation to the national datum but in any case in relation to the levels of the main outfall drain or drains serving the area. The levels of local streets and lanes can then be fixed in relation to those of the main streets to which they connect.

DESIGN

There are two stages in the design of paving schemes. The first is the development of a series of standard cross-sections, pavement designs and edge details to deal with the range of conditions and situations likely to be encountered. The second is the selection of suitable standard designs and details for use in specific streets and lanes. During this stage, it may be necessary to indicate deviations from the standard designs and cross-sections to suit particular conditions.

It is normally advisable to include the development of standard cross-section and pavement designs at the overall planning stage. This enables costs to be estimated and alternatives to be compared.

Typical cross-sections

The cross section adopted for a particular street will be influenced by the street width, the traffic to be carried and the proposed drainage system. A range of typical cross-sections are shown in Figures 7.3 and 7.4.

Figure 7.3 shows typical cross sections for areas with sewerage. Cross sections (a) to (d) show possible arrangements for streets which are to be completely paved. It is advisable to provide a cross fall except where either:

◆ the lane width is less than about 1.5m; or
◆ the longitudinal fall is less than about 1 in 300.

For narrow lanes, the benefits derived from a cross-fall are not great enough to justify its provision. Where there is little longitudinal fall and the surface is impervious, irregularities in the surface will result in standing water after rain, The water will remain for longer if it is concentrated in one spot by the cross-fall, especially where infrequent street cleaning allows dirt and rubbish to gather at the low point of the cross-section. With a flat cross-section, water will stand over a wider area but the depth will be less and the speed with which the water will either evaporate or percolate away will be greater. Standing water problems will be further reduced if joints in brick and block pavements are grouted with sand rather than cement mortar.

A development of the theme of using sand-grouted brick joints is shown in (d). In this, the cross-fall directs water to a shallow channel with a pervious base located above a french drain (ie. a trench containing an open jointed pipeline and filled with stones to allow the passage of water). A similar arrangement, suitable for use in a wider street, is shown in (g). These arrangements have not been used in practice but offer the theoretical advantage that they should require less maintenance than conventional drains, both open and covered.

Cross-section (e) also removes the need for drains by allowing water to run on the road surface. The size of the area which can be drained by this method will depend on the rainfall, catchment characteristics and longitudinal fall. the remarks already made about standing water where there is limited longitudinal fall also apply to this cross-section. Further information on drainage design will be given in Chapter 8.

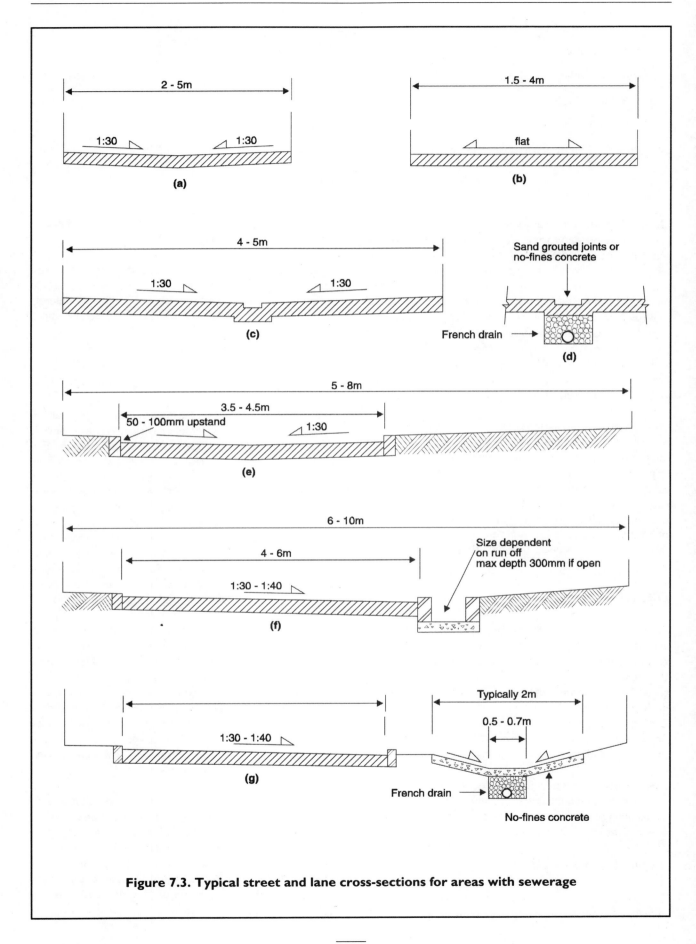

Figure 7.3. Typical street and lane cross-sections for areas with sewerage

Cross-section (f) shows a conventional arrangement with a cross-fall to a drain. This will be required where run-off flows are too great to be carried on the road surface alone but the size of the drain may be reduced by allowing for the drainage capacity of the road in the design. Again, further information will be given in Chapter 8.

Figure 7.4 shows typical cross-sections for areas which do not have sewers and thus require drains in all streets. All the arrangements shown are already found in Pakistan. Cross-section (d) is suitable for short lanes and those with sufficient fall to give self-cleansing velocities in covered side drains laid at the street gradient. This detail may be used

either as a first step towards sewering an area or for short lanes in sewered areas.

Pavement design

Pavement depth

The first step in pavement design is to determine the overall depth of pavement required. This depends on the loading, the subgrade strength and whether the pavement is intended to be rigid or flexible. In general, the overall depth of a flexible pavement will be more than that of a

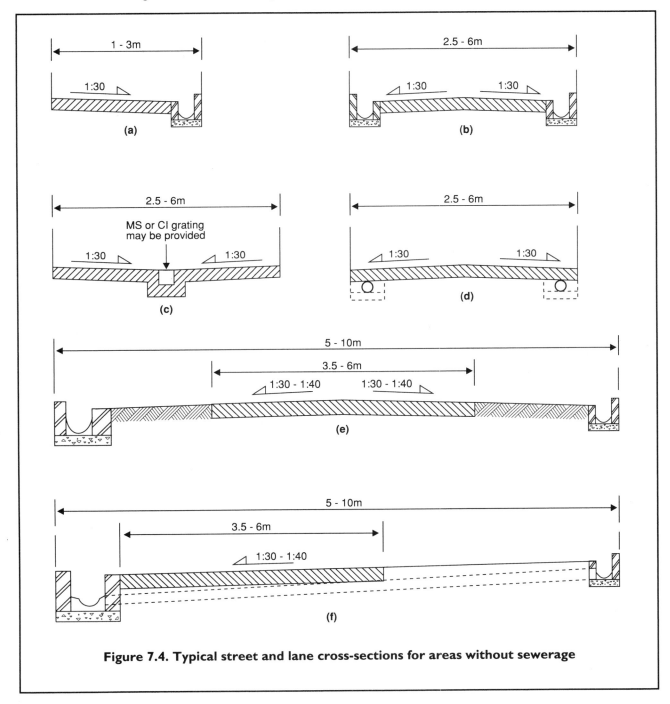

Figure 7.4. Typical street and lane cross-sections for areas without sewerage

LOCATION	TRAFFIC INTENSITY	CALIFORNIA BEARING RATIO (%)					
		1.5	2	3	5	8	12
Lanes < 2.5m	Light	150	125	100	75	60	50
Local access lanes and streets > 2.5m	Light	210	170	130	100	75	55
Minor through routes	Medium	325	275	230	160	125	90
Major through routes	Heavy	610	525	425	300	225	175

Table 7.2. Minimum pavement thickness

pavement in the same situation. The depth and construction details for pavements in most upgrading schemes are decided on the basis of experience and on what 'feels right'. This is reasonable given the fact that most conventional design methods are intended primarily for more heavily trafficked roads, indeed the typical pavement structures given in Figure 7.5 were all developed empirically and have proved successful in practice. Nevertheless, it is useful to provide a rational approach to pavement design and an empirical method for determining overall pavement depth is given in Annex 2. Table 7.2 gives guidelines for pavement depth based on this design method.

The pavement depths given in Table 7.2 are related to the subgrade strength as measured by the Californian Bearing Ratio (CBR) test. It will not be practical and should not be necessary to carry out CBR tests for every scheme. The aim should rather be to obtain representative values for various areas and to incorporate these in design guidelines. CBR results for low strength materials tend to be very variable. For this reason, it may be better to measure the plasticity index of clay subgrades and estimate the CBR using Table 7.3 which is given in Annex 2. In many informal areas, streets and lanes have been made up using a variety of materials including, in some cases, solid waste. In such instances, it will be difficult to obtain a reliable overall CBR value. In the absence of reliable field data, a CBR value of 3 should be assumed. (1.5 for fill material containing solid waste).

It can be seen that the pavement depth required can theoretically be less than 50mm for subgrades with a high CBR. In practice, a minimum depth should be specified. Suitable figures are:

- for access streets and lanes carrying little traffic
  - 100mm
- for minor through routes
  - 150mm

Pavement construction

Once the overall pavement depth has been decided, the details of the pavement construction must be decided. The following minimum construction standards are suggested:

Lanes < 2.5m wide

- 50mm 1:2:4 concrete on 60mm 1:4:8 dry concrete base.
- Bricks laid flat on 20mm mortar on 25mm sand.

(Bricks laid flat give a rather uneven surface and brick-on-edge may be preferable.)

Access streets and lanes greater than 2.5m wide

- Brick-on-edge on 50mm sand bed.
- Brick-on-edge on 20mm mortar on 25mm sand.
- 50mm 1:2:4 concrete on 100mm 1:4:8 dry concrete base.

Minor through routes

- 50mm dense bitumen macadam on 100mm rolled stone base on 100mm rolled stone or broken brick sub-base.
- Double surface treatment on 200mm rolled stone base.
- 125mm 1:2:4 concrete over 80mm stone base.

The pavement construction for major through routes will be dependent on the amount of traffic carried and should follow National or State standards for highway design.

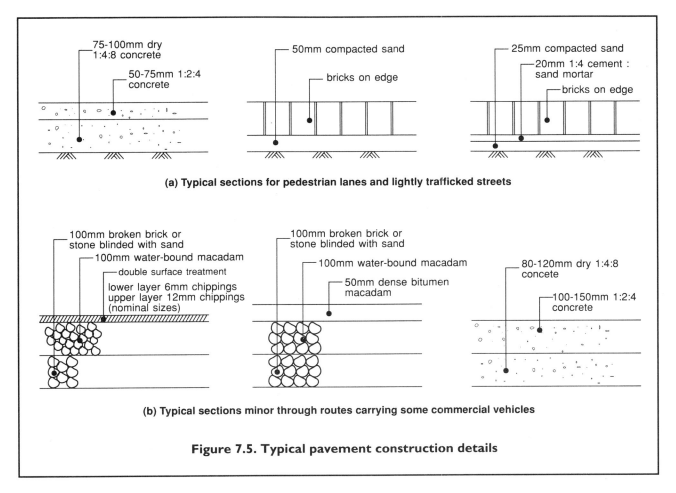

(a) Typical sections for pedestrian lanes and lightly trafficked streets

(b) Typical sections minor through routes carrying some commercial vehicles

Figure 7.5. Typical pavement construction details

Figure 7.5 shows typical pavement construction details for a range of situations and using a variety of materials.

Edge details

Most street pavements in upgrading areas are bounded by either property walls or brick masonry drains. Where this is the case, no special edge detail is required other than to perhaps provide a raised strip or tega to contain stormwater. Such raised strips are typically a half brick (112mm) wide and 75-100mm high. There are places, however, where streets run alongside unbuilt plots and public open spaces which may be at a lower level than the pavement itself. In such cases, the pavement must be contained by a continuous edge strip which prevents local failure when either heavy loads are imposed at the pavement edge or there is local erosion. Figure 7.6 gives some typical edge details.

Application of standard designs to particular areas

The first task in designing a surfacing scheme for a particular area is to decide the hierarchy of access. In other words, through streets must be distinguished from those that will be used for purely local access. In many cases, the

hierarchy will be obvious with the wider streets taking through traffic. In others, it may be appropriate to prevent through traffic from using certain streets, using bollards or other forms of barrier to prevent access. Where a planning process such as that described in Chapter 3 has already been undertaken, the hierarchy of streets should have already been decided by the detailed design stage. In any event, it is important that any schemes to restrict access are discussed with the local community.

Appropriate pavement designs can then be selected for the various categories of street and lane, using the approach already described. For large schemes, located mainly on virgin ground, representative CBR tests should be carried out if possible and used as the basis of design. For small schemes and those where pavements are to be constructed on made-up ground of variable quality, judgement may be required, where possible based on experience with other schemes in the same area. Where solid waste has been used as fill, it may be necessary to replace the top 100-300mm of fill with compacted sand. However, our experience is that this is not necessary with lightly loaded cement-grouted brick pavements. There is much to be said for building trial sections of paving and monitoring their performance at the beginning of large upgrading projects.

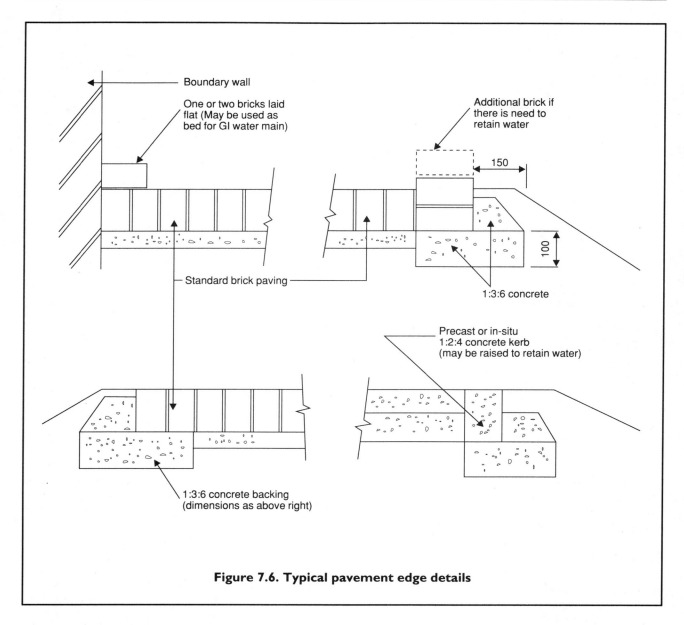

Figure 7.6. Typical pavement edge details

The paving scheme should be shown on a suitable scale plan on which the limits of the different types of paving proposed are shown. A scale of around 1:500 will be required if pavement levels are to be shown on the drawing. Where there are good falls so that levels do not have to be specified, a smaller scale may be used. In flat areas, the cross-fall should be taken into account when considering levels. Where the paving is not to extend the full width of a street or lane, this should be made clear either on the drawing or in accompanying notes. Further information on the presentation of paving schemes is given in Chapter 11.

CONSTRUCTION

This section gives a brief introduction to the most important aspects of good pavement construction practice.

Preparation of subgrade

This is perhaps the most important task in the pavement construction process and is also the most frequently neglected. Where the pavement is to be laid on fill the subgrade must always be compacted well before construction begins. Failure to do so will result in premature pavement failure because of excessive settlement.

The first task in subgrade preparation is to excavate to the correct levels. It is always worth doing this as accurately as possible since excess excavation results in a need for additional fill and this increases costs. The best procedure is to work from levels marked on the walls bounding the street or lane. If a cross-fall or camber is required, a profile board as shown in Figure 7.7 may be useful in ensuring accurate cross-sectional profiles. Setting out and construction procedures are shown in Figure 7.8. Where there is little fall, say less than 1:100, it will be necessary to specify longitudinal profiles accurately and fix level marks using a surveyors level. Where the fall is greater, it may be sufficient to specify levels in relation to existing ground levels and dispense with the use of a surveyors level.

The options for compaction of the subgrade are:

◆ hand-held rammers; and

◆ small vibrating rollers.

In most cases, the first will be sufficient. In dry weather, the subgrade should be watered before compaction begins.

Where a sewer or water main has been laid before paving the street, special care should be taken to ensure that the trench backfill material has been properly compacted. If there is any doubt the trench should be re-excavated and refilled in compacted layers not exceeding 225mm in depth.

A good specification should include a clause stating that any soft spots in the subgrade must be excavated and filled with sand or selected material, placed in layers and compacted. Where pavements are laid on poor quality fill, as is often the case in upgrading areas, strict application of such a clause would mean that almost all the existing fill would have to be replaced, an impractical course of action. A compromise course of action will be to remove the poor quality material to a depth of 100-300mm and replace it with compacted sand or hard-core, as already indicated.

Brick pavements

Paving should start from a straight edge which may be an edge restraint or a string-line. Whole pavers should be laid first with any edge make-up pieces being marked and cut as a follow-on operation behind the advance of the laying face. Where anything more than light traffic is expected, bricks should be laid in a herringbone pattern. (See Figure 7.9). Running bond and basketweave bond are usually used for paving of lanes in Pakistan. The former is preferable where there is to be occasional light traffic, with the long axis of the pavers being laid across the street or lane.

If a sand bed is used, this should be placed in layers of about 35mm compacted to 25mm. Bricks should be laid dry with joints not more than 5mm wide. They should then be grouted either with sand brushed into the joints or a 1:4 cement:sand slurry. In European countries, bricks or pavers are then compacted into position using a vibrating compactor. This is not done in Pakistan, partly because of the absence of suitable compactors. Another factor may be the inferior quality of bricks available and a consequent fear that they may be damaged by any attempt at compaction. Hand compaction using a wooden compactor might provide an inferior but acceptable alternative.

Concrete pavements

A dry lean concrete sub-base has the advantage that it is easy to handle and does not require shuttering.

The concrete slab itself should be cast in lengths not exceeding 4.5m in length so that the construction joints can function as contraction joints. Alternate slabs should be cast and the intervening slabs filled in later. It is important to ensure that the mix proportions and depth of slab are correct. Mix proportions can be controlled by insisting on the use of standard measuring boxes for aggregate and cement. These can easily be made on site. Site engineers should check the construction at regular intervals to ensure that the slab base is at the correct level and the full slab depth is being provided.

Flexible pavements

The base and sub-base for flexible pavements should be rolled well in accordance with the specification. The procedure for laying waterbound macadam base courses is the same as that given in the section on unbound pavements in Annex 1. It is not possible to roll right up to

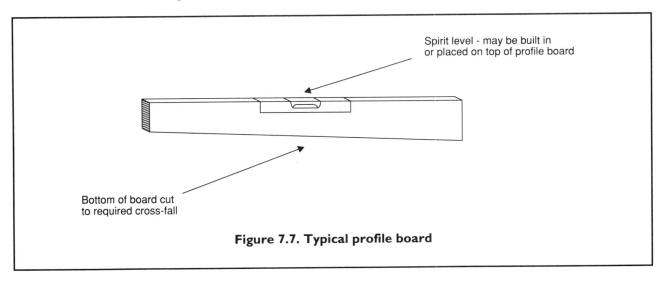

Figure 7.7. Typical profile board

Spirit level - may be built in or placed on top of profile board

Bottom of board cut to required cross-fall

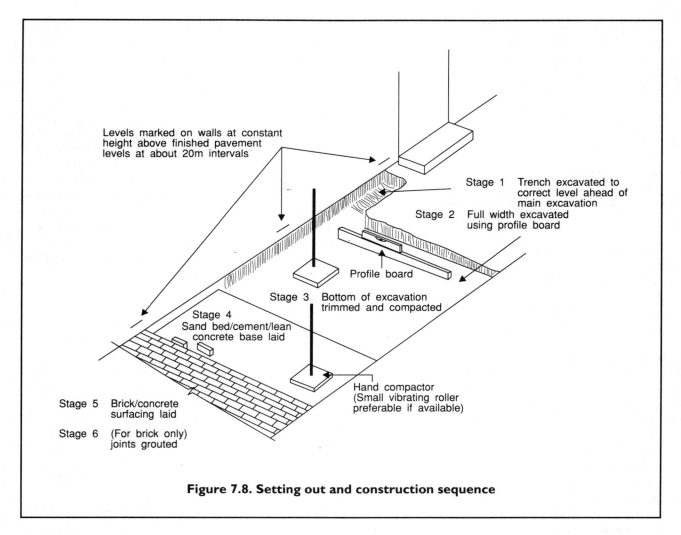

Levels marked on walls at constant height above finished pavement levels at about 20m intervals

Stage 1 Trench excavated to correct level ahead of main excavation

Stage 2 Full width excavated using profile board

Profile board

Stage 3 Bottom of excavation trimmed and compacted

Stage 4 Sand bed/cement/lean concrete base laid

Hand compactor (Small vibrating roller preferable if available)

Stage 5 Brick/concrete surfacing laid

Stage 6 (For brick only) joints grouted

Figure 7.8. Setting out and construction sequence

existing buildings and so consolidation of the edges of the pavement is often difficult. Where they are available, small vibrating rollers may be used for these lengths. An alternative may be to design the street cross-section to provide a strip of concrete along each side of the street but this will tend to increase costs.

Site engineers should check that the sub-base and base are to specification both in the type and size of material provided. There is sometimes a tendency for contractors to supply over-size stones for the base course.

The final surfacing should be provided as quickly as possible after the base has been laid and rolled to avoid the build up of mud on the surface of the base. Where some build-up of mud is unavoidable, the base course surface should be brushed thoroughly before the bituminous material is laid.

The thickness of the bituminous surface course and the temperature of the surfacing material should be regularly checked to ensure that they are in accordance with the drawings and specifications.

ANNEX I

ADDITIONAL INFORMATION ON PAVING OPTIONS

Unbound pavements

Unbound pavements can be formed from gravel, hardcore or water-bound macadam. The latter consists of coarse aggregates, mechanically interlocked by rolling and bound together by screenings and/or stone dust and water. Whichever material is used, it should be rolled to achieve consolidation, using a 6-8 tonne roller. This will not be possible in narrow streets and lanes although reasonable results might be obtained using a small vibrating roller. When considering the provision of unbound pavements by community action, the need to roll the pavement must be remembered.

Gravel roads should consist predominantly of stones in the size range 6mm-20mm, with about 10% of fine material to act as a binder. Where washed gravel is used, fine river sand may be used as the binder. For lightly trafficked roads, the total consolidated thickness should be at least 150mm, laid in two 75mm layers. For more heavily trafficked roads, the total thickness may be increased up to about 300mm.

For lightly trafficked roads a water-bound macadam thickness of 115mm, laid on 75mm of gravel or clinker, will be appropriate. The maximum size of aggregate should not exceed three quarters of the total consolidated thickness of any one layer of construction. Suggested size ranges for different types of aggregate are:

- ◆ soft stone/broken brick   40-63mm
- ◆ hard stone   20-50mm

The first stage in constructing a waterbound macadam road is to spread and roll the dry aggregate until it is well compacted. Screenings of crushed rock, brick kiln dust or similar, graded from about 12mm down, are then spread over the surface, brushed into the gaps between stones, sprinkled with water and rolled until the coarse aggregate is well bonded and firm for its whole depth. For hard aggregates, fine grained binding material should be spread watered and rolled into the surface after application of the screenings.

Flexible Pavements

Conventional flexible pavements consist of a weather-proof surface layer laid over a granular base. The base, in turn, will usually be laid over a sub-base. Surfacing materials fall into two main categories. These are:

- ◆ surface dressings; and
- ◆ premixed bituminous materials.

Surface dressings

These consist of a layer of stone chippings bonded to the road surface by a thin continuous film of bitumen or tar binder, usually the former. They can be used for surfacing new roads, when it is usual to apply two or occasionally three layers, and for rehabilitation of existing road surfaces. Surface dressing is frequently used to pave through roads in informal areas. It is cheaper than bituminous surfacing but has a shorter design life, typically about 6 years as opposed to 10 years or more for a bituminous carpet. Surface dressing will not normally be an option for narrow lanes, partly because other pavement options are cheaper and partly because the rolling which is essential if the surface is to be of good quality will be difficult or impossible.

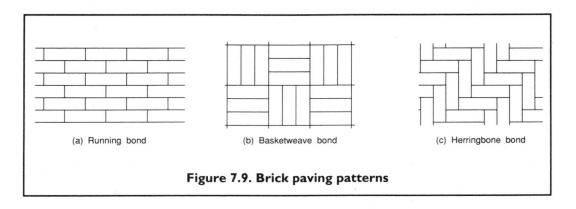

(a) Running bond   (b) Basketweave bond   (c) Herringbone bond

Figure 7.9. Brick paving patterns

Premixed bituminous surfacing

There are various types of bituminous surfacing. Those used in Pakistan at present are coated macadams. In these, graded aggregate is coated with a bituminous binder with the aggregate interlock providing most of the strength of the material. In Lahore, LDA specify a dense bitumen macadam which is sometimes referred to as asphalt concrete. This material is produced by LDA at its own plant so there is reasonable quality control and similar premixed material is used in many informal areas to pave through routes.

A single bituminous layer, laid by a mechanical paving machine, is normally specified with a granular base and sub-base. It is not suitable for use on small contracts in narrow streets and lanes because of its cost and the physical difficulties involved in using mechanical equipment in restricted areas.

Movable small scale 'donkey' plants may be used to prepare coated macadams on site but it is hard to ensure quality control of site mixed material. For this reason, brick and block pavements will be a better option than bituminous pavements for tertiary streets and lanes.

Rigid concrete pavements

Rigid pavements must have sufficient beam strength to bridge localised failures of the subgrade and withstand the stresses that develop. They must also be able to withstand the stresses caused by the concrete curing and temperature variations. There are three types of pavement. These are:

◆ jointed unreinforced concrete pavement;

◆ jointed reinforced concrete pavement;

◆ continuously reinforced concrete pavement;

The function of the reinforcement is to resist temperature induced stresses rather than those caused by traffic loading. In unreinforced pavements, the former are controlled by the provision of frequent joints. Unreinforced concrete is often used to pave pedestrian access ways and lightly trafficked streets in upgrading areas. Reinforced concrete pavements provide few advantages in the conditions found in such areas and are considerably more difficult to construct. They should not normally be used in upgrading schemes.

Spacing of expansion and contraction joints.

For pavements less than 150mm deep, contraction joints are basically the same as construction joints. The method of laying a pavement to provide construction joints at a maximum of 4.5m intervals has already been described.

Theoretically, expansion joints should be provided in concrete pavements laid at any time other than the height of summer at a spacing of 40m. In practice, these are rarely provided on the thin concrete slabs currently used in pedestrian lanes. More research is needed on this subject to discover whether the absence of expansion joints decreases the life of the pavements.

Brick and block pavements

Where they are readily available, bricks are often used in informal areas to pave lightly trafficked areas. Such pavements are durable, reasonably cheap and have the advantage that they can be laid without expensive equipment. Another advantage, particularly with sand grouted bricks, is that the paving can easily be removed and reinstated to allow installation of services. If the bricks are grouted with cement mortar, such pavements can be assumed to act rigidly. Sand grouted bricks have some rigidity if they are placed close together to prevent rotation of individual blocks under load. However, it is assumed here that sand grouted brick pavements behave in a flexible way. Where bricks are not available, the option of using concrete block pavers should be considered. They are commercially produced in Pakistan but are more expensive than bricks in areas where bricks are manufactured.

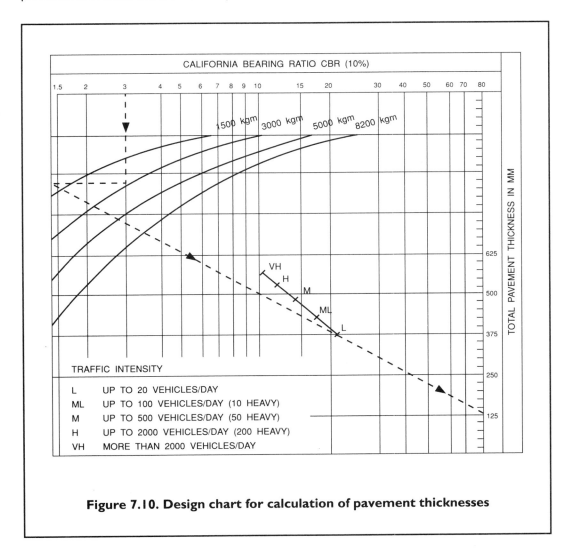

Figure 7.10. Design chart for calculation of pavement thicknesses

ANNEX 2

DETERMINATION OF PAVEMENT DEPTH

Pavement design is empirical. The design method used in this manual is based on that developed by the American Asphalt Institute. This has the advantage over other methods that it makes allowance for a range of design axle loads. It is strictly applicable to flexible pavements but, in the absence of similar methods allowing for a range of axle loads, may also be used for concrete and brick/block pavements. The method requires information on the design load and the subgrade strength as measured by the CBR value.

Loading

Most conventional design methods specify the design loading in terms of the number of standard 8200kgm (18000lb) axle loads that the pavement can carry before failure. This relates to heavy commercial vehicles and is clearly inappropriate for the design of a lane used only by pedestrians, motorcycles and perhaps motor-rickshaws. It also seems unnecessarily conservative for access streets where the largest vehicles regularly passing will be cars. Bearing in mind that the laden weight of a private car is less than 2000kgm, the following design axle loadings are suggested:

◆ for lanes less than 2.5 m in width   -   1500kgm

◆ for access lanes and streets, 2.5m-5m in width   -   3000kgm

◆ for minor through routes, up to 7m road width   -   5000kgm

◆ for through routes carrying buses, trucks daily   -   8200kgm

Subgrade strength

The CBR test is the commonly accepted method of measuring subgrade stength. The testing procedure is described in standard textbooks. Typical CBR values for a range of soil types are given in Table 7.3.

Procedure for determining pavement depth

Soil Type	Plasticity Index	CBR Value (%)	
		Ground water depth < 600mm	Ground water depth >600mm
Heavy clay	70	1.5	2
	50	2	2.5
	40	2.5	3
Silty clay	30	3	5
Sandy clay	20	4	6
	10	5	7
Silt (unconsolidated)	-	1	2
Sand (poorly graded)	Non-plastic	10	20
Sand (well graded)	-do-	15	40
Sandy gravel	-do-	20	60

Table 7.3. Typical CBR values

Once the design loading and the CBR value of the subgrade have been determined, the pavement depth can be obtained from Figure 7.10.

The procedure for using the figure is as follows:

(1) Select the appropriate CBR value for the subgrade.

(2) Draw a vertical line to the curve which represents the loading appropriate to the location of the pavement.

(3) Draw a horizontal line from the intersection point obtained from (2) to the left hand side of the chart.

(4) Decide whether the likely volume of traffic can be classified as light, medium etc. This will require some judgement as traffic figures will not normally be available. The volume of traffic in access streets can almost always be assumed to be light and anything more than a medium volume of traffic will be unlikely in most through streets in upgrading areas.

(5) Draw a line from the point on the left-hand margin obtained from (3) through the appropriate pivot point obtained from (4). The required overall pavement thickness can be read off from the scale on the right- hand side of the chart.

The dashed line on Figure 7.10 shows the process for a CBR value of 3 and a 4m wide lane carrying occasional light vehicles.

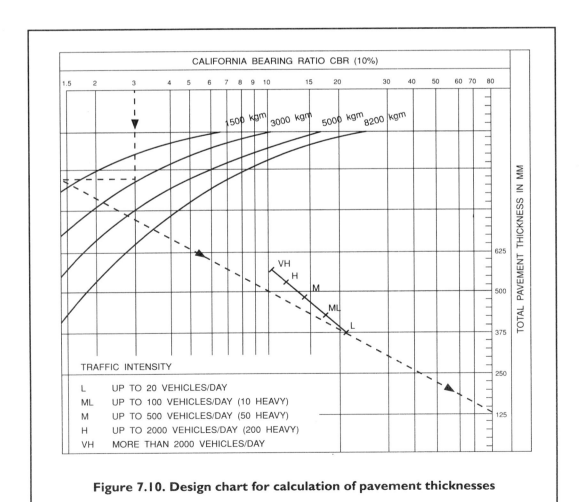

Figure 7.10. Design chart for calculation of pavement thicknesses

8.

DRAINAGE

SUMMARY

The chapter begins with an examination of the causes of flooding in informal areas and the harmful effects of flooding. This leads to a section on the objectives of drainage improvements after which three aspects of drainage planning are considered; initial appraisal of the situation, the choice of approach and the determination of system layout. The section on choice of approach examines the conventional option of discharging water quickly, together with those of delaying run-off and relying on percolation from soakaways and infiltration areas. The option of holding and delaying run-off is shown to be attractive in many of the situations commonly found in informal areas. Attention is next turned to detailed design. The calculation of run-off flows and total run-off quantities is examined, followed by the processes for deciding drain slopes and sizes. Construction details and practice are then discussed. Annex I examines the components that might be included in a drainage scheme, noting their advantages and disadvantages. Annex 2 provides information on run-off coefficients and rainfall intensities.

KEY POINTS

◆

The objective of drainage improvements is to contain and limit flooding so that it causes minimal damage and disruption.

◆

Drainage schemes which seek to retain water in order to reduce the rate of run-off should be considered where the off-site drainage facilities are inadequate.

◆

Unlined ditches have limited uses in upgrading schemes because of their need for constant maintenance.

◆

Both open and covered drains give rise to maintenance problems and their total length should be minimised. This can be done by designing streets to act as drains wherever possible. In general, the run-off from areas up to about 5ha in area can be carried on the street surface where the annual rainfall is in the range 500-1000 mm/yr.

◆

Drainage schemes in informal areas should normally be designed for a return period of 1 year or less.

◆

Covered drains should not be smaller than about 500mm square in cross-section.

◆

The raising of road surfaces along primary and secondary drainage routes should be avoided unless absolutely necessary.

◆

Combined sewers may be used provided that there are strong reasons why they are preferable to separate facilities and there is sufficient fall to provide overflow facilities before any treatment or pumping facility.

BACKGROUND

Most informal areas experience flooding during and after rainfall and improved drainage is therefore often a priority in upgrading schemes. The flooding may result from some or all of the following.

◆ Increased amounts of rainwater running off the land rather than percolating into it as a result of the increase in hard surfaces caused by urbanisation

◆ The lack of planning in informal areas. Main collector drains are rarely adequate and local problems arise because piecemeal improvements have been made without regard to their effect on the general situation.

◆ The fact that many informal areas are located in low-lying areas which tend to flood during storms.

◆ Low levels of maintenance and encroachment of those drains which do exist.

Inadequate drainage has obvious harmful effects when it results in flooding of properties, erosion of land or damage to buildings. Less obvious but equally important are the consequences for health. Standing water is invariably polluted. It provides breeding grounds for mosquitoes and may thus increase the incidence of malaria, dengue fever and filariasis. The latter, which is common in urban areas on the Indian subcontinent, is spread by the culex pipiens mosquito which breeds in polluted water.

Flooding of roads may prevent movement within and between areas, causing inconvenience and loss of income.

OBJECTIVES

Drainage improvements should aim to reduce the problems identified above. This means that they must:

◆ minimise the incidence of flooding of houses;

◆ prevent erosion and the consequent risk of damage to property;

◆ eliminate standing water and the consequent danger from mosquito-carried diseases and

◆ reduce the extent and duration of flooding of streets and rights of way to acceptable levels.

It is necessary to define what constitute acceptable levels of flooding. Ideally, the drainage system should prevent flooding completely in all but the most severe storms. However, this ideal will be unattainable in many informal areas. In general, some flooding of streets and public spaces can be tolerated if:

◆ the flooding does not prevent movement of pedestrians and vehicles;

◆ flood levels are below most house plinth and yard levels;

◆ the flooding clears quickly, say within 30 minutes of the ending of heavy rainfall; and

◆ the flood water does not include sewage.

In unsewered areas, drains usually carry sullage water as well as stormwater. In this case, drainage also has the objective of removing this sullage water from the housing areas in a controlled and hygienic manner.

PLANNING

The planning of drainage systems moves from an appraisal of the existing situation, through choices on the system or systems to be adopted to decisions on the drainage layout. Each stage is dependent on the outputs from the previous stages. They will now be considered in turn.

Initial appraisal

The aim of initial appraisal is to establish the extent and capacity of existing facilities and to identify problems and their causes. A plan of the area under consideration is required at a scale between 1:2000 and 1:5000. The procedures for preparing plans have already been discussed in Chapter 4. Overall drainage plans should be consulted where they are available.

A visual survey of the site should be made in order to:

◆ establish existing drainage routes and boundaries;

◆ identify the places where flooding is a problem. and

◆ identify any restrictions and encroachments that restrict the capacity of main drainage routes.

In the case of flooding, it will usually be necessary to obtain information by talking to local people and officials. This may be done formally using the in-depth interview and group discussion methods described in Chapter 2.

The likely causes of flooding are likely to be found among the following:

◆ inadequacy of main drains;

◆ reduced capacity of main drains due to encroachments, restrictions or lack of maintenance;

◆ unplanned development which leaves some low lying areas into which flow storm and foul water drains; and

◆ inadequacies in local drainage.

In many cases, this initial survey will provide a clear indication that existing main drains are inadequate. In other cases, it will be necessary to produce calculations to determine their capacity in relation to design flows. This is a task for specialists as is the design of new main drainage facilities and so neither is covered in this manual. The important things from the point of view of upgrading are to establish that a problem exists and to ensure that appropriate action is taken by the concerned agency.

As far as local problems are concerned, the links between causes and effects will usually be fairly obvious and so there should be a basis for deciding on remedial action.

Approaches to drainage

The type and size of drainage facilities required will depend on what the drainage system is intended to do. Drainage systems may be designed:

- to remove all storm water from an area as quickly as possible;
- to hold some water and allow the remainder to drain away in a controlled manner;
- to hold water and allow it to percolate and evaporate away after a storm;

The advantages and disadvantages of these three basic approaches are considered below..

Rapid removal of stormwater

Most conventional drainage systems use this approach. Drains and storm sewers are designed to have enough capacity to carry the peak run-off flows generated by heavy rainfall. While the approach is conceptually simple, it has several disadvantages when applied in informal areas, particularly those which are flat. These can be summarised as follows:

- It is dependent on the provision of off-site drains. This may be prohibitively expensive in many informal areas.
- It requires a degree of coordination and planning which may be difficult to achieve, particularly in schemes which rely on community action to provide local level facilities.
- Maintenance of conventional drains, both open and covered, is often inadequate. This results in blockages and ultimately in failure of drainage systems.

Temporary retention of stormwater

Systems which reduce flows in drains and sewers by holding water and allowing it to discharge over an extended period reduce the peak run-off flow and thus the

required size of off-site drains. This will be an important consideration where off-site drains are grossly inadequate. Such systems, which may be referred to as hybrid systems, are also less dependent on soil permeability than completely on-site systems. For these reasons they offer an attractive option for upgrading schemes. Their main problem is that they are difficult to analyse and more work is needed to develop simple design guidelines for the hybrid approach.

Storage on site

Systems which drain to soakaways and areas specially provided to hold storm water fall into this category. The main advantage of the approach is that it is not dependent on off-site facilities. However, the serious disadvantages listed below limit its usefulness.

- systems will not deal with two storms occurring in quick succession, particularly where ground permeability is low as is the case in most urban areas in Pakistan.
- systems which provide open storage are not suitable for use where storm flows are combined with either sewage or sullage flows.
- System capacity will tend to reduce with time as surfaces become clogged with fine material. An associated problem is that soakaways will gradually fill with silt, particularly where street surfaces are dirty or dusty.

Despite these disadvantages, there may be scope for encouraging the provision of soakaways and other facilities by plotholders to improve the drainage of their plots.

Conclusions on appropriate approach

From the above the following conclusions can be drawn:

- conventional drainage is only appropriate where adequate off-site drains exist or can be economically provided.
- Wholly on-site systems are unlikely to be appropriate in upgrading schemes although the provision of on-plot soakaways may be encouraged on larger plots.
- Systems which hold stormwater and allow it to run off over an extended period are likely to be an attractive option, particularly in flat or steeply sloping areas.

System components

The possible components of drainage systems are as follows:

Unlined ditches
Open drains
Covered drains
Combined sewers
Streets and lanes acting as drains
Soakaways
Percolation basins
Infiltration trenches

The first five are all used to transport stormwater and so may be components in conventional drainage systems which aim to remove water as quickly as possible. However, they will all provide storage to a greater or lesser extent and can therefore be used in systems intended to reduce maximum run-off rates. Soakaways, percolation basins and infiltration trenches can all be used to dispose of stormwater on-site but they will normally be used in upgrading areas as components in systems designed to control and reduce run-off. More information on the various possible components, together with their advantages and disadvantages, is given in Annex 1.

Drainage layout

The drainage layout may be affected by the approach adopted; for instance, a layout that incorporates local storage/infiltration basins may be different from that for a conventional system. Nevertheless, the principles that follow can be employed for all but the most self-contained drainage systems.

The drainage layout is largely determined by topography. A good guide to the likely drainage layout can be obtained from existing drainage routes but it is preferable to base layout decisions on survey levels, particularly in flat areas. Longitudinal sections should be drawn along the routes of collector drains. Typical scales for these sections should be in the range 1:1000-1:2500 horizontally with a 10 to 20 times vertical exaggeration. (Normal practice is to use a vertical exaggeration of 10 but a greater amount may be justified in flat areas). There will be some places, for instance where an existing inadequate drain runs in a narrow right of way between plots, where a new drain cannot be located along the lowest possible route. In such cases, it should be located as closely as possible to the lowest route.

The length of drains should be reduced as far as is possible by allowing water to be held and/or drain on the surface for some distance before entering the drain. In places with annual rainfalls between 500mm and 1000mm, it is reasonable to assume that drains will only be required for areas greater than about 5ha. This assumes that streets can be graded to provide a slope, no matter how small, to the drains and that some temporary flooding of access streets and lanes is permissible. It is reasonable to allow larger areas without formal drains in dryer areas, providing that

streets and lanes are designed to deal with stormwater. To avoid erosion problems, this approach should be used with some caution where not all the right of way is paved and average falls are greater than about 1:100.

Any low-lying areas which might be retained and used to hold stormwater and thus reduce run-off should be identified at the planning stage. The scope for providing temporary storage in shallow ditches, infiltration trenches and depressed areas should also be assessed.

The decision on the approach to be adopted will depend on both the topography and the adequacy or otherwise of main drains. Where either the average ground slope is less than about 1:500 or main drains are inadequate, the aim should be to hold stormwater within the area for as long as possible. The further consequences of the design approach for detailed design are considered in the next section.

Pumping of stormwater should be avoided except where there is absolutely no other option. Where it cannot be avoided, stormwater should be collected in a holding pond connected to the pumping station sump. This will have two benefits; it will balance flows so that the required pumping rate can be less than the peak discharge rate and it will settle any solids and thus reduce the likelihood of pumps being blocked.

DETAILED DESIGN

Once the drainage layout has been decided, detailed design is required to determine the size of the drains and other drainage facilities required. Because of the lack of data and the complex conditions which occur in informal areas, it will often be necessary to simplify conventional drainage theory to make it appropriate for use in upgrading schemes.

Bearing these general points in mind, the steps in the detailed design process will now be outlined. More detailed information relating to design is given in Annex 2 The steps in the design process are:

◆ calculate flows at intervals along the proposed drainage routes;

◆ calculate the falls available along those routes; and

◆ design drains and other facilities to carry or store the calculated flows.

Calculation of run-off flows

Basic principles

The simplest formula for the calculation of run-off flow is the Rational Formula which states that:

$$Q = 2.78CIA$$

where **Q** is the run-off flow in litres/second;
C is the run-off coefficient. This defines the percentage of stormwater that runs off rather than soaking away or standing in surface depressions;
I is the rainfall intensity in mm/hr;
A is the total area drained in hectares.

Typical 'C' values for urban areas are in the range 0.5-0.8. Selection of a suitable value is discussed in Annex 2.

The drainage area at any point on a drain or drainage route can be measured once the catchment boundaries have been determined and marked on a suitable map.

Conventional theory states that the value of **I** to be used in the Rational Formula can be obtained from a formula of the form:

$$I = a/(b+T)^n$$

where T is the rainfall duration in hours and a,b and n are constants for a given location and return period. (The return period is the average interval between occurrences of rainfall of the given intensity and duration.) It can be shown that, for normal catchments, the maximum run-off occurs when the rainfall duration T is the same as the time of concentration of the catchment. (The time of concentration is the time after the beginning of the storm before run-off from the farthest point in the catchment contributes to the flow.)

Normal practice is to design drainage facilities to cope with a 2 year or even 5 year return period storm. In upgrading areas, it will normally be more appropriate to design for a return period of 1 year or less.

Figure 8.1 gives the set of intensity-duration curves for Lahore.

Design intensities for small areas

It can be seen from Figure 8.1 that design rainfall intensity decreases with increased duration. This means in effect that the smaller the drainage area, the larger the intensity assumed in design. In practice, the run-off from short periods of rainfall will usually be less than that predicted using the intensity obtained from the intensity/duration curve with a constant run-off coefficient. This is because water gathers in small depressions in the surface and thus reduces the short-term run-off coefficient. To allow for

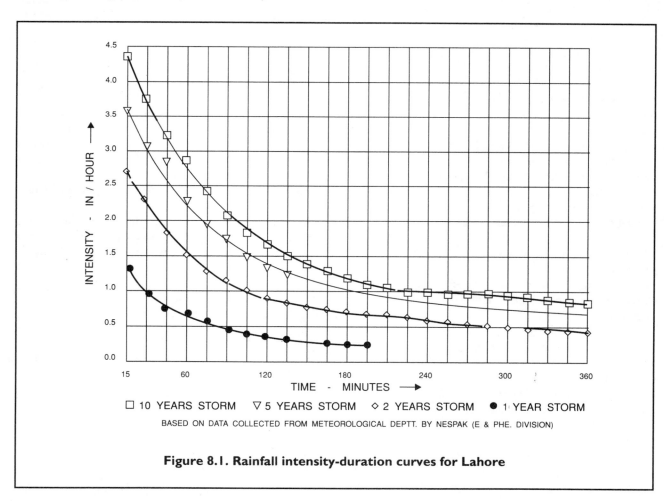

□ 10 YEARS STORM   ▽ 5 YEARS STORM   ◇ 2 YEARS STORM   ● 1 YEAR STORM

BASED ON DATA COLLECTED FROM METEOROLOGICAL DEPTT. BY NESPAK (E & PHE. DIVISION)

Figure 8.1. Rainfall intensity-duration curves for Lahore

this effect, a constant intensity can be assumed for times of concentration of 15 minutes and less. (In effect, the adjustment for the reduced run-off is then made in the intensity assumed rather than the run-off coefficient). In practice, this will mean for catchment areas of about 15ha. and less, in other words for tertiary level facilities. Further information on rainfall intensities is given in Annex 2.

Effect of storage on run-off

The Rational Formula is intended for use with conventional schemes in which the aim is to remove water from the site as quickly as possible. It does not allow for storage of water in the drainage system and therefore tends to overestimate run-off, particularly in flat, slow-draining areas. In areas with average slopes less than about 1:250, the effect of storage on road surfaces will be significant but this effect cannot be quantified simply.

It is probable that the best way to deal with this situation will be to use reduced run-off coefficients to compensate for storage and this is the approach which is followed here. Table 8.1 in Annex 2 gives suggested relationships between run-off coefficients and average ground slope. However, it must be emphasised that these figures are estimates only and more research is needed on this subject.

For wholly on-site and hybrid systems that rely heavily on storage, the critical factor is not so much the instantaneous run-off flow as the total volume of run-off. Analysis of these systems is complex, indeed the necessary theory is not available in any simple usable form. If a site contains a substantial area of potential stormwater storage, for instance a low-lying park or playing field area, the advice of a specialist drainage engineer should be obtained.

Estimation of available falls

The first step in estimating available falls is to prepare longitudinal sections of the main drainage routes, showing existing ground levels and noting the bed level and top water levels of receiving drains or watercourses. Sections already prepared when deciding the drainage layout may be used. Possible drain profiles can then be added to these sections, together with road profiles where it is planned that the road may occasionally carry stormwater. (This will be the case in most informal areas.) When planning street and drain profiles, the following rules should be observed:

◆ raising of road surfaces along primary and secondary drainage routes should be avoided;

◆ variations in longitudinal fall that result in flat lengths of street and drain should be smoothed out. This will be particularly important where a flat length of street is located upstream of a length with a good fall. This point is illustrated in Figure 8.2.

◆ The aim should always be to slope tertiary streets towards drainage routes.

◆ covered drains and storm sewers should have sufficient fall to ensure self-cleansing velocities. This requirement is less important for open drains since they can be cleaned more easily. Nevertheless, it should be achieved where possible.

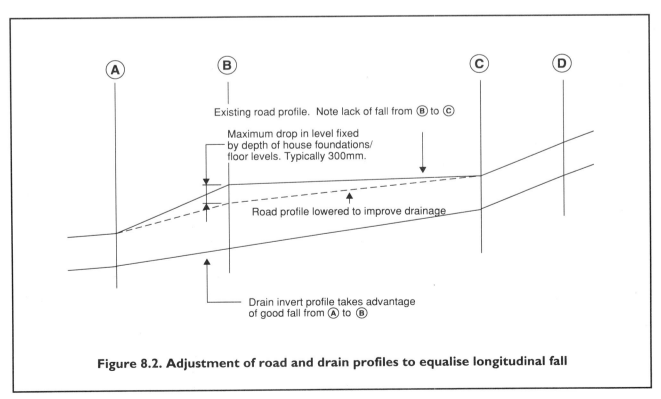

Figure 8.2. Adjustment of road and drain profiles to equalise longitudinal fall

they can be cleaned more easily. Nevertheless, it should be achieved where possible.

Drain design

Tertiary drainage routes

Specific design calculations are not required for individual tertiary drainage routes. Rather, standard design tables and charts should be prepared to show the maximum areas that can be drained by standard street/lane and drain cross-sections at different slopes. The appropriate standard street and/or drain details can then be specified for any smaller drainage areas. Specific calculations will only be required where the drainage area is greater than that specified in the standard charts/tables. This will only be the case for secondary drains. Thus location specific calculations will only be required for primary/secondary systems.

Primary/secondary drains

The drain design procedure is similar to that already described for foul sewers in Chapter 6. For each length of drain, starting at the head of the system, a size is assumed and the velocity when the drain is running full is calculated using Mannings Formula,

$$V = \{(A/P)^{2/3}S^{1/2}\}/n$$

where **V** is the velocity in metres/sec; **A** is the cross-sectional area of the flow in m²; **P** is the wetted perimeter which is made up of the sides and bottom of an open drain and the sides, bottom and top for a covered drain; **S** is the slope; and **n** is Mannings coefficient, typically 0.015 for concrete and asphalt, 0.017 for brick paving and 0.025 for unlined channels free of vegetation.

Note that for sheet flow on street pavements, the value of (A/P) approximates to the average depth, measured in metres.

There should be sufficient slope on lined drains to ensure velocities of at least 0.75 m/sec and ideally over 1.0m/sec when the drain is running full. Velocities in unlined drains should not exceed about 1m/sec.

The capacity Q = VA. If the capacity is not within about 10% of the design flow or the velocity is too low, different assumptions must be made about plan dimensions and slope until a reasonable match is reached.

It is normal to carry out calculations for secondary drains on standard sheets such as that shown in Figure 8.3. Columns 1-13 of the sheet are concerned with the calculation of design flows in the drain. Columns 8-12 are concerned with the calculation of the rainfall intensity, using rainfall intensity/ duration curves such as that given in Figure 8.1. For areas up to about 15 ha, the procedure may be simplified by assuming a constant rainfall intensity. Columns 14-24 are concerned with the calculation of the velocity and quantity of flow in the drain. For each drain leg, starting at the head of the system, in the same way as for foul sewers, the design flow is calculated, drain dimensions are assumed and the drain full flow velocity and quantity are calculated. Calculation is an iterative process. If the velocity obtained in column 23 is too low, a greater drain slope must be assumed. If the capacity calculated in column 24 differs by more than 10% from that obtained from column 13, revised drain dimensions or slope should be tried. If the calculated velocity obtained in column 23 differs by more than about 20% from that assumed in column 9, it may be necessary to recalculate the rainfall intensity based on a revised time of concentration. Once

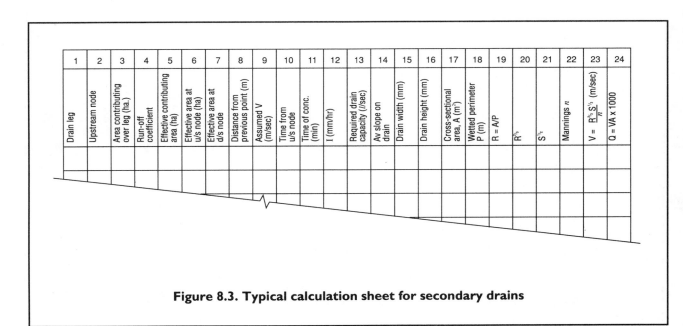

Figure 8.3. Typical calculation sheet for secondary drains

CONSTRUCTION

Construction details

Some typical drain details are shown in Figure 8.4. These are, on the whole, self-explanatory but some additional comments will help to explain particular points.

Formal drains may be constructed in brick, in-situ concrete, precast concrete or a combination of materials. In general, brick will tend to be cheaper for smaller drains where it is available but reinforced concrete should come into its own for deeper drains for which thick brick or mass concrete walls will be required to resist lateral earth pressures. For larger covered drains, the cover slab can have an important structural effect, converting the walls from cantilevers to propped cantilevers and reducing the wall thickness required.

The hydraulic performance of a drain with a curved bed will be better than that with a horizontal bed, particularly

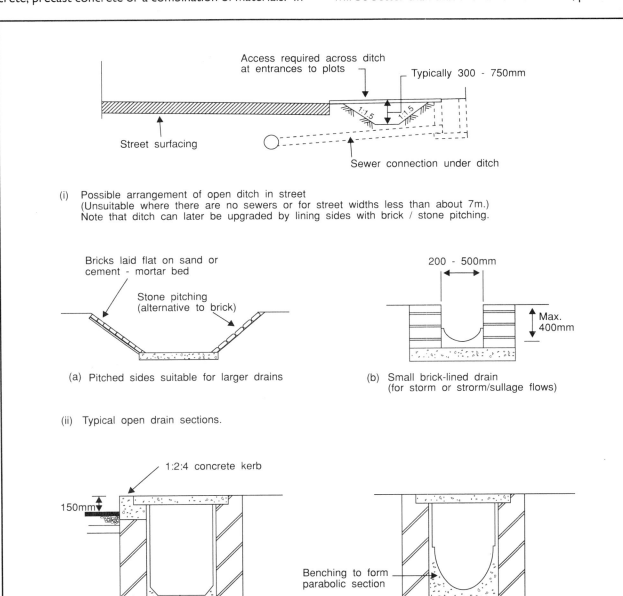

(i) Possible arrangement of open ditch in street
(Unsuitable where there are no sewers or for street widths less than about 7m.)
Note that ditch can later be upgraded by lining sides with brick / stone pitching.

(a) Pitched sides suitable for larger drains

(b) Small brick-lined drain
(for storm or storm/sullage flows)

(ii) Typical open drain sections.

(a) Under footpath

(b) Under road

(iii) Typical covered drain details.

Figure 8.4. Typical drain cross-sections

if the bed shape is parabolic. However, cost is increased and capacity decreased by the benching required to provide the desired bed shape. Because of this, flat bottomed drains with minimal benching will probably be the best option in many situations.

Half-round and parabolic benching for small drains can be produced in-situ using a wooden hand-held former up to about a metre long.

Access requirements for drains will normally be similar to those for sewers although the spacing of manholes can possibly be increased for drains in which it is possible for a man to walk or crawl. However, manhole spacings of greater than about 150m should not be used even when the drain is big enough to walk in.

Construction practice

Care should be taken to ensure that the ground under drains is graded to the correct fall and is well trimmed and consolidated before construction starts. Techniques for establishing drain levels are similar to those already described for sewers in Chapter 6.

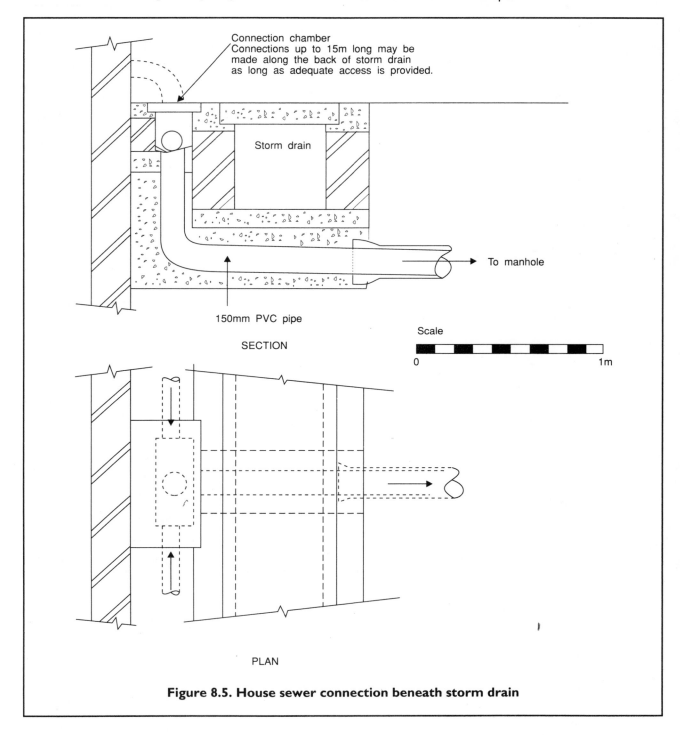

Figure 8.5. House sewer connection beneath storm drain

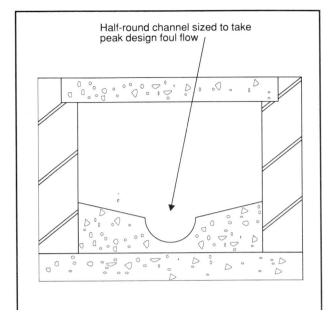

Half-round channel sized to take
peak design foul flow

**Figure 8.6. Invert arrangement for drain
carrying both foul and storm flows**

Drains must be cleared of all debris when construction is completed. If this task is neglected, a build up of solids against debris left in the drain is likely after commissioning, leading to a reduction in capacity and eventual blockage.

A likely problem with nominally separate drains is that people will tend to make foul connections to them. To avoid this, nominally separate drains should normally only be provided in areas where there are foul sewers. Where there are houses which do not yet have a sewer connection, it is important to provide sewer connections beneath the storm drain to chambers at which future foul connections can be made. A typical arrangement is shown in Figure 8.5.

Where the storm drain is also required to carry foul or sullage flows, a half round channel sized to take the design foul or sullage flow may be provided in the flat bottom of a larger drain, as shown in Figure 8.6. This will help to ensure that an acceptable velocity and depth of flow is maintained during low flows but that the capacity is sufficient to deal with high flows.

Average plot size	Typical population density	Average ground slope	Typical run-off coefficient
< 50m²	400 and over	<1:500	0.65
		1:500-1:200	0.70
		>1:200	0.80
100m²	200 - 400	<1:500	0.50
		1:500-1:200	0.55
		>1:200	0.65
250m²	50 - 200		0.45

Table 8.1. Suggested run-off coefficients

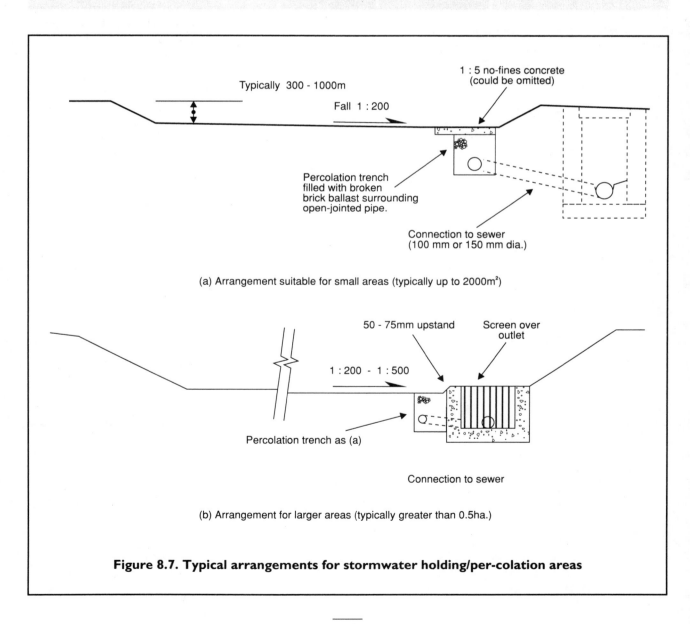

(a) Arrangement suitable for small areas (typically up to 2000m²)

(b) Arrangement for larger areas (typically greater than 0.5ha.)

Figure 8.7. Typical arrangements for stormwater holding/per-colation areas

ANNEX I

COMPONENTS OF DRAINAGE SYSTEMS

Unlined ditches

Unlined ditches are the cheapest form of drain to construct. However, they require constant maintenance and this limits their usefulness in informal areas. They are not suitable for carrying sullage flows and should therefore only be considered in sewered areas. In practice, they will only be an option in the rare situations in which streets are at least 7 metres wide. The slope on unlined drains should not be greater than about 1% (1 in 100) to avoid scouring. The side slopes should normally be about 1 in 2.

Open drains

Brick-lined open drains intended to carry both storm and sullage flows are used in informal areas throughout Pakistan. Their main disadvantage is that it is easy to throw rubbish into them, reducing their capacity and eventually blocking the flow. On the other hand, they are much easier to clean than covered drains and the equipment presently used by municipality sweepers is intended for use with them. Open drains over about 400mm deep are a hazard in that people, particularly children, may fall into them and injure themselves. Large open drains may be appropriate where space is available so that sides can be pitched or where access can be restricted. The former may be the case where the drain runs in a wide right of way. For main drains, access may be restricted by providing walls on either side of the drain.

Covered drains

It is more difficult to gain access to covered drains than to open drains. This means that it is more difficult to throw solid waste into them so that they do not become blocked as quickly. Conversely, it means that they are more difficult to clean and experience in Lahore and Peshawar shows that municipalities are often not equipped or prepared to clean them.

An advantage of covered drains is that it is possible to use the area above them. This may be important where the available right of way is limited. Against this must be set the additional cost of covering the drain. (For large drains, this will be partly offset by the reduction in wall section required for the covered drain).

As a general rule, drains smaller than about 500mm x 500mm should not be covered. Larger drains should be covered except where access to them can be prevented.

Combined sewers

Conventional wisdom on the design of sewerage and drainage systems is that combined sewers, carrying both foul and storm water, should not be used. However, we have already seen in Chapter 6 that there are situations in informal areas where a combined system may be the best option. The important thing, where sewers discharge to a treatment works or an existing nominally separate trunk sewer, is to be able to provide a storm overflow at some point downstream.

Streets acting as drains

For separate systems, tertiary drains can be eliminated by designing streets and lanes to carry stormwater. This reduces both the capital cost of drainage and the need for maintenance and the approach should therefore be used in upgrading schemes wherever possible. Most of the typical street and lane cross-sections given in Chapter 7 allow for stormwater to be drained on the surface. Where streets are designed to act as drains, surfacing materials such as brick and concrete, which are not damaged by stormwater, should be used.

Average annual rainfall		Average rainfall in wettest month		Design rainfall intensity	
mm/yr	in/yr	mm	inches	mm/hr	in/hr
0-250	0-10	0-75	0-3	15	0.6
250-500	10-20	75-125	3-5	25	1.0
500-750	20-30	125-175	5-7	35	1.4
750-1000	30-40	175-225	7-9	40	1.6

Table 8.2. Suggested rainfall intensity figures for use with small schemes

Soakaways

Although these are not appropriate for general use in upgrading schemes, there may be a case for encouraging individual plot-holders to construct soakaways to drain their property, particularly in low-lying areas.

Percolation basins

These have two advantages over soakaways. The first is that they are accessible for maintenance and the second that the storm water is held at a relatively high level. This means that it should be possible to provide an outlet drain or sewer so that percolation can be augmented by a controlled run-off during and after rainfall. The basin thus becomes a percolation/holding basin and can form part of a system designed to hold stormwater and reduce the rate of run-off to manageable levels.

In practice, the scope for using percolation/holding basins will be limited in informal areas by the lack of land on which to site them. (Much of the open land in informal areas is in private ownership and will not be available). However, there is a case for developing parks and public playing fields which are designed to hold stormwater after heavy rain. This will only be appropriate where foul flows are dealt with separately. It requires a fair degree of planning and public cooperation but would appear to be a worthwhile objective of upgrading efforts.

Infiltration trenches

There is theoretically scope for providing infiltration trenches filled with stones or broken bricks in streets and lanes to store stormwater and release it slowly to a drain or sewer. However, it will be difficult to ensure that the top of the drain is kept clean and the effectiveness of the system is likely to be greatly reduced by clogging in a relatively short time. Figure 8.7 shows how a layer of no-fines concrete, ie. concrete without any sand, could be used to give a hard surface over the infiltration trench. The advantage of this is that it could be swept regularly, thus reducing the problem of clogging. However, the system has not, to our knowledge, been tried in practice.

ANNEX 2

INFORMATION ON RUN-OFF COEFFICIENTS AND RAINFALL INTENSITY

Run-off coefficient 'C'

Typical 'C' values for different types of surface are as follows:

Impervious road surfaces	0.9
Sand grouted brick surfaces	0.6
Sloping roofs	0.9
Flat concrete roofs	0.75
Paved yards	0.6
Gravel paving	0.5
Grass and unpaved areas	0.25

It is theoretically possible to work out a composite 'C' value for an area by multiplying the areas of different types of surface by their appropriate 'C' values and then dividing by the total area. This could be done for a number of small areas and then applied to whole homogenous areas. In practice, the information on areas and run-off coefficients will rarely justify such an approach and it will usually be sufficient to assume overall run-off coefficients as given in Table 8.1.

The run-off coefficients given in Table 8.1 are based on the following assumptions:

◆ that the area is fully developed; few informal areas will not develop fully within the design life of a drainage scheme;

◆ that all roads and lanes are paved with an impermeable material (surface treatment, dense bitumen macadam, concrete or cement mortar- grouted bricks);

◆ that the majority of plots are above the level of streets and lanes.

Some reduction in run-off coefficient is justified if the paving consists of sand-grouted bricks or some other semi-permeable material. An overall reduction of about 10% of the run-off coefficients given in Table 8.1 would seem to be appropriate where the majority of streets are paved with semi-permeable materials.

The run-off coefficient will be further reduced when measures are taken to retain stormwater on-site.

Rainfall intensity

Rainfall intensities vary widely but meteriological records show that for any given location, heavy rainfall tends to last for a shorter time than light rainfall. Where good rainfall records exist, ideally based on data from recording rain gauges, statistical analysis can be used to produce intensity-duration curves to represent this phenomenon. Figure 8.1 shows the set of intensity-duration curves for Lahore. The significance of the curves is that each represents the maximum intensities of rainfall of different durations which will occur on average once in the stated return period.

A problem arises because rainfall-intensity curves are at present available for only a few cities in Pakistan. Production of curves for other cities will require analysis of data which may be inadequate, particularly where records from recording rain gauges are not available. Another problem is that the use of intensity duration curves will tend to result in overestimates of run-off flows for small areas since high short- term intensities will tend to be balanced by low run-off coefficients for short-duration storms.

In view of the above, a simplified design method is suggested for small systems. The design rainfall intensity is related to either the average annual rainfall or the average rainfall in the wettest month according to Table 8.2. The design intensities given in Table 8.2 are consistent with those commonly recommended for use in drainage calculations in India.

9.

SOLID WASTE COLLECTION

SUMMARY

Solid waste collection services in informal areas are rarely adequate. Efforts to improve the situation must pay attention to both the technologies used and the way in which services are organised. The chapter considers both in an integrated way. It begins by summarising the background situation in Pakistan, then states the objectives of solid waste disposal, before moving on to the planning of solid waste management services. The stages in the collection and disposal process are defined and the options for local and district level collection services are examined. Management options for local level services are considered and the issues to be addressed when considering community management options are listed. Guidelines for investigating existing conditions, practices and attitudes are given next and the planning section ends by examining the choices to be made between options, emphasising the need to take into account the existing situation. The final section of the chapter considers design factors and options. It starts with an examination of the various types of communal storage container, moves on to consider transfer stations and ends with a brief introduction to collection vehicles and equipment. An annex outlines the procedure for determining the amount of household solid waste produced.

KEY POINTS

◆

Successful solid waste management is only possible if an efficient operational system is available from the outset.

◆

Solid waste should be collected at least three times a week in hot climates and preferably daily.

◆

Improvements in local services will only be effective if reliable services are present at the district and citywide levels.

◆

In densely populated informal areas, problems are likely to occur with systems that rely on communal containers. Such systems should only be considered if residents agree to the bin locations and regular collection can be guaranteed.

◆

Roadside collection options in which residents either leave containers outside their houses or bring them out when the sweeper rings a bell can work in informal areas if sweepers work to a regular timetable.

◆

Collection from houses may be possible where people are willing to pay a small amount directly to the sweeper for the service.

◆

Community management of local services has advantages but responsibilities must be defined and accepted by the concerned individuals and organisations from the outset.

◆

Container systems are the best option for district level collection if they can be operated and maintained. Modified systems, based on the use of small vehicles may be appropriate for use in informal areas with poor access.

◆

Planning decisions should take into account the findings of investigations into the existing situation. These should cover the amount of waste produced, existing responsibilities and services, attitudes and priorities and any informal recycling practices that exist.

◆

The amount of household waste generated in informal areas in Pakistan is typically around 0.25 kg per person per day. Street sweepings may add a further 0.1 kg per person per day to this figure.

BACKGROUND

Solid waste or refuse is generated by many human activities. In residential areas, it comprises kitchen waste from food preparation, a wide variety of materials for which no further use can be found within the household and street sweepings. Commercial, industrial and institutional activities will also generate solid waste and particular attention may have to be paid in upgrading schemes to the wastes generated by food shops and markets.

Few informal areas in Pakistan have adequate solid waste management systems. Studies for several cities suggest that less than 50% of the solid waste generated throughout the cities is collected and observation suggests that the situation is worse in low-income informal areas. The result is that solid waste is deposited and accumulates along roadsides, on undeveloped plots and in drains, causing unpleasant smells, encouraging the breeding of flies and rats and blocking drains and sewers. Apart from the obvious deterioration in the environment caused by this situation, there are potentially serious consequences for health.

Solid waste management differs from all other components of physical infrastructure in that it depends upon an efficient operational system being established from the very outset. (Other services, such as roads or drainage, can operate adequately for a considerable period of time after construction with practically no input on the maintenance side until something actually goes wrong). Thus solid waste management is concerned more with operation than with design and construction. In this respect, it is worth noting that solid waste management may consume between 20% and 40% of municipal revenues. In India, for example, it employs between 3 and 6 people per 1000 population. At present, street cleaning usually comprises a significant proportion of the solid waste management budget. Nevertheless, good design, leading to more efficient operation, is important.

It is rarely possible to dispose of solid wastes within the boundaries of an upgrading area; the wastes must be collected and transported away from the site, usually to a municipal disposal area on the fringes of the town or city.

OBJECTIVES

The objectives of solid waste management services are to ensure the satisfactory storage, collection and disposal of solid wastes and the cleaning of streets and other public places. More specifically, the aim should be to:-

◆ collect solid waste from houses or communal collection points, preferably on a daily basis but at least three times per week (longer periods between collections are undesirable in hot climates since organic material putrefies quickly at high temperatures);

◆ eliminate solid waste from drains, roadsides, open plots and around solid waste storage facilities;

◆ dispose of the solid waste in an economic and hygienic way;

◆ allow for recycling of useful materials.

Achievement of these objectives will bring about obvious improvements in the aesthetic quality of the environment. It will also have an important effect on public health. Elimination of heaps of putrefying waste will remove a breeding medium for flies and a home for rats. At the same time, the number of places where mosquitoes can breed will be reduced as stagnant pools of water caused by solid waste-induced drain blockages are eliminated.

An important overall objective of solid waste management improvements should be to provide services at a cost which is affordable to both the consumer and the organisation responsible for managing services. At present, most services are heavily subsidised and expansion and improvements in them are unlikely unless this situation is changed.

PLANNING

A successful solid waste management system requires that adequate facilities and procedures exist at all points in the collection and disposal process. There are four broad stages in this process:

storage in the house;
local collection;
district/citywide collection; and
final disposal.

Collection and disposal systems must deal with street sweepings and wastes from commercial premises as well as household wastes.

This manual is primarily concerned with what happens at the local level but experience shows that local services will quickly break down if they are not linked with efficient district level services. A discussion of the options for district level collection is therefore included. The options for final disposal do not affect decisions at the local level and so these are not covered by the manual.

Bearing in mind that the organisation of solid waste collection services is as important as the techniques used, management issues will be addressed in parallel with technical issues throughout the chapter.

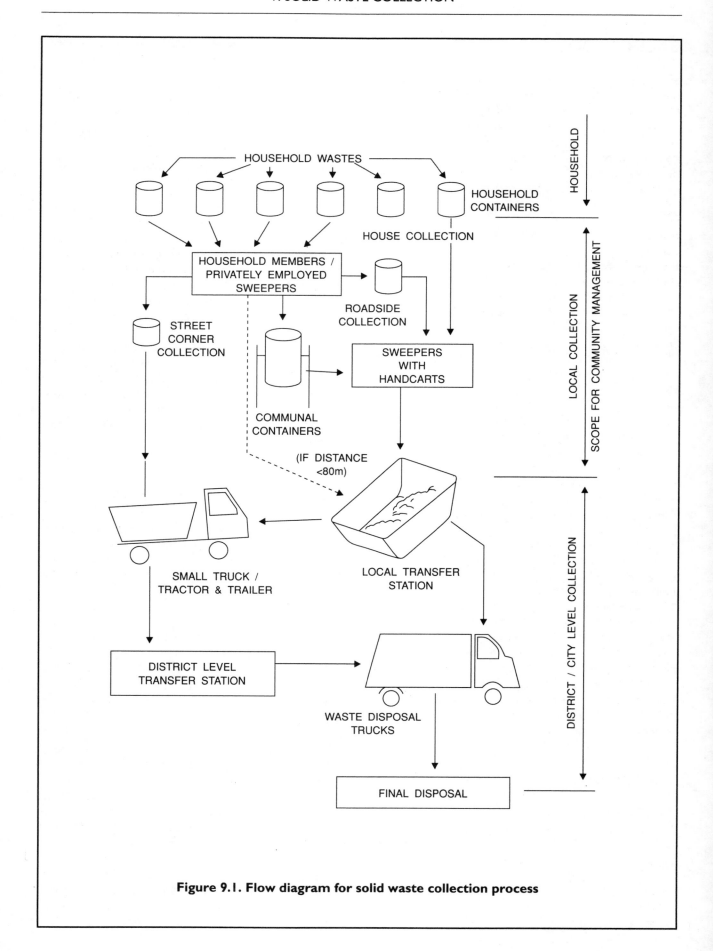

Figure 9.1. Flow diagram for solid waste collection process

Planning must start from a consideration of the possible options in relation to existing conditions and the available resources. With this in mind, technical options at the household, local and district levels will now be described and possible management arrangements will be introduced. The subjects to be covered in the investigation of existing conditions will then be considered and the factors which will influence the choice between technical and management options will be discussed. Figure 9.1 shows the way in which the various options at each stage of the process can be integrated together.

Household storage options

Household waste should be stored in a sturdy container or containers with sufficient capacity to deal with the maximum amount of solid waste in the house at any given time. These should be easy to empty and clean and should ideally have a well-fitting lid. Galvanised steel and plastic bins can satisfy these criteria but are not affordable in most low-income communities. Many houses use small containers for which no other use can be found. Surveys in Lahore and Faisalabad indicate that people use old ghee tins of about 5 litres capacity, emptying them daily.

In general, action at the household level should be aimed at getting people to improve their own storage facilities. The provision of containers by collection authorities will rarely be affordable and experience shows that such containers are often used for purposes other than storing solid waste. Under no circumstances should there be any attempt to introduce systems which depend on the collecting authorities supplying plastic storage bags to householders on a regular basis.

Local level collection options

There are four basic options for collection of household solid waste. These are:-

Communal storage, in which householders or sweepers employed by householders carry waste from the house to a communal storage container.

Street corner collection, when a collection vehicle halts at predetermined places and householders carry their solid waste to the vehicle.

Roadside collection, when the householder leaves the household storage container by the side of the road at an appointed time and it is emptied by the sweeper.

House collection, when the workers collect the waste container from within the boundaries of the plot; this involves the minimum effort on the part of the householder.

Each system is briefly discussed below.

Communal storage

This system requires maximum effort on behalf of the household, members of which have to carry the solid waste from the house to the communal storage container. Surveys in Faisalabad indicate that family members walk up to 40 metres to deposit waste and that privately employed sweepers carry waste an average distance of 80-100 metres. The implication is that containers should not be located further than 80m from any house. The communal brick dustbins and steel skips commonly used in formal developments are often unsuitable for use in upgrading areas because:

◆ narrow rights of way restrict access for emptying vehicles;

◆ with a high housing density, people do not want bins outside their houses.

Bins have been designed which are more appropriate to conditions in upgrading areas and examples are given later in this chapter. However, the most appropriate design of bin will only prove acceptable if:-

◆ residents use the bins properly and do not leave rubbish strewn around; and

◆ a regular collection can be guaranteed.

Achievement of these conditions requires both that people are educated in the importance of hygienic disposal practices and that those employed in solid waste collection have the motivation, resources and equipment to provide a better service.

Street corner collection

This option eliminates the problem associated with siting communal storage bins. It has two disadvantages in relation to informal areas. The first is the difficulty that will often be experienced in arranging collection points within 80 metres of every house. This can be overcome to some extent if small pickups are used for collection rather than conventional trucks. The second disadvantage is that the operational cost of allowing a vehicle to stand for several minutes while people bring their solid waste is likely to be high. In any event, the system will only work if vehicles work to a regular reliable schedule and people know when to expect them.

Roadside collection

This system overcomes the problems associated with street corner collection and it would appear to be a good option for use in informal areas. A variant, in which the sweeper rings a bell and people bring their waste out and deposit it in his or her cart, has been used successfully in the Lahore Walled City and elsewhere. However, the system will quickly break down unless sweepers work to a regular and reliable timetable. Another point is that it will take rather more of the sweepers time than a system which relies on communal containers.

House to house collection

This requires greater inputs from sweepers than other systems and for this reason is often assumed to be too expensive for use in low-income areas. However, it may be an option where surveys show that the majority of house-holders either already pay or are willing to pay to have solid waste removed from their houses. In such cases, it will be necessary to formalise existing payments in some way and build them into the new collection system.

Street cleaning

The sweepers who deal with household wastes are usually also responsible for street cleaning. This is an important aspect of local solid waste management that cannot be ignored without risking problems with blocked drains and a dirty environment. The materials to be dealt with include:

◆ waste dumped by householders in the street or drains;

◆ waste which spreads from communal waste bins;

◆ sand and silt on paved roads and in open drains;

◆ leaves and vegetation;

◆ animal dung, especially where bullocks and goats roam freely and along routes used to take buffaloes out to the fields. (It is common to keep buffaloes in urban fringe areas in Pakistan);

◆ silt removed from drains and sewers.

Street cleaning is a major item of expenditure for many urban local authorities and may account for 30-50% of the budget for urban solid waste management. However, the work requires the most basic equipment, typically:

◆ long handled brooms having stiff bristles for paved surfaces and soft bristles for unpaved surfaces;

◆ flat-front shovels;

◆ two flat boards for picking up and transferring waste, especially leaves; and

◆ handcarts.

For normal residential areas, it is unrealistic to aim for streets to be cleaned more frequently than once a week.

Market areas should be swept more frequently, preferably at least once daily. When planning solid waste collection services, it is important to consider how the collection of household wastes and street cleaning can be integrated.

Management options for local collection

The two basic options for local collection of wastes are:

◆ management by the municipality; and

◆ management by the local community.

In either case, the possibility of contracting out the service exists.

Management by the municipality

This is the normal management approach at present. The main advantage of municipality managed services is that the same organisation is responsible for all aspects of the collection and disposal process. Against this must be set the fact that municipality managed services rarely prove to be adequate in informal areas. The main reasons for this are usually:

◆ inadequate finances;

◆ the difficulties experienced in managing a large programme employing a large number of unskilled and unmotivated people.

Improvements in efficiency are essential if better use is to be made of limited finances. One option which should always be considered is the devolution of as many respon-sibilities as possible to the local level. The ward structure may provide a suitable framework for such devolution.

Community management

When community management options are considered, it is essential to establish the following:

◆ who will be responsible for day to day management;

◆ who will control finances;

◆ to whom will residents have recourse in the event of there being problems; and

◆ what arrangements have been made to ensure that the district level service necessary for successful functioning of the local community managed service will be provided by the municipality.

It is possible that sweepers could continue to be paid by the municipality but managed by the community, perhaps through the local councillor. The important questions to ask about arrangements based on political boundaries and personalities are:

- will they will be local enough; and
- will they favour some areas against others because of the overt political control.

District level collection options

The options for district level collection can be divided into two main categories:

- those that transport waste directly to the disposal point; and
- those that incorporate an intermediate district level transfer point.

The first option should be used whenever possible since it minimises the number of times that waste has to be handled. This has obvious benefits to workers but reduction in the amount of handling required also reduces costs. However, direct transport may prove to be impractical in areas which are remote from the final disposal point and dependent on small or slow moving transport vehicles. Where this is the case, as it often is in low-income areas, there may be a need for an intermediate transfer point at which the waste can be transferred to larger and faster vehicles.

The second broad division in the options available is between those that rely on conventional bins, enclosures and collection vehicles and those which are containerised. The latter have obvious operational advantages in that they minimise handling and intermediate transfer of waste. However, they are more expensive and require more sophisticated equipment, in particular trucks have to be fitted with hydraulic lifting equipment to hoist containers. They may thus be too expensive and should certainly be discounted if the equipment and/or spare parts required to maintain the hydraulic equipment are not available. It is also important to discuss proposed changes in equipment and practices thoroughly with those who are responsible for operating systems. In some places where containerised systems have been introduced, the containers function solely as fixed bins because either lifting equipment has broken down or operators do not use it. This can actually make operational conditions worse since the containers are harder to empty by hand than conventional bins.

Conventional container systems may in any case be inappropriate for use in informal areas because conventional trucks are too wide to use in narrow congested streets. Modified containerised systems, based on the use of small trucks, dumper chassis and pick-up trucks have been introduced in some countries to overcome this problem. While these systems appear to have advantages, their economics and maintenance requirements should be examined carefully before they are adopted.

An option that might be considered where the distance to the disposal point or a district-level transfer point is not too great is to provide trailers at transfer points which can be replaced and taken to the disposal/district transfer point for emptying at regular intervals. The system could work as follows. A tractor would take an empty trailer to the transfer point, leave it and pick up the full trailer. Upon reaching the disposal or district transfer point, the full trailer would be left for unloading and a recently emptied trailer would be taken to the next transfer point, exchanged for a full trailer and so on. One tractor could work in this way with 6-10 trailers, serving 4-8 transfer points depending on the journey distances involved.

Investigation of existing situation

Planning for improved solid waste collection services must take into account existing conditions, organisational structures, practices and attitudes. Investigations should cover the following specific subjects:-

- the amount and characteristics of solid waste;
- present responsibility for solid waste collection services;
- existing solid waste collection services;
- any financial incentives or other financial consideration which affect the quality of service provided;
- attitudes of householders and solid waste collectors;
- any informal recycling practices.

Once these factors are understood, it is possible to evaluate the options available. However, if the preliminary investigation is omitted, there is a grave danger that any proposals made will be inappropriate and unworkable. The specific subjects to be investigated are considered in more detail below.

Amount and composition of solid waste generated.

In order to estimate storage requirements and collection frequencies and devise suitable collection methods, it is important to know the volume, density and weight of solid waste produced. Knowledge of its composition will be required when considering disposal methods and the possibilities for recycling. The generation rate of solid waste is usually given in kilograms per person per day (kpd) and its density in kilograms per cubic metre (kg m^{-3}). The volume in litres per day (lpd) is then equal to the mass divided by the density. The typical range of characteristics of solid waste is as follows:

Generation rate	:	0.25 - 1.0 kpd
Density	:	100 - 600 kg m^{-3}
Putrescible matter (which decomposes)	:	20 - 80% by weight

Examples of generation rates from Pakistan are:

Faisalabad (residential only ,1991)
low income   :   0.20 kpd
middle income   :   0.23 kpd
high income   :   0.25 kpd

Lahore (residential only, 1981)
city-wide average   :   0.43 kpd

In India, a countrywide average generation rate of 0.35 kpd has been estimated for domestic solid waste.

Based on these figures an amount of 0.25 kpd plus an allowance of 0.10 kpd for street sweepings giving a total of 0.35 kpd should be allowed for upgrading areas if local information is not available. (The procedure for sampling to obtain local figures is briefly described in Annex 1).

The volume generated, which is important in planning the local storage and collection on the site depends upon the density of the solid waste. In low-income communities much material is salvaged either for sale or reuse; the same material would be thrown away by richer people. As income levels rise, the mass of waste produced increases and its density decreases, leading to marked increases in the volume.

Density increases during the collection and disposal process; typical densities based on data from Faisalabad are shown below.

Location	Density kg m^{-3}
Household storage containers	210
In collection trucks	600
In tractor-trailer	450
6 months after disposal	850

Based on these figures, the density in communal bins is likely to be in the range 250-400 kg m^{-3}, depending on the time between collections.

It is therefore reasonable to assume a volumetric generation rate of about 1.7 lpd (including street sweeping) at the site level and about 1.2 lpd at the household level.

The composition of solid waste does not have a significant effect on the choice of collection method.

Present responsibilities

Solid waste management is almost always the responsibility of municipalities. In the larger cities, it normally comes under the Chief Medical Officer. The investigation of present responsibilities should concentrate on establishing:

◆ whether there is a zonal structure with day to day management responsibilities decentralised to zonal offices;

◆ the extent to which services are organised on a ward basis, with collection staff answerable to elected representatives.

It will also be worthwhile to investigate whether there is any informal or formal involvement of community groups and others in local collection and disposal services.

Existing collection services

Once administrative boundaries and present responsibilities have been ascertained, it is possible to assess existing collection services. There are three aspects to this:-

◆ what vehicles, equipment and manpower are available;

◆ what level of service is being provided; and

◆ how efficient is the use of vehicles, equipment and personnel.

The investigation of vehicles and equipment may be at a zonal and citywide level but the allocation to the area being considered for upgrading should be established if possible. The types, condition and capacities of available vehicles should be established, as should the capacity and performance of workshop facilities. Manpower resources should be established at the ward level or more locally if at all possible. Field studies should be carried out to determine the way in which personnel, vehicles and equipment are used. It will usually be advisable to carry out a thorough study of collection practices in either the area to be upgraded or one that has similar characteristics. This should cover collection routes, times and methods and the working practices of the sweepers and supervisors employed in the area.

Attitudes of householders and sweepers

Information on the attitudes of householders may be obtained at public meetings and through the social survey methods described in Chapter 4. The particular subjects to be covered in such surveys include:-

◆ whether people pay for solid waste to be removed from the house and, if so, how much;

◆ whether people who do not pay at present would be prepared to pay and, if so, how much;

◆ whether there is an awareness of the health risks associated with poor solid waste disposal practices.

The options for improving services should be discussed with the sweepers and supervisors who are responsible for the day-to-day operation of the services. Any potential changes in working practices should be explained and particular note should be taken of any serious concerns that are expressed about these changes. Workers on low incomes are unlikely to cooperate in any changes that threaten their overall income and initiatives will fail without this cooperation. Conversely, workers should welcome improved methods which allow them to earn more because of increased productivity. It is quite possible that workers will have ideas that could improve services and it is always worth listening to the ideas of those who actually do a job.

Scavenging and recycling

Many authorities and officials regard scavenging as a problem which needs to be eliminated. However, the reality is that in many towns and cities, scavenging is something which is going to remain for the foreseeable future. Scavenging may in fact have a number of important benefits, including:

◆ resource recovery from waste;

◆ provision of substitute materials for the poorest people;

◆ reduction in the quantity of solid waste to be collected.

Existing scavenging practices should be investigated to find out what materials are recovered, where the scavenging takes place and who does the scavenging.

Transfer stations are likely to attract scavengers; whilst this can be an effective way of recycling waste materials it is important to prevent the waste being scattered about indiscriminately. Ideally, a transfer station should be manned to exercise some control over scavenging and to oversee waste transfer from handcarts or portable bins into trailers.

On a city-wide basis there may be considerable informal sector involvement through intricate networks of scavengers, middle-men, and users of waste products. Informal waste recovery should be viewed as an integral part of the city's solid waste management service, and the design and operation of collection, transfer and disposal should facilitate the operation of scavenging.

Choice of approach

Local level

The choice of approach at the local level will depend largely on the findings of the investigation into the existing situation and discussions with the local community.

Where locations for communal containers can be agreed, the communal storage option has attractions because it maximises the area that can be covered by a given number of sweepers. Design options for storage containers are considered later.

The roadside collection option should always be considered as an alternative to the communal storage option. If it is well organised, savings in handling time may largely offset the longer collection routes and waiting time that it requires. The attractiveness of the approach is further enhanced if responsibility for management can be devolved to the community and small weekly or monthly payments can be collected from householders. This is perhaps the most generally attractive option for use in low-income areas with poor access. However, it does require the cooperation of sweepers and will be more likely to work if they are given some incentive to operate it.

House to house collection should be considered where surveys and community meetings show that a majority of householders already pay or are willing to pay for waste to be collected from their houses. The system is only likely to work if:

◆ management responsibility is devolved to the local level; and

◆ sweepers and other collection staff benefit directly from the payments that are made.

As for roadside collection, this option will have more chance of success if management responsibilities can be devolved to the community.

Where road access is limited, all three options considered above are dependent on the presence of areas/enclosures/ containers at which the waste is transferred from handcarts or other local collection vehicles to larger vehicles. The option of street corner collection may be considered where:

◆ locations for such transfer points cannot be agreed; and

◆ there is vehicular access to within 100m of most houses.

However, street corner collection should be avoided whenever possible because it ties up expensive vehicles for long periods and is thus more expensive than other options.

District level services

It cannot be emphasised too often that local level services will fail unless adequate district level collection is available. Waste should be collected from local transfer points at least three times per week.

The choice of district level collection system will depend on:

street widths;
available vehicles and plant;
the distance to the disposal point;
the maintenance requirements of the various options; and
the economics of the various options.

Where the funds available for capital investment are limited, it may be necessary to consider systems using existing vehicles and equipment in the first instance with improved containerised systems delayed until the necessary finances and maintenance facilities are available.

DESIGN

Communal storage

Communal storage containers should:

- be spaced at intervals which ensure that people are prepared to carry their solid waste to them;
- have sufficient capacity;
- be designed to minimise the time taken to empty them; and
- restrict access of flies, rats and other pests as far as is possible.

As already indicated, the maximum distance from any house to a storage container should not exceed 80m. Where possible, maximum walking distances should be less than this.

The required capacity will depend on the container spacing, the population density, the rate at which solid waste accumulates and the collection frequency. To estimate requirements, the best approach will be to calculate the storage capacity required per hectare. This is given by:

$$C = PRI$$

where C is the capacity in litres;
P is the population density/ha.
R is the waste generation rate (lpd)
I is the emptying interval (days)

The number of individual containers per hectare can then be obtained on the basis of the spacing standards adopted. The volume of each container is given by $V = C/N$ where V is in litres and N is the number of containers per hectare. The emptying interval allowed when calculating storage requirements should be one day longer than the longest interval which will occur under normal operating condi-

tions. This will allow for irregularities in the collection service. (This means that the storage provided for a daily collection service will cater cater for two day's waste, that for a three times a week service will cater for four days waste).

Brick enclosures

The traditional design for storage containers is a brick-built enclosure as shown in Figure 9.2. These typically have capacities in the range 1-10 cubic metres. Problems with this type of storage include:

- the full capacity of the enclosure in rarely utilised because people throw their waste from just outside the entrance, forming a heap which tends to overflow into the street;
- the removal of wastes from the enclosure is difficult, unpleasant and unhygienic with all wastes having to be lifted into the receiving vehicle.
- scavenging animals have unlimited access; and
- a large enclosure may be used for defecation and urination.

For all these reasons, brick enclosures are less than ideal. Moreover, there will rarely be space to locate them within densely developed informal areas and their locations will therefore normally be restricted to main roads. Their one advantage is that they are cheap and constructed of materials that are unlikely to be stolen. Brick enclosures may be provided as a temporary measure for medium size transfer stations but the aim should be to replace them eventually with some form of containerised system.

Fixed storage bins

Fixed storage bins differ from enclosures in having no direct entrance. The walls are normally less than 1.5 metres high so that waste can be dropped inside. An

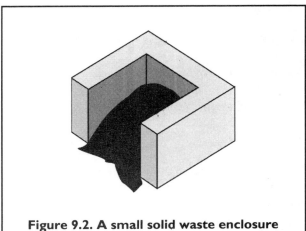

Figure 9.2. A small solid waste enclosure

opening covered by a flap is placed in one of the walls to enable wastes to be raked out. The theoretical advantages that this design offers in terms of restricting access for animals are more than offset by the obstacles that the design places in the way of quick and efficient emptying. In practice, the flap is likely to be quickly removed to facilitate access, so removing the one theoretical advantage of the system. Fixed storage bins are not recommended. The same is true of their simple variants, concrete pipe sections and oil drums placed upright along the roadside. These have the added disadvantage that they have limited capacity.

Various designs for steel bins incorporating features that allow them to be empied quickly and easily have been developed over the years. Figure 9.3 shows two such designs, one of which has been tried in Lahore and the other in Peshawar. Such bins can be made with capacities in the range 150-250 litres. They have the theoretical advantage that they can be fitted with a lid to keep out flies and vermin but the the function of the lid will have to be explained to users if it is not to be quickly removed for the sake of convenience. Potential problems with such bins include their cost, their height above the ground and the fact that they are liable to be stolen for their scrap value.

Portable bins

Small portable steel or plastic bins, ideally with fitted lids, could provide hygienic storage if the collection frequency is high. However, they are expensive and are likely to be stolen for their resale value or for alternative uses. In Lahore, portable containers have been produced by cutting used tar/bitumen barrels in two. These do not have fitted lids but they have no resale value and are cheap. Such containers could be carried on hand carts such as that shown in Figure 9.6 and changed at daily intervals, an empty container being used to replace a full container. This option is limited by the fact that the weight of one container should not be more than one person can lift, in practice around 25 kgm at the most. This would suggest that one container would be required for every 4-5 houses and the system will only be viable if there are frequent transfer points at which containers can be emptied.

Transfer stations

The simplest form of transfer station is an open space at which waste is deposited from handcarts and picked up by collection vehicles. There are obvious problems with this system in that waste is not contained and there is free access for animals and insects. Some people argue that open spaces are nevertheless better than brick enclosures because the latter are more difficult to empty so that solid waste tends to be left in the corners for considerable periods. Whichever option is considered the better, both are far from ideal and should only be considered as a temporary measure. An advantage of enclosures may be that they can be built with a slightly raised floor that allows waste to be shovelled or pushed directly into the back of a low pick-up.

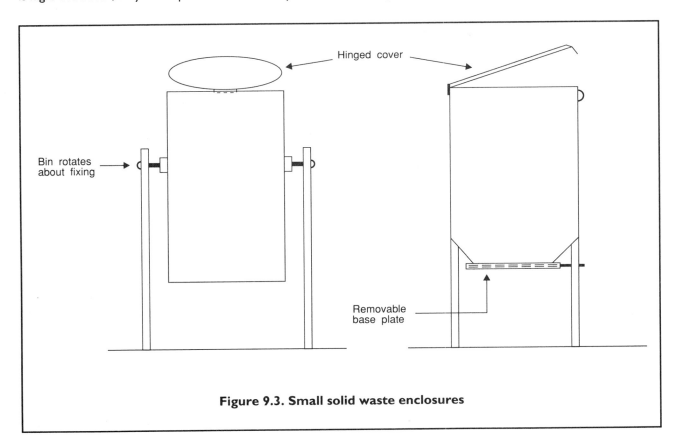

Figure 9.3. Small solid waste enclosures

Where the local authority possesses the necessary equipment, portable containers and skips which can be hoisted onto standard vehicles when full present the best option at transfer stations. The sides of the containers should not be too high unless it is possible to provide a ramp up which carts can be pushed to allow them to be tipped into the containers.

Another option, already suggested for district level collection, is the use of tractors and trailers. Transfer stations for this option need to have enough space to allow trailers to be parked and exchanged. Where possible, a ramp should be provided to allow handcarts to be wheeled onto the trailer so that the solid waste can be easily unloaded. Figure 9.4 shows a possible arrangement.

Collection vehicles

Careful consideration must be given to the vehicles and equipment that are used to transfer solid waste from one location to another. Access widths and the type of waste storage in use will influence the design. Indeed, the design of storage facilities and transport should always be considered in relation to one another. In steep or inaccessible places, it may be necessary to carry waste manually, using baskets or shoulder panniers connected by a bar. However, in most cases some form of cart or vehicle will be required. The various types of vehicle are briefly described below.

Handcarts

The simplest form of handcart consists of an open box on wheels with a capacity of 200-500 litres. Such handcarts are widely used in street and general cleaning and can be used for transporting waste from communal containers and in roadside and house collection services. They are suitable for areas having narrow streets and high population densities but loading and unloading can be messy as it frequently involves emptying the contents of the cart onto the ground when transferring the waste. The problems of transfer can be reduced if the cart can be designed either to tip froward or with a removable panel that allows waste to be shovelled out on the level rather than over the sides of the cart. A typical cart is shown in Figure 9.5.

A variation on the basic handcart idea is to make the cart a platform on which containers can be placed. A design of this type, developed in Lahore, is illustrated in Figure 9.6. Similar carts, carrying two 200 litre containers are used in Rabat, Morocco as part of a roadside collection system. The large containers are possible because they are unloaded at a central transfer station at which help is always available to lift them.

Tricycles

The use of either pedal or motorised tricycles to power a frame carrying portable containers speeds up the collection operation and increases the radius of collection. They are appropriate in flat areas of low population density, provided that roads and lanes are well surfaced.

A possible development of this idea is the use of customised auto-rickshaws to carry solid waste. However, the fairly high cost of these vehicles, combined with their limited capacity means that there will usually be better options.

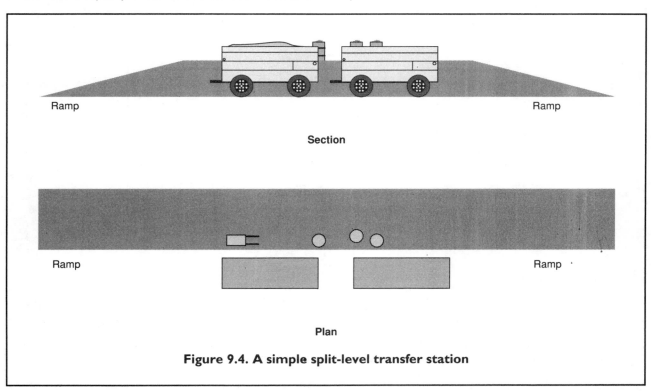

Figure 9.4. A simple split-level transfer station

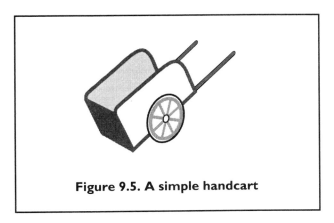

Figure 9.5. A simple handcart

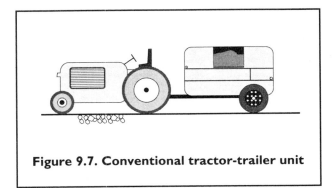

Figure 9.7. Conventional tractor-trailer unit

Animals

Donkeys may be saddled with baskets and used for collection in areas where access is difficult because of steep slopes or narrow lanes. Carts drawn by bullocks, horses or donkeys can pull much larger loads over longer distances than tricycle systems although they are very slow.

Tractor-trailer units

These are much quicker than animal carts and may be appropriate for moving waste short to medium distances, typically up to about 5km. As already indicated, a single tractor can be used with several trailers that are left in turn at transfer points. In countries such as Pakistan, tractor and trailer units have the advantage that they can be purchased in-country and maintained using components available in the local market. The small single axle 'mini' tractor units common in south-east Asia can carry between 1000 and 3000 litres, depending on the trailer design. Conventional tractors can carry larger payloads.

Small pick-ups

Small pick-up trucks provide an attractive option in congested areas. Such pick-ups can penetrate streets with usable widths as small as 3 metres. Their capacity is limited to perhaps 1000-3000 litres depending on the design, but they are quicker than tractor and trailer combinations. Standard pick-up truck chassis have been fitted with hydraulics and used as the basis of mini-container systems.

Larger vehicles

The range of vehicles available for long-range movement of waste is large and careful selection of appropriate vehicles is essential. While this is a problem to be faced by the municipality, it is important to ensure that the design of communal containers and transfer stations enables the local authority to adopt the most efficient overall solution.

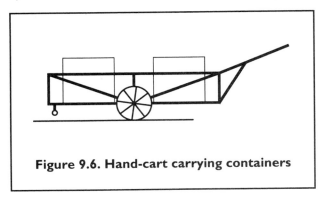

Figure 9.6. Hand-cart carrying containers

ANNEX I

PROCEDURE FOR MEASURING AMOUNT OF SOLID WASTE PRODUCED

In order to estimate the amount of solid waste produced, a sampling programme is desirable. The programme should cover representative areas and should normally be restricted to a representative sample of the houses in these areas. (For instance, every fifth house along a street might be sampled). The survey should ideally cover at least 100 households.

After selection of the houses to be sampled, each householder should be interviewed to explain the purpose of the sampling exercise. This should be done by community facilitators whenever possible. At the interview, information on family size and, if required, socio-economic details of the household can be obtained.

The sampling programme should extend over eight successive days with waste collected on the first day being discarded as it may have been accumulated over more than one day. The remaining days will give data covering a whole week. The collector should carry a supply of plastic bags, one of which should be handed in at each dwelling in return for the full one collected. Each full bag should be labelled before being taken for analysis so that its source can be identified.

Each sample should be weighed and its contents should be analysed as required. Information on per-capita generation rates can then be obtained by dividing the household generation rates by household sizes. The data obtained should be analysed to determine whether there is any pattern of waste production over the week.

The average density of the waste at various points in the system can be obtained by measuring the weight of a known volume of waste.

10.

STREET LIGHTING

SUMMARY

This chapter addresses the problems of providing lighting for access ways in low-income areas which will be principally used by pedestrians and occasional slow moving vehicles. Different types of light sources and lamps are described. The terminology used by lighting engineers is defined and lighting levels appropriate for areas to be upgraded are considered.

A simplified design procedure for determining the spacing of street lights is outlined; consideration is then given to electrical supply requirements, including power, switching and fixtures. The chapter ends with a brief summary of maintenance requirements.

KEY POINTS

◆

The objectives of street lighting in upgrading areas with minimal traffic are to facilitate pedestrian movements, recognition of obstacles and other pedestrians and to provide a degree of security.

◆

The principle of street lighting is to make objects appear dark against a brighter road surface.

◆

Fluorescent tubes are likely to be the most appropriate lamps for streets less than about 7 metres wide.

◆

For streets up to 3 metres wide, lanterns can be mounted on the walls of buildings 3 metres above ground level.

◆

For streets up to 7 metres wide, lanterns may be mounted either as above or on poles 5 metres above ground level.

◆

For wider streets carrying substantial traffic flows, high pressure mercury lamps may be used.

◆

Single phase power supply is required.

◆

All live power lines should be insulated or inaccessible for reasons of public safety.

◆

An inventory of the installation and maintenance records should be kept.

◆

Maintenance activities include regular night inspection, lamp cleaning, replacement of lamps on a regular basis, periodic inspection and testing of the installation.

INTRODUCTION

The objectives of street lighting are to provide safety, security and well-being on roads and access ways; the requirements for lighting depend upon the principal use of the road. The driver of a vehicle needs sufficient light to enable him to perceive obstructions and to stop safely when required. Pedestrians do not have to react as quickly to distant objects as drivers, and the overall lighting level can be lower.

The principal of street lighting is to make objects appear dark against a brighter road surface, or in silhouette. The bright surface is obtained by using street lighting to direct light up and down the road so that sufficient light is reflected off the surface to reveal objects.

This chapter concentrates on the problems of providing lighting for access ways in low-income areas which will be principally used by pedestrians and occasional slow moving vehicles. National standards exist for the provision of lighting on heavily trafficked roads; these are not considered here.

LIGHTING

Lamps

The lamp is the source of light and converts electrical energy into radiation to which our eyes respond. The main types of lamp in use are:

◆ tungsten lamps (designated GLS), in which a small wire contained in a glass bulb is heated to a high temperature in a vacuum;

◆ fluorescent lamps (designated MCF & TL), in which ultra-violet radiation causes phosphor powder to glow inside a tube;

◆ discharge lamps, in which an electric current is passed through a mixture of gases in a sealed tube. Examples are low pressure sodium, high pressure sodium, high pressure mercury (designated SOX, SON, MBF or HPL-N respectively).

Light from the lamp is usually reflected by mirrors; together with the lamp housing and some electrical fittings, the assembly is known as the luminaire. Those luminaires specifically designed for street lighting are called lanterns.

Lighting theory terminology

The luminous flux represents the quantity of radiation which comes from a lamp, measured in units of Lumens.

The intensity of light emitted is measured in units of Candelas.

The illuminance of a point on the road surface which is receiving light from a lantern equals the intensity of light emitted divided by the square of the distance from the source to the point considered. Note that illuminance relates to the incident light falling on a surface. It is measured in units of Lux (which equal lumens per square metre). Illuminance forms the basis of the adopted design method and will be discussed further.

The luminance is a measure of the intensity of the light reflected from the road surface and is measured in units of Candelas per square metre. Note that luminance relates to reflected light from a surface; the relationship between light falling on a surface and the amount reflected in any direction depends upon the physical properties of the surface as well as the lantern. Luminance is now commonly used to assess lighting requirements for heavily trafficked roads.

LIGHTING LEVELS

For the lighting of areas used principally for pedestrian access such as galis and narrow streets, it is important to provide a level of lighting which is sufficient to permit safe movement and recognition of obstacles and other pedestrians. Lighting also provides a degree of security, whereby potential intruders can be noticed. An additional benefit is that the attractiveness of an area is enhanced by lighting. Whilst it is desirable to provide an adequate level of lighting, the capital and operational costs increase with increasing illuminance and these must be kept to a minimum.

The following values of illuminance are recommended.

Illuminance	Comments
0.2 lux	Minimum in order to positively detect obstacles
I lux	Satisfactory recognition of obstacles and irregularities
5 lux	Human features are recognisable
10-20 lux	Attractive lighting

Selection of suitable lighting levels is made difficult because the above guideline figures refer to an 'overall' or 'average' level of lighting. From the definition of illuminance and Figure 10.1 it is clear that the illuminance at different distances from the lantern varies enormously.

It is recommended that the design criteria for areas used principally by pedestrians and a limited amount of very slow moving traffic should be to provide a minimum illuminance of 0.5 lux at any point.

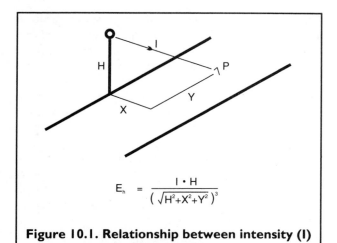

$$E_h = \frac{I \cdot H}{\left(\sqrt{H^2+X^2+Y^2}\right)^3}$$

Figure 10.1. Relationship between intensity (I) and illuminance (E_h)

Adopting this approach should mean that in most cases the 'average' illuminance from the lanterns is in excess of 1 lux.

DESIGN PROCEDURE

Having selected an appropriate level of lighting in terms of illuminance (lux), the problem is to specify:

◆ lantern type;

◆ lantern height;

◆ lantern spacing;

in order to give the required illuminance in an access way of a known width.

For streets less than about 4 metres wide it will be cost effective to mount the lanterns on the walls of houses at a minimum height of 3 metres. Whilst this can also be used for streets up to 7 metres wide, better overall illumination will result from mounting the lanterns on poles which are 5 metres high. It is assumed that lanterns will be located along one side of the street only.

In Pakistan, fluorescent tubes are likely to be the most appropriate lamps for streets less than about 7 metres wide. For wider streets carrying substantial traffic flows, high pressure mercury lamps may be used in accordance with highway lighting guidelines.

Street Width (m)	Light source
2-4 metres	Two No. 20 watt fluorescent tubes Wall-mounted (3 m)
4-7 metres	Two no. 40 watt fluorescent tubes Wall (3 m) or pole (5 m) mounted

It is important to obtain the lamp characteristics from the manufacturer, as the following steps require the lamp intensity to be known. Approximate values are:

Two No. 20 watt fluorescent = 200 candelas

Two No. 40 watt fluorescent = 500 candelas

The lantern spacing can be estimated if it is assumed that the minimum lighting level of 0.5 lux occurs at the mid point (X) between two consecutive lanterns (L1 and L2) separated by a distance 'S' as shown below.

L1 _____ X _____ L2

       S/2   S/2

Use the 'Distance Factor (DF)' from Table 10.1 below to estimate the required spacing (S) for a given mounting height for a lamp intensity (I) as follows.

Step 1: Calculate DF = 25/I

Step 2: Read off the value of Spacing (S) corresponding to the value of DF in the table below.

Note that the maximum spacing has been assumed to be 40 metres; unless the lamps are exceptionally powerful, larger spacings will result in parts of the lighted region receiving extremely low illumination.

Table 10.1. Distance Factor (DF)

Mounting Height	3m	5m	8m
Spacing (m)	Distance Factors		
10	1.51	1.41	0.95
12	1.00	1.05	0.80
14	0.68	0.79	0.67
16	0.48	0.60	0.55
18	0.35	0.46	0.46
20	0.26	0.36	0.38
22	0.20	0.28	0.32
24	0.16	0.23	0.27
26	0.13	0.19	0.23
28	0.10	0.15	0.19
30	0.08	0.13	0.16
32	0.07	0.11	0.14
34	0.06	0.09	0.12
36	0.05	0.08	0.11
38	0.04	0.07	0.09
40	0.04	0.06	0.08

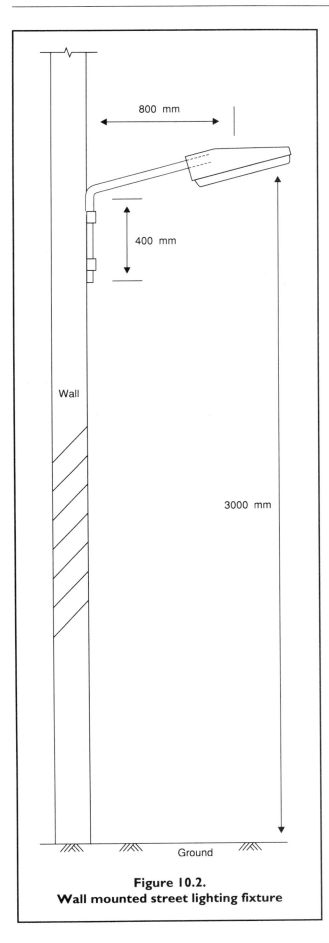

Figure 10.2.
Wall mounted street lighting fixture

Example Estimate the required spacing between lanterns which are providing lighting for a street 3 metres wide. Each lantern comprises 2 No. 20 watt fluorescent tubes having a total intensity of 240 candelas which are to be wall mounted 3 metres above ground level.

Step 1: Calculate DF = 25/I = 25/240 = 0.104

Step 2: Read down the '3 metre mounting height' column in the distance Factor table until DF = 0.10 is reached at a spacing of 28 metres.

Therefore the lantern spacing should be 28 metres.

Note, however, that this theoretical spacing may have to be amended in practice to allow for bends in streets, incorporation of existing street lights etc.

ELECTRICAL

Power supply

Street lighting usually requires single phase power supply, that is, one live and one neutral line. It is essential that live power lines be insulated if they are run along the walls of buildings or if they are otherwise easily accessible. Other metal parts of the lanterns such as the lamp housing and other fixtures should be earthed to ensure automatic disconnection of the supply in case they become live. Fuses or circuit breakers are normally installed so that the power supply is automatically disconnected in the event of power surging or overloading.

Switching

Manual operation: at a suitable location, for example on a power pole, a main switch is connected between supply lines and is turned on and off at the appropriate time. Up to 100 lanterns can be operated from a single switching point.

Time switching: these are electrically operated switches, but should also be fitted with either a reserve spring-wound time switch or a battery back-up to operate the switch in the event of power failure.

Fixtures

When fixing to a wall it is important to ensure that the structure is strong enough to support the lantern and bracket; in some cases backing plates may be needed to spread the load. Where lanterns are fixed to power poles, the requirements of the power utility must be followed.

Any control gear which is not inside the lantern should be housed in strong containers which are waterproof and difficult to tamper with and are secured to the wall or pole.

Any wiring between the control gear and lantern should be protected by galvanised steel conduit in accordance with the requirements of the power utility.

MAINTENANCE

The objective of street light maintenance is to ensure efficient, safe and reliable working of the installations. This requires the following activities.

1. Night inspection to identify failed lamps. Between 30% and 70% of lanterns are likely to fail during the course of one year. Routes should be pre-planned and faults reported and attended to as soon as possible; it is not usually economical to attempt 'on the spot' repairs.

2. Lamps should be cleaned regularly as surface dirt on the lamp can significantly reduce the effective illuminance.

3. The replacement or repair of defective equipment, which might include:

◆ fuses;

◆ switches;

◆ luminaires and wiring;

◆ lamps;

◆ igniters;

◆ control gear.

4. The replacement of lamps can be done on either a regular basis, or when an individual lamps fails. All lamps will fail eventually, but planned cyclic replacement or 'bulk changing' can be cheaper than responding to individual lamp failures. Transport costs are reduced, and there are likely to be fewer random failures between bulk changes.

5. Visual inspection of the electrical equipment, wiring, lantern brackets and fixings should be carried out every three years.

6. The electrical installation should be tested at least every five years.

7. An inventory containing accurate records of the installation and the maintenance work carried out are essential to the effective management of the lighting system. Record cards should give full details for each lantern.

11.

DOCUMENTATION

SUMMARY

This chapter provides a brief review of the documentation required to implement upgrading schemes. The first part deals with points that apply to the documentation for all infrastructure services. It is divided into three sections, the first covering drawings, the second measurement and bills of quantitities and the third specifications. In each section, the documentation required for conventionally managed schemes is covered first and any adjustments required for community managed schemes are then described. The second part of the chapter deals with the particular documentation requirements for specific services, starting with street paving and drainage and moving on to cover water supply, sewerage and, briefly, solid waste collection facilities and street lighting.

KEY POINTS

◆

Standard contract documentation, including drawings, bills of quantities and specifications, is required for upgrading works built by contractors.

◆

Drawings show what is to be built, schedules and bills of quantities enable the work required to be measured and specifications define acceptable construction procedures and standards of workmanship and materials.

◆

Drawings, both layout plans and standard details, should always be available on site to those responsible for the construction and supervision of schemes.

◆

Bills of quantities may not be required for small community managed schemes but there will be a need to produce simple schedules of quantities so that costs can be estimated and materials can be ordered.

◆

Standard schedules can be used for calculating quantities and costs for frequently repeated items such as manholes. For linear items such as drains, the schedules should give quantities and costs per unit length.

◆

For larger schemes, streets and lanes should be numbered and the quantities for each street or lane should be calculated separately and entered on standard summary sheets.

◆

Specifications should always be as simple as possible. For small schemes, it will be appropriate to produce special standard specifications which cover only the works included in the scheme.

◆

The method of carrying out a task rather than the end result required should be specified where measurement of the end result is not possible using readily available equipment.

◆

The reasoning behind specifications should be clearly explained to community members involved in the implementation of schemes.

INTRODUCTION

All upgrading schemes require some form of documentation in order to:

◆ show those providing the facilities what is required; and

◆ provide information to those responsible for monitoring the work.

The documents required fall into three broad categories, drawings, estimates of material quantities and specifications. Drawings provide information on what is to be built. Schedules of quantities based on the drawings enable the total requirement for materials and the cost of schemes to be estimated. Specifications define what is acceptable with regard to procedures and the quality of workmanship and materials.

Where a contractor is employed, the drawings, quantities and specification should be presented in a formal way. Quantities should be presented in the form of standard bills of quantities and these, together with the drawings, specification and standard conditions of contract should form the basis of the contract between the client and the contractor. The question of what forms an acceptable level of documentation will be considered later but for the moment the point to be stressed is that there should be adequate documentation. Without this, the contractor will not know what he has to do and those responsible for supervising the work will not have a benchmark against which to measure its adequacy.

It is possible that contractors will be used to implement community managed schemes, in which case it is necessary to have formal documentation although every effort should be made to keep it as simple as possible. Where community managed schemes use community resources, together with directly employed tradesmen, there will not be formal contracts as such. Nevertheless, there will be a need to provide drawings, estimate quantities and specify the materials and standard of workmanship required.

REQUIREMENTS OF 'GOOD PRACTICE'

Drawings

Upgrading proposals should be represented by a series of layout plans supported by standard details.

Layout plans should normally be at a scale of 1:500, 1:1000 or their imperial equivalents and should be based on base plans produced using the survey techniques described in

Chapter 4. Where plans for several services are required, draughting time can be saved by preparing one base negative and then adding details of proposals on copy negative or 'sepia' prints of this negative. However, this procedure is not cheap and depends on the availability of good quality copy negative paper and for these reasons it will not always be practical or economic. The next best option will be to produce a number of tracings of the base drawing and add the information on one service to each tracing. For larger schemes, it is not advisable to try to save effort by showing more than one service on a single drawing although this may be acceptable for simple small schemes. In general, the temptation to show services on prints of base drawings should be avoided since every copy of the drawing will have to be produced separately. (A possible exception to this rule is for small schemes for which the necessary information can be provided on a plan which is small enough to be photocopied).

For small schemes, simple sketch plans will be adequate provided that lengths and average street/paving widths are shown reasonably accurately. Levels may or may not be required as discussed later.

Standard details should be produced at scales, typically 1:10, 1:20 and 1:50, that enable all the necessary detail to be shown. It may be worthwhile to produce these details in booklet form, copies of which can be issued to contractors and community groups. A full set of drawings should be available on-site to the contractor, government workers or community group responsible for construction. Those responsible for site supervision should also have copies.

For community managed schemes, the drawings must be made available to the managing group and explained at the beginning of the work. It may be appropriate to combine typical details with simple specifications and guidelines on how to work out quantities. The appropriate local language should be used in all this documentation and other ways of making drawings and instructions easy to understand should be investigated.

From the point of view of the community, it may be argued that this procedure leaves control of key decisions in the hands of the professionals and assigns only a reactive role to community members and representatives. Despite the commonly held view among professionals that lay-people lack the knowledge to make technical decisions, experience suggests that community members often do have valuable insights and knowledge. One possible procedure for making use of this knowledge in a structured way would start with the production of rough proposal drawings at a meeting between community representatives and professionals. The drawings would then be worked up by the appropriate professionals and finalised at a subsequent meeting involving the community.

Quantities

The estimation of quantities and costs for items like manholes, chambers and drains which comprise several components can be simplified by preparing a schedule of quantities for a single item and costing each component. The total cost for one item can then be calculated from the schedule and entered against the appropriate item in the main bill of quantities or work estimate. A typical schedule for a manhole is shown in Box 11.1. Note that for linear items such as drains, the cost schedule should provide quantities per unit length.

For larger schemes, it is advisable to prepare information on quantities in the form of a schedule, providing all the required quantities for each street and lane. An example is shown in Box 11.2. This approach has two advantages. First, it provides a simple way of setting out the calculations for quantities and can easily be computerised, reducing the calculation time needed and the scope for error. Second, it enables changes during construction to be recorded easily and payments to contractors to be adjusted accordingly. By its very nature, upgrading is a process which requires many small adjustments at the implementation stage and without itemised lists of quantities for each street or lane it may prove difficult to keep track of changes.

For community managed schemes, it will usually be unnecessary to produce a formal bill of quantities. However, it is desirable that simple schedules of the work to be undertaken are produced so that costs can be estimated and materials ordered. In this respect, it is useful if facilitators have some basic technical knowledge so that they can provide guidance to community groups. Some information on quantities is given in Annex 1 at the end of this chapter.

Specifications

The purpose of specifications is to regulate the quality of the work carried out on site. This may be done in three basic ways:

◆ by specifying the type and quantity of the materials to be used;

◆ by specifying working practices and the standard of workmanship to be achieved; and

◆ by specifying the end result to be achieved by an operation;

An example in the first category would be a clause specifying that cement should be ordinary portland cement produced in accordance with relevant government and/or internationally accepted standards. Clauses specifying the way in which cement should be stored and concrete should be placed fall into the second category. A clause stating the cube strengths to be achieved after 7 and 28 days for various classes of concrete falls into the third category.

The tendency in modern specifications is to specify the result to be achieved whenever possible. However, this will not always be advisable in upgrading schemes where there is limited access to appropriate testing facilities. For instance, it is probably unrealistic to include a clause requiring that fill material be compacted to 95% of maximum dry density. Such a clause is commonly used in specifications for major highway schemes but a better approach for upgrading would be to specify the maximum thickness of layers, the type of compaction equipment to be used and something about the compaction procedures. In effect, the specification is then concerned with what has to be done rather than what has to be achieved. In other cases, such as the specification for bituminous surfacing material, it may be appropriate to specify the source and say that the supplier must provide evidence that the composition and grading requirements are met.

Regardless of the above, specifications should not be longer or more complicated than they have to be. For instance, a surfacing specification should be available for small schemes in tertiary lanes containing only information on techniques such as brick-paving, in-situ concrete and, where appropriate, hand-laid asphalt. Such a specification need only be a few pages long.

It is useful to monitor the way in which specifications are used on site. If a clause appears not to be used, it should be reviewed and possibly replaced by one that is easier to use and achieves the same result. On the other hand, it may be necessary to insist on improved site supervision where essential clauses in the specification are being ignored.

Where possible, specifications should be related to the relevant national and international standards. (For instance, government specifications in Pakistan require that 150m and 225mm dia. concrete pipes are manufactured to BS5911 and larger sizes to ASTM standards). However, caution is needed where satisfactory materials which have not been produced to such standards are available. It is possible, for instance, to produce satisfactory small diameter concrete sewer pipes in small casting yards, even though the pipes are not strictly to national specifications.

Simple specifications are also required for community managed schemes. It is important that the reasons for specified standards and procedures are explained to the community members who will be involved in implementation. Only if they are understood will they be observed properly. In particular , it is necessary to make clear:

SCHEDULE 8.7-IVMANHOLE TYPE 'C' (EACH)

DEPTH 1.5 METRE TO INVERT AND 450mm DIA PIPE

For greater depths to invert, add costs from supplementary schedule.

Item No.	Description	Qty	Unit	Rate	Amount
1.	Excavate in any kind of material for manhole to depth as required, including removal of surplus material to an approved dumping place within 6.0 kilometre from the site.	9.30	M³	265.40	2,468
2.	Provide and place Class-C (1:3:6) concrete base slab as per details shown on the drawing.	1.50	M³	863.48	1,295
3.	Provide and lay in (1:4) cement-sand mortar selected bricks to form manhole walls including access shaft as shown on the drawing.	2.00	M³	615.99	1,232
4.	Render both faces of wall with 13mm thick plaster in 1:3 cement sand mortar.	20.40	M²	19.40	396
5A	Provide and fix in position, manhole cover slab in Class B (1:2:4) concrete as per details shown on the drawing excluding cost of standard WASA cover.	0.68	M²	1612.56	1,097
5B	Provide and fix in position standard WASA heavy duty cover slab (26" size).		Item	435	435
6.	Provide and fix C.I angle iron frame as per WASA specifications embedded in concrete for fixed manhole cover slab as shown on the drawings.		Item	435	435
7.	Provide and securely fix in position in precast concrete slab, steel reinforcement as per details shown on the drawing.	48.0	Kg.	13.05	626
8.	Provide and place Class-B (1:2:4) concrete in benching as per details shown on the drawing.	0.62	M³	1005.46	623
9.	Provide and fix malleable cast iron steps in masonry works as per details shown on the drawing.	4	Nos.	101	404
	Total Rs:				9,011

(to be used as bill rate).

Box 11.1. Standard schedule of quantities for manhole

1	2	3	4	5	6	7	8	9	10	11	12	13	14	15	16	17	18	19
Lane no.	Lane length (m)	Average lane width (m)	Average depth of fill required (m)	Total volume of fill required (m³) (2x3x4)	Length to be paved (m)	Width to be paved (m)	Total area to be paved (m²) (6 x 7 - MH area)	Total sewer length (m)	Sewer diameter (mm)	Number of manholes Type A	Number of manholes Type B	Number of manholes Type C	Length of sewer billed (m) (9-int.MH lengths)	Average sewer depth (m)	Excavation for sewer (m³)	Number of house connections	Average length of house connection	Length of house connection
													/					

Box 11.2. Part of standard sheet for calculating quantities for individual streets and lanes

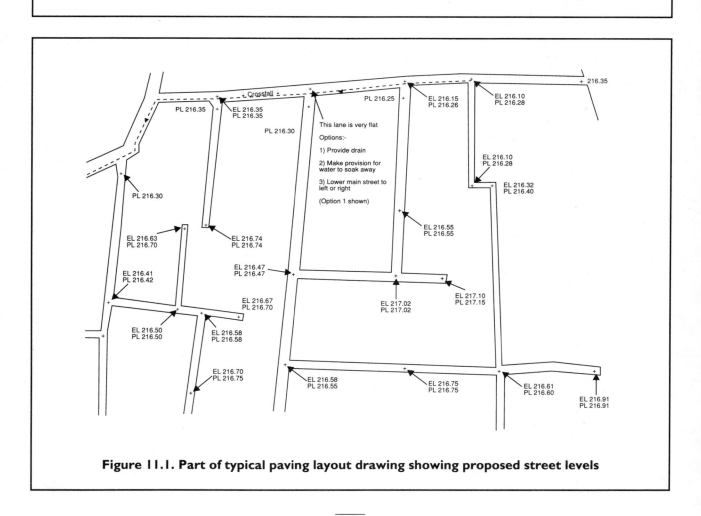

Figure 11.1. Part of typical paving layout drawing showing proposed street levels

◆ where failure to adhere to specifications will lead to future problems, for instance in the backfilling of trenches; and

◆ the reasons why different qualities of material are acceptable in different situations, for instance why blinding concrete does not have to have the same mix as that in a structural slab.

It is important to set up proper procedures where community members have a role in checking the quality of work done by contractors. Any comments and complaints should be channelled through a limited number of community spokespersons. If this is not done, recriminations between community members, government employees and contractors staff are likely to arise. On-going technical advice and guidance is likely to be required for community managed schemes, at least in the early stages.

POINTS RELATED TO SPECIFIC SERVICES

Paving and drainage schemes

Most paving proposals can be represented by standard cross-sections , typically at a scale of 1:20 to 1:50, together with plans at 1:500 or 1:1000 which show the streets to be paved and the required pavement levels. It is probable that pavement levels as such will not be required where there are good average falls, say greater than 1:50 on average. It is also possible that levels can be omitted from drawings for individual lanes less than about 150m long even in flatter areas, provided that a fall is provided towards the outlet point.

Figure 11.1 shows a typical paving drawing for part of North East Lahore. Both the existing ground level and the proposed pavement level are shown, enabling quantities for fill and excavation to be calculated.

For small schemes, it should be possible to decide levels relative to the point at which the tertiary level streets or lanes to be paved meet a through street. Figure 11.2 shows the stages in deciding and setting out the levels for a paving scheme implemented by the community without access to sophisticated surveying equipment.

Information on the route and levels of drains should be provided on drawings, each showing a plan of a length of drain under which is a longitudinal section of that length. It is important to show plan and section on the same drawing. By providing standard cross-sections, including both the drain and the street surface, it will often be possible to use one drawing to show levels for both the drain and the street. The normal procedure will be first to construct the drain to the levels shown on the drawings

and then to relate levels across the street cross-section to the drain levels. Additional levels may be shown on the plan at points where the arrangement diverges from a simple cross-section, for instance where the drain crosses from one side of the street to the other. Figure 11.3 shows a typical plan and section for a length of drain.

Construction details for drains are provided by standard cross-sections and details of features such as access arrangements for covered drains. These should normally be produced at a scale of about 1:20.

Water supply

The routes of proposed water mains should be shown on plans with scales in the range 1:500 - 1:2000. The positions of all valves, wash-outs, fire hydrants and air-valves should also be shown on these drawings, together with the locations of any tubewells and elevated reservoirs. It will also be advisable to show the expected locations of any bends, tees and other fittings, except in the case of small diameter GI mains. In the case of valves, the drawing should indicate whether the installation is to be in a chamber or using a surface box.

Standard details should be given of all standard components of the system, for instance, thrust blocks, bedding arrangements, house connection arrangements etc.

When taking off quantities for water supply schemes, a provisional allowance for additional bends and other fittings should be made. Typically this should be about 10% of the recorded fittings in the case of fairly large schemes. It may also be advisable to include provisional items for realigning some existing lengths of main in congested areas where sewers and other underground services are to be laid.

Sewers

Conventional practice for sewers is to provide a plan and longitudinal section for each length of sewer. For tertiary sewers, this is not necessary since all the required information on sewer routes, sizes, slopes and invert levels can be shown on layout plans. The invert level and cover level of each manhole should be shown, and the size and slope indicated against the sewers running between manholes. Where a branch sewer enters a manhole at a different level to the main sewer or there is a change in the main sewer invert at the manhole, this must be clearly indicated on the plan.

The manhole types required can be deduced from the cover and invert levels shown on the plan and the location. The type of each manhole should then be indicated on the plan. Figure 11.4 shows a typical finished sewer layout plan.

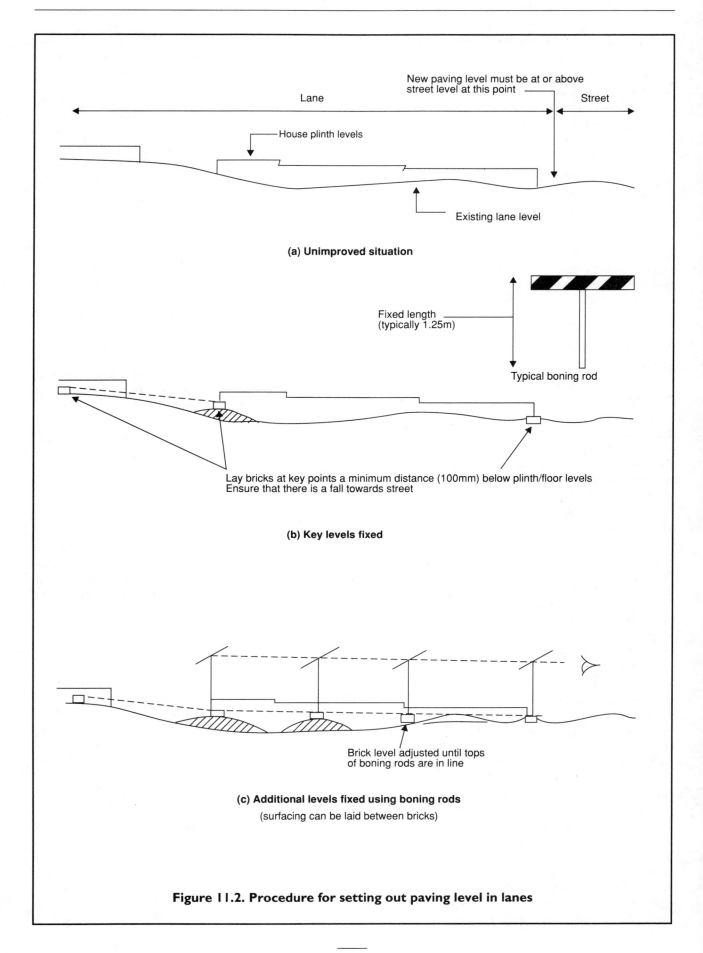

Figure 11.2. Procedure for setting out paving level in lanes

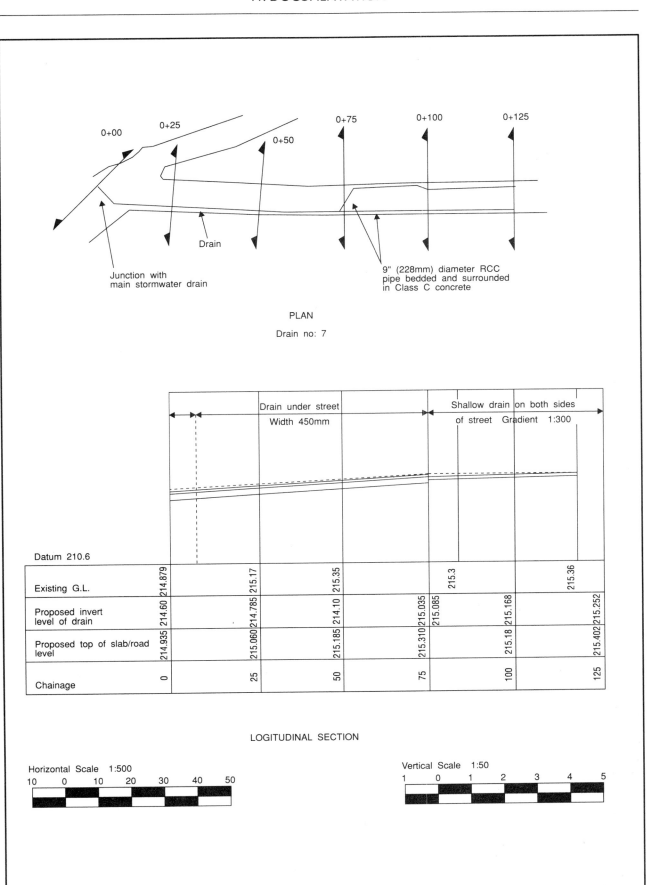

PLAN

Drain no: 7

Figure 11.3. Typical plan and section drawing for secondary drain

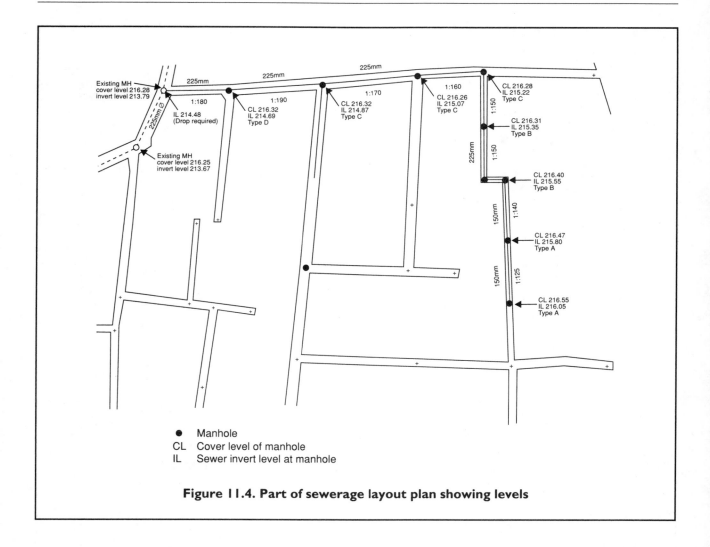

● Manhole
CL Cover level of manhole
IL Sewer invert level at manhole

Figure 11.4. Part of sewerage layout plan showing levels

For small schemes constructed by municipalities and community groups, it may be possible to work on the basis of slopes rather than absolute levels provided that either:

◆ ground slopes are greater than about 1: 100;

◆ the depth to the collector sewer which is to receive the flow is such that there will be no danger of the branch sewer being laid too low.

Standard details are required for each manhole type, typical house connections and pipe bedding arrangements. A schedule of trench widths may also be included with the drawings.

Specifications should include clauses on pipe quality, laying procedures and jointing methods and procedures. Most specifications in use at present also require that a water test is carried out to ensure that the pipe is sound. In practice, these tests are rarely carried out,partly because of the frequent shortage of water with which to make the tests and partly because of the non-availablity of sound pipe stoppers to prevent leakage of water from the ends

of pipes during the tests. In practice, it may be better to specify the way in which the pipe is to be laid and rely on good site supervision to ensure a satisfactory quality of work.

Flexible pipe joints should only be specified if it is certain that properly formed grooves can be produced in pipe spigots to receive the rings and that good quality rings of the correct size are available. In practice, this will mean that the majority of tertiary sewers will continue to be laid with rigid joints for the foreseeable future.

Solid waste collection

Drawings, bills of quantities and specifications in the same form as those required for other services will be required for fixed facilities such as enclosures. For vehicles and bins fabricated from steel, the procedure is likely to be rather different. Manufacturers should be approached with a specification of the duties which the equipment is required to perform, together with sketches or general arrangement drawings of the proposed equipment as appropriate.

They should be asked to give an outline design for the required equipment and to produce a price for manufacturing it. On the basis of this, a preferred supplier should be chosen and asked to produce detailed fabrication drawings and or samples of the equipment to be produced. Once these have been approved, they and the quoted price will form the basis of a contract between the supplier and the client. The client, which should normally be the operating authority or organisation, should reserve the right to request amendments in the design to incorporate lessons learnt during operation.

Street lighting

The drawings and specifications used for street lighting should normally be in accordance with those used by the electicity supply authority. The drawings produced should include those for standard poles and wall fittings. Specifications should cover safety requirements and the type and size of conductor wires and other fittings to be used. Street lighting is a specialised subject and it will normally be necessary to obtain the advice of a specialist in this field when preparing proposals to upgrade facilities.

ANNEX 1

INFORMATION FOR USE IN ESTIMATING QUANTITIES

Concrete

Table 11.1 gives approximate material quantities required to produce one cubic metre of finished concrete. The exact quanties required depend on the type, size and grading of aggregate and sand, the quantity of water used and the mixing method. The cement quantities given are for machine mixed concrete using a gravel or shingle aggregate. For machine mixed broken stone aggregate, about 20kg more cement will be required for all mixes. For all aggregates, cement quantities should be increased by about 10kg/m³ when mixing is by hand.

For small jobs, one 50kg bag of cement will make approximately:

    0.13m³ of 1:1½:3 concrete;
    0.17m³ of 1:2:4 concrete;
    0.25m³ of 1:3:6 concrete;
    0.33m³ of 1:4:8 concrete;
    0.50m³ of 1:6:12 concrete.

Mortar

Table 11.2 gives information that may be used in estimating the quantities of materials required to make various cement:sand mortar mixes. The quantities of cement given are averages and slightly more cement should be used for fine sands. Quantities are given to make 1m³ of cement and for the amount of sand required per 50kg bag of cement.

Brick paving

The approximate numbers of standard bricks required for paving a 1 m² area, assuming that all joints are 4-6mm in width are as follows:

    For Bricks laid flat   -   38
    For bricks laid on edge   -   57

Mix (Nominal)	Cement (kg)	Dry sand(m³) (m³)	Aggregate (graded av. 12-25mm)
1:1:2	550	0.40	0.80
1:1½:3	370	0.42	0.84
1:2:4	290	0.45	0.90
1:3:6	190	0.46	0.92
1:4:8	140	0.47	0.94
1:6:12	100	0.49	0.98

Table 11.1. Quantities in concrete mixes

Mix proportions (Cement:sand)	Cement kg	Sand m³	Sand per 50kg bag of cement
1:1	1020	0.71	0.035
1:2	680	0.95	0.07
1:3	510	1.05	0.105
1:4	380	1.05	0.14
1:5	310	1.05	0.17
1:6	250	1.05	0.21
1:7	220	1.05	0.24
1:8	200	1.05	0.27

Table 11.2. Material quantities for cement: sand mortars

12.

COSTS, COST RECOVERY AND AFFORDABILITY

SUMMARY

The chapter starts with an introduction to economic analysis, financial analysis and affordability analysis and then reviews the costs associated with upgrading projects. Capital costs for both conventionally managed and community managed schemes are considered, as are recurrent costs and the split between on-site and off-site costs. A section on least cost analysis follows, giving brief introductions to the time value of money, discount rates, present values and shadow factors. This is followed by a section on affordability which begins by explaining how the total annual cost per household (TACH) can be used to estimate the per-household payment required to ensure full cost recovery. This leads to a review of the factors that influence the ability and willingness of beneficiaries to pay for upgrading works. Possible methods of recovering costs from beneficiaries are reviewed and the chapter ends with a brief introduction to cost/benefit analysis. Annexes give examples of the various analyses described in the chapter.

KEY POINTS

Economic analysis is concerned with the value of a project to a country or region and should be undertaken at the time when upgrading strategies are decided.

Financial analysis examines the effects of upgrading initiatives on the finances of organisations, communities and individuals. It should be used to gauge the affordability of upgrading schemes in terms of the total annual cost per household (TACH).

It is desirable to seek cost recovery from the intended beneficiaries of upgrading schemes. Without it, upgrading on the scale required to address overall problems is unlikely to be affordable to government. Affordability of charges to the beneficiaries should be assessed.

Construction costs for new schemes should be estimated on the basis of actual costs from recent schemes whenever possible.

In the absence of specific information, an allowance of 10-15% of the construction cost should be made to cover the cost of the planning and design of a scheme and its supervision on site.

The construction costs of community managed schemes using small contractors are likely to be less than those of conventionally managed schemes (typically 75% of the cost). Greater savings are possible where some or all of the construction is undertaken by the community.

Discount rates which reflect the time value of money are used to compare costs incurred at different times. For economic analysis, the discount rate used is the opportunity cost of capital, typically 10-15% in developing countries. For financial analysis, the discount rate approximates to the prevailing interest rate less the level of inflation.

The ability of beneficaries to pay must be assessed on the basis of socio-economic surveys. The total shelter-related expenditure should not normally exceed 20-30% of income.

Willingness to pay will depend on the beneficiary's perceptions of need for the upgrading works and the degree to which cost recovery is attempted on similar schemes in the vicinity.

For a scheme to be viable, it should be possible to show that its economic benefits are greater than its costs but in practice it is often difficult to measure the benefits of upgrading schemes.

INTRODUCTION

All development projects should aim to make the best use of available financial, physical and institutional resources. This is especially true for upgrading work, for which the available resources are usually limited in relation to the total need. It is therefore important to minimise the cost at which services are provided while ensuring that agreed minimum standards are achieved. It is also important to ensure that costs, both capital and recurrent are affordable to the households and/or organisations which are expected to bear them. Three types of cost analysis are considered in this chapter, economic analysis, financial analysis and affordability analysis.

Economic analysis is concerned with the value of a project in relation to the overall economy of a country or region. It takes into account all costs to the economy, financial and non-financial, no matter who incurs them. The purpose of economic analysis is to show that the project is both viable and the least-cost option in relation to the economy as a whole. It is of interest mainly to central governments and lending agencies which must take into account the overall economic situation and choices in a country. Local government organisations may theoretically be required to examine the economic costs and benefits of alternative strategy choices; an example is that between upgrading and other approaches to shelter provision. In practice, it will usually be better for such strategy decisions to be made at a national or provincial level.

Economic analysis is required at the time when upgrading strategies are decided. It should be particularly concerned with issues such as levels of service and the methods and materials to be used in upgrading. A problem arises in that the information on which decisions are made may be rather unreliable at the planning stage. This is particularly true with regard to estimates of the benefits to be gained and the useful life and maintenance requirements of facilities. (Experience suggests that, because of poor maintenance, the life of facilities is often less than that initially assumed). It is therefore very important to update economic analyses in the light of information obtained from evaluation of completed schemes. In some cases, such information may lead to major revisions in overall strategies. Where accurate information is not available at the time when strategies are initially developed, figures which are estimates should be clearly identified in analyses and the assumptions on which they are based should be stated.

Financial analysis, as its name suggests, deals purely with finances and does not concern itself with the level of economic benefit obtained from a project. It is of particular interest to the organisations which are responsible for the implementation of upgrading schemes and their subsequent operation and maintenance. Financial analysis may be used to compare the costs of different upgrading options and to establish whether these costs are likely to be affordable to the concerned organisations. Any costs incurred directly by individuals and community groups can be omitted from the analysis.

The affordability of proposals to beneficiaries must be assessed where either they incur costs directly or government intends to recover part or all of its costs from them. Affordability analysis will be required in both cases.

COSTS

The costs to be considered when appraising upgrading proposals fall into two basic categories, capital costs and recurrent costs. It is also normal when considering both upgrading and new shelter schemes to further subdivide capital costs into 'on-site' and 'off-site' costs. Each of these is discussed in more detail below.

Capital costs

Capital costs are the costs incurred at the beginning of a project, between its inception and its completion on the ground. They include:

◆ the cost of planning and designing the work;

◆ construction costs;

◆ supervision costs; and

◆ overheads.

Capital costs for conventional schemes

In the absence of more accurate data, an allowance of 5-7.5% of the construction cost is usually taken for the cost of planning and designing upgrading projects. However, the actual costs of planning and designing schemes should be collected where possible and used as the basis for future costing exercises.

Construction costs can be estimated by multiplying estimated quantities by unit rates taken from either standard government schedules of rates or the rates quoted by contractors for recently let contracts. The latter is preferable, although the former may be the method required by government regulations.

In the absence of specific information, supervision costs for conventionally managed projects may be taken as around 5% of construction costs. However, actual costs should be collected from ongoing schemes and used for subsequent schemes wherever possible. Because of their complex nature, integrated upgrading schemes may require a higher level of supervision than conventional engineering projects.

For conventionally managed projects, overheads include the senior management and head office costs which are attributed to the project. For larger schemes, it may also be necessary to include for items such as insurance, performance bonds etc. where these are required. In most cases, the latter will be borne by the contractor and included, either implicitly or explicitly, in his tender. Allowance for overheads are often included in the percentages of construction cost allowed for design and supervision but explicit allowance will have to be made when design and supervision costs are estimated directly from actual projects.

Capital costs for community managed schemes

For community managed schemes, the actual capital costs incurred will be different in some respects from those incurred on conventionally managed contracts. Government will still incur costs relating to overall planning and the design of secondary and tertiary facilities. However, its expenditure at the tertiary level will tend to be for advisors and extension workers rather than for design. This may result in some cost saving but in the absence of firm data, it will be advisable to assume the same costs as for conventionally managed schemes.

Savings in construction costs will occur wherever schemes are implemented directly by the community since there will be no payments for labour or contractors profit. While it is probably true that specialist tradesmen and/or small contractors are used on most community managed schemes, there should still be cost savings since the overheads of individual tradesmen and small firms will be low compared with those of larger organisations. The costs of materials can be obtained from the market, but other costs of community managed schemes should be monitored at the beginning of any programme and used as the basis for future cost estimates. As a first estimate, the cost of community managed schemes executed by small contractors may be assumed to be 75% of those incurred for conventionally managed schemes. Greater savings will be made if some or all of the work is done by community members and/or local tradesmen.

There is some evidence that the level of technical supervision required for community managed schemes is greater than that for conventionally managed schemes. In the absence of firm data, this may be allowed for by increasing the supervision cost allowance to around 7.5% of the estimated construction cost. However, efforts should be made to record actual supervision requirements in the early stages of any community managed project.

National and international costs

For many projects, it is necessary to allow separately for those costs incurred locally and those that require foreign currency to pay for imported goods or services. This is necessary for economic analysis, since the true 'economic' value of a scheme may be different from its 'financial' cost if exchange rates fluctuate or are overvalued. It may also be of direct interest to the implementing organisation if it has difficulty in obtaining access to foreign currency. In practice, most materials and services required for upgrading schemes in Pakistan can be obtained within the country, the possible exception being vehicles and equipment for district level solid waste collection.

Recurrent costs

These include the costs of power and the equipment, materials and labour required for routine operation and maintenance. As with capital costs, it may be appropriate to include relevant overheads, for instance the cost of operations and maintenance supervision, in the total allowed. Where community organisations or individual householders are responsible for operation and maintenance of facilities, financial costs to government organisations and agencies will be reduced.

Estimates of recurrent costs may be based on the records of the organisations responsible for operation and maintenance of facilities. However, these will often give misleading information since current budgets may be insufficient to ensure adequate maintenance levels. A better approach will be to build up information on recurrent costs from observation of the performance of facilities and the activities of those responsible for operation and maintenance.

On-site and off-site costs

The terms on-site and off-site in relation to costs incurred in upgrading are a little misleading since some 'off-site' facilities may actually pass through the area to be upgraded. In general, on-site facilities are those that will benefit only the people living in the area to be upgraded while off-site facilities are those that also benefit a wider area. All tertiary facilities can certainly be taken as on-site as can some at the secondary level. Primary facilities can almost invariably be taken to be off-site. The definition of what is on-site and what is off-site may be influenced by the size of a scheme and the limits of areas of responsibility. In most instances, the aim should be to recover the capital and recurrent costs of on-site works directly from beneficaries. Utility service charges should also include an appropriate amount towards the cost of operating and maintaining off-site facilities. Where community managed and financed services are connected to facilities belonging to central agencies, it will be necessary to consider the split between maintenance costs for the two systems so that adjustments can be made to user charges to allow for the self-managed element.

LEAST COST ANALYSIS

Where there is more than one way of achieving an objective, it is important to know the overall costs of the various options. In general, the option chosen should be that which is cheapest, provided that:

◆ it achieves acceptable levels of service;

◆ the knowledge, skills and equipment required for its implementation, operation and maintenance are available;

◆ it is acceptable to the beneficiaries and meets their needs.

The problem is to decide what is the cheapest option overall. A gravel road has has a much lower initial cost than one incorporating a bituminous pavement but will have a shorter life and higher maintenance costs. In order to compare the two options, it is necessary to take into account the time value of money

The time value of money

The time value of money relates to the fact that a return or profit is made when money is invested productively. Thus, a sum productively invested today will be worth more at a future date than the same amount obtained at that date. In order to allow for this, it is necessary to apply a discount rate to future expenditure and income. The discount rate used depends on whether an economic or financial appraisal of a scheme is required.

For economic analysis, the discount rate used is called the opportunity cost of capital. This is defined as the return that could be achieved if the money was used in the next best alternative investment. It can also be thought of as the price (or yield) of capital. In many developing counties, capital is a scarce commodity and therefore has a fairly high opportunity cost and should be used wherever possible in areas which produce high rates of return. Thus a least cost economic comparison of alternatives that differ in their capital intensity should reflect the real cost of capital to the economy rather than the market price of use capital. Real costs of capital in developing countries are typically in the range 10-15%.

Where two options are closely matched in price, economic analysis using a high discount rate will tend to favour that which has the lower capital cost and higher recurrent costs. While this conclusion is correct in economic terms, it is dependent on recurrent costs being available when they are needed. Many upgrading projects have failed because the tariffs and user charges are not sufficient to pay for ongoing operation and maintenance. Economic efficiency therefore demands security of payment for recurrent costs and this is an area which should always be considered when planning upgrading initiatives. A related point is that the existing arrangements for operation and maintenance may, in any case, be deficient. If it is not certain that these deficiencies can be overcome, it is better to avoid options which have a high operation and maintenance requirement since it is uncertain whether they will achieve their intended working life. The choice between gravel and surfaced roads, for instance, may well be significantly affected by the high maintenance requirements of gravel roads.

For financial analysis, the discount rate should be the prevailing interest rate (or its equivalent in an Islamic banking system), reduced by an appropriate amount to allow for inflation. If the interest rate is R and the inflation rate is I, both expressed in percentages, then the real time value of money can be expressed as $(R-I)/(100+I)$. Thus, for instance, if the interest rate is 10% and the inflation rate is 5%, the time value of money is $(10-5)/(100+5) = 0.0476$ or 4.76%. It will be seen that the real time value of money approximates to the interest rate minus the inflation rate. This assumes that future costs are expressed at todays values without allowance being made for inflation. It also assumes that the rates of inflation in different parts of the economy will be roughly the same. (For both economic and financial analysis, all future costs are given at today's prices, in other words they are not increased to allow for inflation).

The theory of economic analysis assumes implicitly that the next best alternative investment could be in any field, for instance industry, transport or agriculture. This, in turn assumes that the best course of action for any country is to maximise investment in the most productive areas of its economy, regardless of issues of balance and distribution. This is a matter for debate but there is strong evidence that social and distributional factors have to be taken into account, particularly in societies where wealth is shared very unequally.

Present value

The costs of the options available may be compared by discounting them all back to a common datum year, normally the present year. The present value of each option is then the sum of the discounted costs.

The present value of an expenditure P made in N years time is $P/(1+i)^N$, where i is the appropriate discount rate. The expression $1/(1+i)^N$ is the discount factor. To save time, discount factors can be read off from sets of tables, such as those given in Table 12.1, which give values for different years and interest rates.

For costs such as operation and maintenance costs which remain the same over a number of years, it is possible to calculate the present value of a series of constant costs running from year 1 to year N by multiplying the annual cost by the expression $[(1+i)^N-1]/[i(1+i)^N]$, which is referred to as the annuity factor. Table 12.1 also gives a range of annuity factors.

Because annuity factors are the addition of discount factors, it is possible to subtract years when there is no expenditure. For instance, if operation and maintenance costs start in year 2 and continue to year 20, the present value of these costs is obtained by multiplying the annual cost by the annuity factor for 20 years less that for 1 year, ie:

$$PV = [AF(20)-AF(1)] \times \text{Annual cost.}$$

If the discount rate is 10% and the annual cost is Rs5M, this equation becomes:

$$PV = [8.514-0.909] \times Rs5M = Rs38.03M$$

Shadow factors

For economic analysis, allowance may have to be made for the fact that the real costs to the economy of some items may be different from their apparent values. The most important examples are foreign exchange costs and labour costs.

The foreign exchange rate can be overvalued and this has the effect of making any imports appear cheaper to the economy than they really are. The adjustment for foreign exchange is made by multipling the cost of imported goods, excluding any customs duties and other transfer payments, by the shadow exchange factor (SEF). This is normally between 1 and 2.

Adjustments for labour rates take into account the 'real' value of labour in the economy. Where there is considerable unemployment or underemployment in the economy, so that the alternative to someone working on a project would be for them to be unemployed, the economy will not suffer any loss from the person working on the proposed project. To allow for this, a shadow factor, typically between 0.5 and 1 may be applied to labour costs.

Calculation of shadow factors is difficult and needs a thorough knowledge of the economy's workings. In general, economic analyses should only be carried out by trained economists who are well acquainted with the national economy.

AFFORDABILITY AND COST RECOVERY

Affordability

There are two aspects to the affordability of upgrading schemes:

- affordability to the implementing and operating agencies; and
- affordability to the beneficiaries.

These are related by the amount either paid directly by the beneficiaries or recovered from the beneficiaries by the government. The higher the percentage of costs paid by beneficiaries, the less likely is there to be a problem of affordability for government. Conversely, higher levels of cost recovery mean that more attention has to be paid to affordability to beneficiaries.

We have already seen that financial analysis can be used to determine affordability to government agencies. The first step in investigating the affordability of a scheme to its intended beneficiaries is to convert its cost into a cost per household. Capital costs per household can be worked out fairly easily by dividing overall capital costs by the number of households served. For small schemes, the number of households served can be counted directly. For larger schemes, it may be necessary to survey typical areas to obtain information on the number of households per hectare and then extrapolate the survey results to the whole area served. In the normal case in which cost recovery is to be achieved over a period of time, some means of calculating the annual payments to be made is required.

Total annual cost per household

The Total Annual Cost per Household (TACH) is a measure of the annual amount which each household has to pay if the full cost recovery is to be achieved from the beneficiaries. The first step in calculating the TACH is to multiply the present value of the project costs by the Capital Recovery Factor. The latter converts a single amount into an annual cost over a number of years, taking into account the time value of money and smoothing out yearly variations in capital, replacement, operation and maintenance costs. The Capital Recovery Factor is given by the expression:

$$[i(1+i)^N]/(1+i)^N-1]$$

where i is the discount rate and N is the number of years over which the cost is to be spread. This should not be longer than either the projected life of the facilities provided or the time over which the implementing authority is required to repay money borrowed for the project.

The total annual cost per household is worked out by dividing the annual cost by the number of households served. The cost per household is used rather than the cost per person because the household is the smallest unit that is likely to pay for any service. For instance, water bills are charged per household connection rather than per person.

Discount Factor – Present Value of payment of 1 unit:

Year	8%	10%	12%	14%
1	0.926	0.909	0.893	0.877
2	0.857	0.826	0.797	0.769
3	0.794	0.751	0.712	0.675
4	0.735	0.683	0.636	0.592
5	0.681	0.621	0.567	0.519
6	0.630	0.564	0.507	0.456
7	0.583	0.513	0.452	0.400
8	0.540	0.467	0.404	0.351
9	0.500	0.424	0.361	0.308
10	0.463	0.386	0.322	0.270
11	0.429	0.350	0.287	0.237
12	0.397	0.319	0.247	0.208
13	0.368	0.290	0.229	0.182
14	0.340	0.263	0.205	0.160
15	0.315	0.239	0.183	0.140
16	0.292	0.218	0.163	0.123
17	0.270	0.198	0.146	0.108
18	0.250	0.180	0.130	0.095
19	0.232	0.164	0.116	0.083
20	0.215	0.149	0.104	0.073
21	0.199	0.135	0.093	0.064
22	0.184	0.123	0.083	0.056
23	0.170	0.112	0.074	0.049
24	0.158	0.102	0.066	0.043
25	0.146	0.092	0.059	0.038
26	0.135	0.084	0.053	0.033
27	0.125	0.076	0.047	0.029
28	0.116	0.069	0.042	0.026
29	0.107	0.063	0.037	0.022
30	0.099	0.057	0.033	0.020
35	0.068	0.036	0.019	0.010
40	0.046	0.022	0.011	0.005
45	0.031	0.014	0.006	0.003
50	0.021	0.009	0.003	0.001

Annuity Factor – Present value of equal annual payments of 1 unit each:

Year	8%	10%	12%	14%
1	0.926	0.909	0.893	0.877
2	1.783	1.736	1.690	1.647
3	2.577	2.487	2.402	2.322
4	3.312	3.170	3.037	2.914
5	3.993	3.791	3.605	3.433
6	4.623	4.355	4.111	3.889
7	5.206	4.868	4.564	4.288
8	5.747	5.335	4.968	4.639
9	6.247	5.759	5.328	4.946
10	6.710	6.145	5.650	5.216
11	7.139	6.495	5.938	5.453
12	7.536	6.814	6.194	5.660
13	7.904	7.103	6.424	5.842
14	8.244	7.367	6.638	6.002
15	8.559	7.606	6.811	6.142
16	8.851	7.824	6.974	6.265
17	9.122	8.022	7.120	6.373
18	9.372	8.201	7.250	6.467
19	9.604	8.365	7.366	6.550
20	9.818	8.514	7.469	6.623
21	10.017	8.649	7.562	6.687
22	10.201	8.772	7.645	6.743
23	10.371	8.883	7.718	6.792
24	10.529	8.985	7.784	6.835
25	10.675	9.077	7.843	6.873
26	10.810	9.161	7.896	6.906
27	10.935	9.237	7.943	6.935
28	11.051	9.307	7.984	6.961
29	11.158	9.370	8.022	6.983
30	11.258	9.427	8.055	7.003
35	11.655	9.644	8.170	7.070
40	11.925	9.779	8.244	7.105
45	12.108	9.863	8.283	7.123
50	12.233	9.915	8.304	7.133

Capital Recovery Factor

Year	8%	10%	12%	14%
1	1.080	1.100	1.120	1.140
2	0.561	0.576	0.592	0.607
3	0.388	0.402	0.416	0.431
4	0.302	0.315	0.329	0.343
5	0.250	0.264	0.277	0.291
6	0.216	0.230	0.243	0.257
7	0.192	0.205	0.219	0.233
8	0.174	0.187	0.201	0.216
9	0.160	0.174	0.188	0.202
10	0.149	0.163	0.177	0.192
11	0.140	0.154	0.168	0.183
12	0.133	0.147	0.161	0.177
13	0.127	0.141	0.156	0.171
14	0.121	0.136	0.151	0.167
15	0.117	0.131	0.147	0.163
16	0.113	0.128	0.143	0.160
17	0.110	0.125	0.140	0.157
18	0.107	0.122	0.138	0.155
19	0.104	0.120	0.136	0.153
20	0.102	0.117	0.134	0.151
21	0.100	0.116	0.132	0.150
22	0.098	0.114	0.131	0.148
23	0.096	0.113	0.130	0.147
24	0.095	0.111	0.128	0.146
25	0.094	0.110	0.127	0.145
26	0.093	0.109	0.127	0.145
27	0.091	0.108	0.126	0.144
28	0.090	0.107	0.125	0.144
29	0.090	0.107	0.125	0.143
30	0.089	0.106	0.124	0.143

Table 12.1. Discount factors, annuity factors and capital recovery factors

Ability and willingness to pay

The total annual cost per household provides information on the level of payment that is required to obtain full cost recovery from the beneficiaries of a scheme. To determine whether it is realistic to aim for this level of cost recovery, it is necessary to consider the beneficiaries ability and willingness to pay for the scheme.

Ability to pay

This is related to the household income of the intended beneficiaries. A problem immediately arises in that there are considerable variations in household incomes. The normal procedure is to conduct a survey of incomes and relate ability to pay to the income exceeded by a set percentage of the households in the project area, typically around 80%. Once an appropriate household income has been determined, ability to pay is estimated by assuming that a percentage of this income will be available to pay for the provision, operation and maintenance of services. It is normally assumed that up to 20-30% of household income is available to pay for shelter and related services, the exact amount depending on local conditions and the level of income. In general, households with higher incomes will be able to devote a higher percentage of their income to shelter-related expenditure. Based on these figures and allowing for expenditure on other aspects of shelter, the aim should be to restrict payments for infrastructure to about 10% of household income.

Willingness to pay

It does not always follow that because someone can afford a service they will be willing to pay for it. It is therefore necessary to consider willingness to pay when assessing the prospects for cost recovery. Willingness to pay may be influenced by:

◆ the perception of the intended beneficiaries of the necessity for and advantages of the proposed upgrading works; and

◆ the presence or otherwise of similar schemes in the area or adjacent areas for which no cost recovery is attempted.

Perceptions of the necessity and advantages of proposed works may be influenced by a variety of factors including the level of service provided and the convenience of use at the point of delivery. If the level of service is perceived as being too low or if cheap alternatives are close at hand, consumers will be less willing to pay for a new service. For example, people are unlikely to pay for an intermittent water supply to a public standpost some distance from their houses if they already have reliable on-plot supplies from shallow wells or tubewells. Even where the level of

service provided is higher than that previously existing, willingness to pay may not be as great as the planner might expect. For instance, where a relatively low value is placed on women's time, existing free water sources may continue to be used even though time can be saved by using a closer source for which a charge is made. In other cases, the perceptions of intended beneficiaries, for instance in relation to public health benefits, may not be the same as those of the planners. The obvious conclusion is that perceptions and priorities must be explored before a project is begun, using the social survey techniques introduced in Chapter 4. Where some lack of awareness of basic benefits from upgrading works is evident, particularly those relating to public health, a programme to raise awareness will be necessary before physical works begin.

The pricing policies for other improvements in or near the project area will have an important bearing on willingness to pay. Householders are unlikely to be willing to pay for upgraded facilities where these facilities are provided in nearby areas without any attempt at cost recovery. This is likely to be true even where a lack of funds means that only a limited number of households can benefit from the free provision of facilities. The clear implication is that cost recovery options need to be considered in relation to the overall situation in an area rather than to specific initiatives.

Methods of cost recovery

Beneficiaries may pay for upgrading works in a number of ways including:

◆ payment of charges for purchase of freehold or leasehold tenure;

◆ payment of betterment charges;

◆ increases in property tax;

◆ utilities charges; and

◆ directly through matching grant and self-managed schemes.

Payment of lease charges in return for regularisation of tenure has until now been the most common method of cost recovery used in katchi abadis. The charges are levied on the plot area, larger rates per square metre being charged on larger plots. The payment made is strictly for the land rather than the services provided but charges are fixed to cover the cost of infrastructure provision. In practice, overall rates of cost recovery average less than 50% because of low charging rates and the failure to get all beneficiaries to pay. Nevertheless, this method is possibly the best option for katchi abadis. It is not suitable for unregulated private subdivisions because there is no need for regularisation of land tenure.

Payment of betterment charges would work in a similar way to that of lease charges with the payment being specifically for the services provided rather than regularisation of tenure. It would thus be suitable for unregulated private subdivisions. New legislation would be required before this method of cost recovery could be attempted in Pakistan.

Payment for upgrading work by increasing property taxes is often recommended by the World Bank and other international agencies. In practice, it presents problems in Pakistan and other countries. The first problem is that most properties in informal areas are assessed to have low rental values and are not eligible for property taxes at present. Even if upgrading schemes result in increases in the assessed values of properties, it is unlikely that anything like 100% will become eligible for tax. This will mean that charges will be levied on only some of those who benefit from upgrading measures. A second problem is that property values are reassessed at intervals and the time of reassessment will not necessarily follow quickly after upgrading work has been completed. There may thus be a delay before increased payments start and this will affect the amount of cost recovery obtained. The third problem occurs where property taxes are collected by a different organisation from that responsible for upgrading. Where this is the case, as it is in Pakistan, it will be difficult to ensure that increases in property taxes are closely related to expenditure on upgrading. For all these reasons, it is wise not to rely on property tax increases for cost recovery.

For water supply and sewerage, some cost recovery may be expected from connection and user charges. The TACH for water and sewerage components of upgrading schemes can be compared with existing user charges to determine the likely level of cost recovery that can be obtained. In general, the aim should be to recover a high proportion of secondary and tertiary system costs, if necessary raising tariff levels to do so.

Direct cost recovery through matching grants and community funded and managed schemes is perhaps the best option for tertiary level facilities. However, it will be necessary to ensure that the legislation and procedures necessary to facilitate this approach are available before it is used.

COST BENEFIT ANALYSIS

Cost-benefit analysis involves the calculation of the ratio of the present value of the lifecycle benefits of a scheme to that of its lifecycle costs. Cost/benefit analysis is an economic tool and the discount rate used is therefore the opportunity cost of capital. If the benefit to cost ratio is greater than one, it suggests that the project is worthwhile to the community and to the nation. If the ratio is less than one, it is necessary to investigate the figures further to see whether all benefits have been evaluated. If so, it will be necessary to look at ways of reducing costs without substantially reducing benefits, in particular examining the approach, standards and levels of service adopted.

Another means of comparing costs and benefits that is commonly used by international agencies is the calculation of the internal rate of return (IRR) on a project. This is the discount rate which makes the present value of the net benefits of the project equal to that of its costs. Lending agencies normally require that a project provides at least a 10% IRR.

Whichever method of analysis is used, a problem arises in that many of the benefits of upgrading are difficult to assess. For instance, it is extremely difficult to assess the effects on health of water supply and sanitation improvements and equally difficult to represent these effects in monetary terms. Similarly, it is difficult to quantify improvements in convenience resulting from improved facilities; the costing of the saving of women's time when water is made available close to the house provides an example. In the circumstances, the best option might seem to be to fall back on estimates of what people are prepared to pay for improved services. The problem with this from an economic point of view is that people may undervalue the services provided and be unwilling to pay their full economic cost. For these reasons, cost/benefit analysis of upgrading proposals should be used with caution and the assumptions made should be clearly stated when presenting results.

ANNEX 1

EXAMPLE OF LEAST COST ANALYSIS

This example provides a comparison between the present values of gravity flow and pumped and treated water supply schemes. The gravity supply scheme has a higher capital cost but lower operating costs. The comparison assumes a discount factor of 10%. A simple analysis ignoring shadow prices is given first. This is followed by an analysis including allowance for shadow prices.

The basic cost data for the two schemes is as follows:

Gravity flow water supply scheme

Capital Cost	Year One	Rs 50 M
	Year Two	Rs 50 M
Annual Recurrent Cost		Rs 1 M

Pumped and treated water supply scheme

| Capital Cost | Year One | Rs 20 M |
| Annual Recurrent Cost | | Rs 5 M |

Gravity flow water supply scheme

All costs in millions Rs

YEAR	Capital Cost	Recurrent Cost	TOTAL ANNUAL COST	Discount Factor of 10%	Present Values
1	50		50	0.909	45.45
2	50		50	0.826	41.30
3		1	1	0.751	0.75
4		1	1	0.683	0.68
5		1	1	0.621	0.62
6		1	1	0.564	0.56
7		1	1	0.513	0.51
8		1	1	0.466	0.47
9		1	1	0.424	0.42
10		1	1	0.386	0.39
11		1	1	0.350	0.35
12		1	1	0.318	0.32
13		1	1	0.290	0.29
14		1	1	0.263	0.26
15		1	1	0.239	0.24
16		1	1	0.218	0.22
16		1	1	0.198	0.20
18		1	1	0.180	0.18
19		1	1	0.164	0.16
20		1	1	0.149	0.15

TOTAL PRESENT VALUE   93.52M

Pumped and treated water supply scheme

All costs in millions Rs

YEAR	Capital Cost	Recurrent Cost	TOTAL ANNUAL COST	Discount Factor of 10%	Present Values
1	20		20	0.909	18.18
2		5	5	0.826	4.13
3		5	5	0.751	3.76
4		5	5	0.683	3.42
5		5	5	0.621	3.11
6		5	5	0.564	2.82
7		5	5	0.513	2.57
8		5	5	0.466	2.33
9		5	5	0.424	2.12
10		5	5	0.386	1.93
11		5	5	0.350	1.75
12		5	5	0.318	1.59
13		5	5	0.290	1.45
14		5	5	0.263	1.32
15		5	5	0.239	1.20
16		5	5	0.218	1.09
16		5	5	0.198	0.99
18		5	5	0.180	0.90
19		5	5	0.164	0.82
20		5	5	0.149	0.75

TOTAL PRESENT VALUE   **56.23**

From this first attempt at analysing the costs more accurately it appears that the pumped system which requires high recurrent costs is cheaper by a significant factor. It is in the nature of discounting that any project with low capital costs and high recurrent costs will have lower present values and is thus apparently cheaper over the life cycle. This result is correct in economic terms but is dependent upon recurrent costs being available when they are needed. Too many projects fail because the tariffs and user charges are not sufficient to pay for the ongoing operation and maintenance. Economic efficiency therefore demands security of payment for recurrent costs - otherwise these results must be questioned.

SHADOW FACTORS

In addition to making an adjustment to financial costs to take into account the time value of money, economists also like to make allowance for other factors. The two main areas for this adjustment in an economic analysis of costs are involved with obtaining the most accurate value for using foreign exchange and labour rates.

The foreign exchange rate can be overvalued and this has the effect of making any imports appear cheaper than they really are to the economy. A good indication as to whether an adjustment has to be made for foreign exchange is if there is a parallel market ('black market') for purchasing foreign exchange.

The adjustment for foreign exchange is made by multiplying the cost of any imported goods (known as 'traded goods' which should not include any customs duties or other transfer payments) by the Shadow Exchange Factor (SEF). This factor is normally between one and two, but can go much higher in countries with very high inflation which have not devalued their exchange rate.

Gravity flow water supply scheme

	National Costs		International Costs	Total Costs
	Labour	Non Labour		
Capital Cost	Rs 10 M	Rs 70 M	Rs 20 M	Rs 100 M
Annual Recurrent Cost	Rs 0.5 M	Rs 0.5 M		Rs 1 M

Shadow Wage Rate = 0.75   Shadow exchange factor = 1.65

Pumped and treated water supply scheme

	National Costs		International Costs	Total Costs
	Labour	Non Labour		
Capital Cost	Rs 5 M	Rs 5 M	Rs 10 M	Rs 20 M
Replacement Cost	Rs 1 M	Rs 1 M	Rs 5 M	Rs 7 M
Annual Recurrent Cost	Rs 3 M	Rs 2M		Rs 5 M

Shadow Wage Rate = 0.75   Shadow exchange factor = 1.65

The two adjustments for foreign exchange and wage rates are incorporated in the solutions shown in the next two pages.

Gravity flow water scheme

All costs in millions Rs

YEAR	CAPITAL			RECURRENT			Total annual adjusted cost **	Discount Factor at 10-% Discount Rate	Present Value Costs
	National Labour (SWR= 0.75) [a]	National Non Labour [b]	Internauo nal (SEF = 1.65) [c]	National Labour (SWR = 0.75) [d]	National Non labour [e]	Internauo nal (SEF = 1.65) [f]			
1	5	35	10				55.25	0.909	50.22
2	5	35	10				55.25	0.826	50.22
3				0.5	0.5		0.88	0.751	0.66
4				0.5	0.5		0.88	0.683	0.60
5				0.5	0.5		0.88	0.621	0.55
6				0.5	0.5		0.88	0.564	0.50
7				0.5	0.5		0.88	0.513	0.45
8				0.5	0.5		0.88	0.466	0.41
9				0.5	0.5		0.88	0.424	0.37
10				0.5	0.5		0.88	0.386	0.34
11				0.5	0.5		0.88	0.350	0.31
12				0.5	0.5		0.88	0.318	0.28
13				0.5	0.5		0.88	0.290	0.26
14				0.5	0.5		0.88	0.263	0.23
15				0.5	0.5		0.88	0.239	0.21
16				0.5	0.5		0.88	0.218	0.19
16				0.5	0.5		0.88	0.198	0.17
18				0.5	0.5		0.88	0.180	0.16
19				0.5	0.5		0.88	0.164	0.14
20				0.5	0.5		0.88	0.149	0.13

Total Adjusted Cost** =   **TOTAL PRESENT VALUE   106.40**
[a]xSWR + [b] + [c]xSEF + [d]xSWR + [e] + [f]xSEF

Pumped and treated water supply scheme

All costs in millions Rs

YEAR	CAPITAL			RECURRENT			Total annual adjusted cost **	Discount Factor at 10-% Discount Rate	Present Value Costs
	National Labour (SWR= 0.75) [a]	National Non Labour [b]	Internauo nal (SEF = 1.65) [c]	National Labour (SWR = 0.65) [d]	National Non labour [e]	Internauo nal (SEF = 1.75) [f]			
1	5	5	10				25.25	0.909	22.95
2				1.5	1.5	2	5.98	0.826	4.94
3				1.5	1.5	2	5.98	0.751	4.49
4				1.5	1.5	2	5.98	0.683	4.08
5				1.5	1.5	2	5.98	0.621	3.71
6				1.5	1.5	2	5.98	0.564	3.37
7				1.5	1.5	2	5.98	0.513	3.07
8				1.5	1.5	2	5.98	0.466	2.79
9				1.5	1.5	2	5.98	0.424	2.51
10				1.5	1.5	2	5.98	0.386	2.31
11	1	1	5	1.5	1.5	2	15.88	0.350	5.56
12				1.5	1.5	2	5.98	0.318	1.90
13				1.5	1.5	2	5.98	0.290	1.73
14				1.5	1.5	2	5.98	0.263	1.57
15				1.5	1.5	2	5.98	0.239	1.43
16				1.5	1.5	2	5.98	0.218	1.30
16				1.5	1.5	2	5.98	0.198	1.18
18				1.5	1.5	2	5.98	0.180	1.08
19				1.5	1.5	2	5.98	0.164	0.98
20				1.5	1.5	2	5.98	0.149	0.89

Total Adjusted Cost** =   **TOTAL PRESENT VALUE   71.84**
[a]xSWR + [b] + [c]xSEF + [d]xSWR + [e] + [f]xSEF

Although an allowance has been added to the pumped and treated scheme in year 11 to take into account the possibility of having to replace the pumps after ten years, the total present value of the pumped scheme is still significantly less than the gravity scheme. Although the difference has narrowed as a result of taking into account these extra factors the effect of the 'time value of money' still overrides these adjustments. But the result is only valid if it is possible to obtain recurrent funds when they are needed.

ANNEX 2

EXAMPLE OF CALCULATION OF
TOTAL ANNUAL COST PER HOUSEHOLD

Once the present values of the schemes considered in Annex 1 have been established, the Total Annual Cost per Household can be calculated once the population to be served is known.

Gravity flow water supply scheme
Present Value Costs = 106.40 M

Pumped and treated water supply scheme
Present Value Costs = 71.84 M

Population to be served = 100,000   Average Household Size = 7
Interest rate = 10%   Assumed pay back time = 20 years

Capital Recovery Factor = $0.1(1+0.1)20/(1+0.1)20 - 1 = 0.117$

Total Annual Cost per Household for the Gravity Scheme =
106,400,000 x 0.117 / (100,000/7) = Rs 871.42

Total Annual Cost per Household for the Pumped Scheme =
71,840,000 x 0.117 / (100,000/7) = Rs 588.37

ANNEX 3

EXAMPLE OF COST/BENEFIT ANALYSIS

The present value of the least cost alternative given in the example in Annex 1 is Rs71.84M. This example shows how the benefits of the having clean water can be equated to either the current costs paid to vendors or the value of time spent gathering water.

Cost of water presently purchased through existing vendors:

Cost of water per 200 litre barrel = Rs 5
Daily use of water in an household = 7 (persons) x 25 (litres per person per day)
  = 175 litres

Annual cost of household water
= 175 litres x Rs 5/200 litres x 365 (days per year) x 100,000/7 (number of households)
= Rs 22.81 M

Present Value of Benefits over nineteen year period (20 year project life minus year 1 for construction)
= (AF20 - AF1) x Rs 22.81 M = 7.605 x 22.81 = Rs 173.47 M

Benefit Cost Ratio = 173.47/71.84 = 2.4

Alternatively, cost of water presently collected from river:

Two hours per day collection time per household
Value of collector's time at unskilled wage rates Rs 15/day
Number of households = 100,000/7 = 14,285.7
Annual costs = 2 (hours per day) x 15/8 (hourly wage rate) x 365 (days/year) x 100,000/7 (number of households)
= Rs 19.55 M

Present Value of Benefits over nineteen year period (20 year project life minus year 1 for construction)
= (AF20 - AF1) x Rs 19.55 M = 7.605 x 19.55
= Rs 148.68 M

Benefit Cost Ratio = 148.68/71.84 = 2.1

It would appear from this simple example that either way of judging the benefits suggests that the water supply project should go ahead as the Benefit Cost Ratio is greater than one.